Contents

APPENDICES

Acknowledgments

This report would not have been possible without the active participation of many people. At the International Gay and Lesbian Human Rights Commission, Rachel Rosenbloom served as project coordinator and editor. Eleven women served as regional coordinators: in Latin America, Gloria Careaga Pérez and Patria Jiménez from El Clóset de Sor Juana; in Western Europe, Maria Pronk and Mirjam Turksma from Nederlandse Vereniging tot Integratie van Homoseksualiteit (NVIH COC); in Asia and the Pacific, B.J.D. Gayatri from Chandra Kirana; in Africa, Midi Achmat, Theresa Raizenberg and Karin Koen from the Association of Bisexuals, Gays, and Lesbians (ABIGALE); in North America, Paula Brantner and Kate Kendell from the National Center for Lesbian Rights. Masha Gessen coordinated the project in Eastern Europe, and Alison Murray helped to coordinate in Asia and the Pacific.

Insightful comments on the country reports and/or introduction were provided by Meg Satterthwaite, Julie Mertus, Susan Allee, Ronalda Murphy, Juan Pablo Ordoñez, Suzanne Goldberg, Alexandra Chasin, Judith Butler, Jim Wilets, and David Angel. Huda Jadallah, Zonny Woods, Charlotte Bunch, Niamh Reilly, Susana Fried, Roxanna Carillo,

Ilana Landsberg-Lewis, Shelley Anderson, and Catherine Saalfield provided information and advice. At the International Gay and Lesbian Human Rights Commission, Julie Dorf, Sydney Levy, Nosrat Khalid, and Mark Harris provided information, documentation, and guidance. Leslie Minot, Nicky McIntyre, Eileen Clancy, Stephen LeBlanc, Lan-Ping Yeh, Jesse Guillen, Ardel Thomas, Susan Evans, Jenni Olson, Ara Wilson, Paul Vander Waerdt, Octavia Morgan, Sarah Murray, and Hinda Seif assisted with fact-checking, editing, proofreading, and other aspects of the report's preparation. Sabrina Brennan, Mary Salome, Arwyn Moore, Kim Compoc and Trinity Ordoña provided assistance with photographs. We would also like to acknowledge the work of several women who do not wish their names to be printed.

The report was designed by Lisa Roth, and typeset by Annette Gaudino. Kathleen Wilkinson copy edited and proofread the entire report. Individual country reports were translated pro bono by Kevin O'Donnell, Gila Svirsky, Kayoko Shirakawa, Mikiko Yamamoto, Ducky Obbink, Jesse Guillen, Kathy Zvanovec, Don Lobree, Lisa Geduldig, Daniel Soto, Frank Banta, and various individuals at Linguanet, Inc.

The International Gay and Lesbian Human Rights Commission gratefully acknowledges the financial support of the Global Fund for Women, the Astraea National Lesbian Action Foundation, Mama Cash, the European Human Rights Foundation, the Fund for a Compassionate Society, the Sister Fund, An Uncommon LEGACY Fund, the Human Rights Program of the Townsend Center for the Humanities at the University of California-Berkeley, and the following individuals: Ise Bosch, Léonie Walker, Shad Reinstein and Jody Laine. Without their generous support we would not have been able to complete this report or to participate in the lesbian organizing for the World Conference on Women.

Foreword

Charlotte Bunch

International Women's Year, MEXICO CITY, JUNE-JULY, 1975 — "What are the lesbians doing here? What can they ask for? Do they want now to inscribe their pathologic irregularity in the Charter of Human Rights? Are they claiming the pathetic 'right' to boast about their sexual aberration? This unawareness of their illness just proves how severe these clinical cases are....They have discredited this Conference and distorted the true purposes of woman's emancipation." Thus, Pedro Gringoire in *Excelsior* (July 1, 1975), the largest circulation newspaper in Mexico, denounced those demanding that lesbianism be included on the agenda at the first United Nations World Conference on Women.

Lesbians have been asserting our fundamental human rights as part of the women's rights agenda in the context of the United Nations World Conferences on Women since their inception in Mexico City in 1975 when the first International Women's Year Conference led to the declaration of a UN Decade for Women (1976-1985). The UN Decade and its world conferences did not create either feminism or lesbian activism, and many of their official proponents have been hostile to both. Nevertheless, they have provided a worldwide public focus on women which legitimized women's activities and sponsored events where women have expanded their international networking and developed greater political savvy. Likewise, women's movements in every region have been both fearful and hesitant about lesbianism. Yet, at the same time, they have provided the theoretical and organizational context for lesbians to become more visible and to challenge homophobia and compulsory heterosexuality as antithetical to the goals of feminism.

Claudia Hinojosa, one of the early lesbian feminist activists in Mexico City, has observed that the emergence of lesbianism at the 1975 conference took everyone by surprise. Yet, she says, it became the frame for the first significant exchange between Mexican lesbians and organized lesbian feminists from other countries. Further while the UN Conference and the NGO (non-governmental organization) parallel event made no official pronouncements on the issue, the scandal that the press made over lesbianism gave it high visibility both in Mexico and among delegates at the conference. Within the NGO Tribune, impromptu lesbian workshops were scheduled which received a large response and also became the only space for discussion by women of their own sexuality of any kind.

At the 1980 mid-decade World Conference on Women in Copenhagen lesbian groups primarily from Western countries proposed six workshops for the parallel NGO Forum which were regularly scheduled and well attended. Some women from Third World countries who did not identify as lesbians also asked for information sessions on the topic, and several lively dialogues were added. But the controversies at this conference focused on the Middle East and on North-South divisions and not on lesbianism. Thus, lesbians moved from outrageous scandal in Mexico to low-key networking and dialogue in Copenhagen. While productive, these sessions were perhaps too quiet as many never knew lesbianism was discussed at the Forum and the governmental conference was not even pushed to consider this as part of its agenda.

In 1985 as 15,000 women prepared to attend the end of the Decade World Conference on Women in Nairobi, rumors were rife that lesbians would not be given visas or allowed to speak at the Forum. Nevertheless lesbians from all regions came and on the first day, the Forum '85 newspaper confirmed "reports appearing in two Kenyan daily papers of the presence of lesbians at the NGO Forum." In spite of some initial misunderstandings, a number of scheduled workshops on lesbianism were suc-

I have asked myself these questions repeatedly over the years. I had the relative privilege of "coming out" as a white middle-class, educated woman in the context of the feminist movement in the United States in 1971. My major fears were that I might lose my job or no longer be able to get visas and travel to other countries. I recall realizing the depth of the isolation that haunts the lives of many lesbians later that year when I was in Tokyo for a meeting of an international student organization and I slipped away to go to a bar for "deviants" (lesbians, gays, and heterosexual couples having extra-marital affairs). As I earnestly struggled through a gay male interpreter to explain the ideas of our newly formed lesbian-feminist collective in Washington D.C. to a bar hostess dressed in an impeccable pin striped suit, she kept asking over and over if there really are women in my country who "love only women." Her astonishment that there were women like her elsewhere was so great that she could not get past that question, compelling me to see the isolation that she felt even in that bar.

This book reminds me once again that while a few of us have found a niche in this homophobic and misogynist world, the lives of most lesbians remain isolated, invisible, and precarious. Yet, the very existence of this book is also testament to the courage, strength, and vision of growing numbers of lesbians who dare to write such essays and to organize groups in spite of the repression they face. While each of us faces different constraints and fears, accepting our identity as lesbians and "coming out" in at least some ways is an empowering experience. The "coming out" process is gradual and ongoing because the world assumes heterosexuality at every turn. No matter how many times one discloses one's sexual orientation, there are always new places and people and times when one must decide again how far "out" to be.

The sense of integration and freedom from hiding that comes with affirming who one is and sharing that with others—whether family, friends, or colleagues at work—is also an energizing force. As the authors of the South Africa report in this book note, many lesbians who are "influenced by their own experiences of oppression are in the vanguard of movements for progressive societal change in numbers far outweighing their proportion of the population." Such lesbian and gay male energy in the human rights coalition against apartheid in South Africa resulted in that country being the first to offer protection against discrimination on the basis of sexual orientation in its new constitution.

Lesbians, both in and out of the "closet," are vital participants in all kinds of struggles for human rights, seeking to end violence against women as well as racial violence and the violence of wars and militarism. But all too often the price of acceptance in this activism has been silence about their own human rights as lesbians. Much psychic energy is lost in this denial of one's own human rights, and the success of any human rights struggle is undermined by denying the rights of others.

The vision suggested by this book is that as more women and men of all sexual identities better understand human rights violations and discrimination based on sexual orientation, they will join forces to end these abuses just as many lesbians are participating in struggles for the human rights of others. The only hope for the future realization of human rights for all is in acting on our understanding that human rights are indeed universal, indivisible, and inalienable. If the human rights of any group are left behind, the human rights of all are incomplete. A women's movement that embraces and works for the most inclusive vision of human rights for all gains not only in vision but also through the energy and commitment of women and men who feel empowered by it to seek to express themselves as full citizens in the global struggle for democracy and human rights.

New York City, July 1995

Introduction

—In an apartment in India, two women commit suicide rather than allow their relationship with one another to be broken up by their families.

—In a house in Zimbabwe, a woman is raped repeatedly with the knowledge and consent of her family so that she will become pregnant, get married, and cease to have relationships with women.

—In a psychiatric institution in the United States, a teenage girl is subjected to coercive "treatment" to "cure" her of her lesbianism.

—In a courtroom in Germany, a woman loses custody of her child because the court finds that her lesbianism disqualifies her as a parent.

—In a prison in Uruguay, a woman is isolated in a cell because her captors know that she is a lesbian.

—In an office in the Philippines, two women are fired from their jobs at a human rights organization because they are in a relationship with one another.

Every day, all over the world, women face violence, harassment, and discrimination because they reject socially imposed gender roles and because they have intimate relationships with other women. The above examples, which are documented in the reports that follow, are drawn from different places and widely varying contexts.

However, they all illustrate the coercion—emotional, physical, legal, and financial—that families, communities, religious institutions, and governments employ in violation of international human rights norms to enforce women's adherence to heterosexuality. In addition, they are all human rights violations that are strikingly absent from the international human rights agenda.

For two years, women around the world worked to ensure that these incidents and other violations of lesbians' human rights would be addressed when the Member States of the United Nations gathered in Beijing, China in September 1995 for the Fourth World Conference on Women. Activists presented declarations at regional preparatory meetings in Asia and the Pacific, Latin America and the Caribbean, and Europe and North America.[1] Petitions calling on governments to "Put Sexuality on the Agenda at the World Conference on Women" were signed by thousands of women from over 60 countries, and by nearly 200 organizations around the world.[2] Many of the documents prepared for the conference by non-governmental organizations (NGOs) included lesbian rights in their recommendations and demands.[3]

At the conference itself, a lesbian caucus made up of activists from every region of the world lobbied government delegates to include language in the conference's Platform for Action recognizing the existence of discrimination based on sexual orientation. The final hours of the conference witnessed a historic debate in which over thirty countries spoke in support of this language, including South Africa, Jamaica, Barbados, Canada, the United States, Cuba, Brazil, Slovenia, Latvia, Bolivia, Chile, the Cook Islands, Colombia, Australia, New Zealand, Switzerland, Norway, Israel and the members of the European Union. Their support was not great enough to overcome opposition from a conservative group of predominantly Muslim and Catholic countries, but it demonstrated that recognition of discrimination based on sexual orientation is growing around the world. A number of countries entered "interpretive statements" declaring that they understood particular sections of the document to apply to discrimination based on sexual orientation. In itself the debate served to raise awareness regarding the exclusion of lesbians from existing human rights guarantees, and laid the groundwork for future action at the local, national, and international level.

One question which lesbian activists encountered repeatedly in the preparations for Beijing was the following: "This is a conference for all women. Why is there a need to speak specifically about lesbians?" As many within the women's human rights movement have argued, women suffer human rights violations not simply on the basis of their gender but also on the basis of their race, nationality, political status, religion, ability, language, sexual orientation, age, and many other factors; no understanding of women's human rights can be complete without consideration of the multiple sources of women's oppression. These reports, compiled as part of the effort to raise awareness in Beijing, give numerous examples of the *particular* ways in which lesbians suffer human rights violations because of their sexual orientation. Further, these reports touch on issues that are relevant to women of all sexual orientations, such as the right of every woman to control her own body and to determine her own sexuality.

SEXUAL ORIENTATION AND HUMAN RIGHTS

This project builds on the important work that has been carried out within both the international lesbian and gay movement and the women's human rights movement in recent years. By integrating questions of gender and sexual orientation into international human rights law, these two movements have laid the groundwork for addressing human rights violations against lesbians.

The International Lesbian and Gay Association, the International Lesbian Information Service, the International Gay and Lesbian Human Rights Commission,[4] and lesbian and gay groups in many countries around the world have demanded in recent years that human rights monitoring agencies begin to address the gross human rights abuses perpetrated against lesbians, gay men, bisexuals, transsexuals, transvestites, and other sexual minorities. Cases that have garnered international attention include the murder of transvestites in Mexico, the imprisonment of gay men under sodomy laws in Romania, and the execution of lesbians and gay men in Iran.[5]

Activists have used letter-writing campaigns, legal challenges, and peaceful demonstrations to exert local and international pressure on offending governments and institutions and have won significant victories in many spheres. Anti-sodomy laws have been repealed in some jurisdictions, and men who have been imprisoned under such laws have been released. A groundbreaking 1994 decision by the United Nations Human Rights Committee found that a Tasmanian law prohibiting sodomy violated the right to equal protection and the right to privacy encompassed in the International Covenant of Civil and Political Rights (ICCPR).[6] Legislation prohibiting discrimination on the basis of sexual orientation has been passed in New Zealand, Israel, and several European countries as well as parts of the United States, Canada, Australia, and Brazil. In 1994, South Africa became the first country to prohibit such discrimination in its constitution, and Poland is now considering a similar constitutional provision. A number of countries have begun to grant refugee status to those who fear persecution on the basis of their sexual orientation in their country of origin.[7]

While human rights organizations have been slow to recognize human rights violations based on sexual orientation as part of their mission, several significant changes have recently taken place. In 1991, after 17 years of pressure from lesbian and gay activists, Amnesty International expanded its mandate to adopt as prisoners of conscience individuals who have been imprisoned solely because of their homosexuality.[8] National human rights organizations in various countries, such as the Romanian Helsinki Committee and the Zimbabwe Human Rights Association, have spoken out on human rights violations based on sexual orientation and collaborated with local lesbian and gay activists.

SEXUAL ORIENTATION
AND *WOMEN'S* HUMAN RIGHTS

The recognition that persecution on the basis of sexual orientation is a violation of basic human rights is an essential first step to addressing human rights violations against lesbians. However, it is not in itself sufficient.

The women's human rights movement has demonstrated a number of different ways in which the dominant human rights discourse fails to address violations of women's human rights. First, the distinction between public and private and the almost exclusive focus on "the public" within mainstream human rights discourse have served to obscure many of the abuses perpetrated against women, particularly those that take place in the "private" sphere of home and family. Further, conventional notions of state accountability overlook the fact that most governments exhibit consistent patterns of failure to intervene in human rights abuses against women—for instance, in domestic violence; this systematic neglect by the state, coupled with the invocation of the sanctity of the family and the private sphere, serves to legitimate the abuse. Finally, human rights bodies can meaningfully address violations of women's human rights only if economic, social, and cultural rights are placed on par with civil and political rights.[9]

Like the broader human rights discourse within which it emerged, the movement for the human rights of sexual minorities has emphasized civil and political rights rather than economic, social, and cultural rights. Likewise, the movement has focused primarily on acts committed by the state against individuals. Where the state has directly infringed upon the rights of lesbians, these violations have received international attention.[10] However, the international community has remained silent when lesbians' economic, social, and cultural rights — such as the right to health care, housing, and education — are at stake, and when abuses are perpetrated by private individuals, particularly within the family. The human rights of lesbians cannot be meaningfully addressed until these violations are taken into consideration.

Laws directly prohibiting lesbianism do exist. For example, in the Bahamas, the Sexual Offences and Domestic Violence Act of 1989 states that "Any female who has sexual intercourse with another female, whether with or without the consent of that female, is guilty of the offence of lesbianism and is liable to imprisonment for twenty years." However, of the over 50 countries in the world that currently prohibit same-sex sexual relations, few have enforced such laws against women. Whether in word or in practice, the majority of such laws have specifically targeted sex between men.[11]

The relative absence of legal prohibitions against lesbianism has led some to believe that lesbians face less severe persecution than gay men. While such legislative silence may lead to a measure of safety, however, it is in itself an indication of other, more hidden, human rights violations. One of the primary reasons that lesbians have not been subject to state persecution is that they are socially invisible. In many places, lesbians are not able to establish communities or participate in public life, and the denial of lesbian existence by governments and society is one of the most profound harms that lesbians endure. As the reports that follow illustrate, these conditions allow society to take no responsibility for the lives of lesbians, and can serve to make political action virtually impossible.

The insights of the women's human rights movement take on particular significance in considering human rights violations against lesbians. Not only do most violations of lesbians' human rights (like violations of women's rights more generally) take place within the "private" sphere, but the silence that surrounds lesbianism adds an additional layer of difficulty in documenting such violations. For example, the barriers that keep women from reporting domestic violence or rape—shame, fear, lack of appropriate services—are well known. Those barriers are even higher when reporting an incident requires that a woman admit to the police or other authorities that she is a lesbian. Whether or not explicit prohibitions against lesbianism exist in the law, women put themselves at great risk—jeopardizing family relationships, friendships, physical safety, employment, housing—if they publicly acknowledge that they are lesbians. In addition to the consequences that they may face, lesbians must also contend with the self-doubt and shame that widespread prejudice engenders. The rules may be unwritten—or even unspoken—but they are very real, and the official silence surrounding lesbianism does not make the prohibition of it any less powerful; it only makes it harder to document, respond to, or resist the abuses that lesbians experience.

LESBIAN RIGHTS, HUMAN RIGHTS

Given the difficulty of addressing human rights violations against women using conventional human rights frameworks, and the particular barriers that lesbians face in attempting to speak publicly about abuses they have suffered, it is not surprising that a central theme of many of the reports that follow is lesbian invisibility: invisibility within the law, within society, within the work of human rights organizations and women's organizations. These reports demonstrate the ways that this invisibility is produced and maintained by means of economic and social inequality, physical violence, religious condemnation, psychological coercion, and other means. Many of the reports argue that this invisibility is in itself a human rights violation; that we must stop seeing silence as signifying an *absence*, but rather see it as signifying the *presence* of a multitude of barriers.

Taken together, these reports suggest ways in which our understanding of the following basic human rights must be transformed if we are to begin to address women's right to control their own bodies and determine their own sexuality:

Life, liberty, and security of person.[12] Several reports contain documentation of lesbians who have been murdered or physically harassed, such as Rita da Silva and her girlfriend Marly, two Brazilian lesbians who were beaten and killed by Marly's relatives in 1983. The Britain report notes a study that found that 31% of the lesbians questioned had experienced homophobic violence at least once in the last five years, mostly by unknown attackers in public places. Those who inflict violence on lesbians often do so with impunity; few governments specifically track hate crimes against sexual minorities, and the silence and shame surrounding lesbianism prevent lesbians from seeking help or speaking out against the violence they experience.

While much of the violence documented here is inflicted by others, self-injurious behavior affects lesbians in great numbers. Many of the reports included here mention the high suicide rates that exist among lesbians—in particular, young lesbians. Some of these are double suicides committed by lesbian couples who cannot face the separation that their families impose upon them, like Gita Darji and Kishori Shah, two women in their mid-twenties whose deaths are documented in the India report. The Thailand report discusses the suicide of a young woman whose family would not accept her relationship with another woman; the reaction of the villagers to her death—that she "deserved to die"—demonstrates how such suicides can continue to occur. A 1989 United States government report found that lesbian and gay teenagers are two to three times more likely to commit suicide than their heterosexual peers, a result of the isolation and rejection that they encounter within a homophobic society.[13] Suicides such as these are more than individual acts; they are the result of social attitudes and actions that can be altered through education and information. This loss of life is, in other words, preventable. Redefining such acts as human rights violations requires that we rethink notions of accountability and look at the complicity of governments in the conditions that lead to such deaths.

Freedom from Torture.[14] Although the standard legal definition of torture requires that the role of the state be clearly identifiable, the women's human rights movement has shown that domestic violence is a form of torture—usually perpetrated by non-state agents but sanctioned by the state's unwillingness to intervene—and must be treated as such by human rights monitoring agencies. Many of the country reports that follow discuss the particular forms of abuse to which lesbians are subjected within their families. The extremes to which this abuse can be taken can be seen in the personal testimony of T.M. from Zimbabwe, who describes the process by which her family sought to keep her from living her life as a lesbian:

> When they found out that I was a lesbian, they tried to force me to find a boyfriend but I could not fit in with what they wanted.... My parents decided to look for a husband on my behalf so they brought several boys home to meet me but I was not interested so in the end they forced an old man on me. They locked me in a room and brought him everyday to rape me so I would fall pregnant and be forced to marry him. They did this to me until I was pregnant after which they told me I was free to do whatever I wanted but that I must go and stay with this man or else they would throw me out of the house.... Now I am always on the run. As soon as I know my parents have found out where I am staying, I move on to another place. They are still after me. I have not seen my family in about seven months. I am scared this time they will put chains on me so I am in hiding.

Another form of torture to which young lesbians are subjected is psychiatric incarceration, which can involve shock therapy and medication with mind-altering drugs. Although homosexuality has been removed from the diagnostic manual approved by the World Health Organization and from similar documents in several countries, many manuals and medical textbooks continue to list homosexuality as a disease or abnormality. Julie Dorf and Gloria Careaga Pérez have suggested that in some countries, punitive psychiatry is used to persecute lesbians in the same way that imprisonment is used to persecute gay men.[15] The Russia report documents several cases of young lesbians who have been committed to psychiatric institutions and treated with mind-altering drugs. Women who have undergone such "treatment" are forced to register with local authorities after their release; their status as mental patients bars them from any vocation that would put them in contact with people. In the United States, young lesbians can be committed to institutions under a variety of diagnoses, including "gender identity disorder." Governments become complicit in these acts when they allow doctors and institutions to confine lesbians and subject them to shock treatment and medication.

Freedom of expression and information.[16] There are numerous examples documented here and elsewhere of governments violating lesbians' right to free expression through traditional means of state censorship. In Austria, Article 220 of the Criminal Code, which bans the promotion of homosexuality, has resulted in the seizure of lesbian and gay publications; in Zimbabwe, the *Penguin Book of Lesbian Short Stories* has been banned by the censors.

What many of these reports bring out are the less direct but equally powerful ways in which lesbians are denied the ability to express themselves and denied vital and sometimes lifesaving information. As the report from Jordan states, "[W]e live our lives deprived of healthy and free chances, deprived of a forum in which we can express ourselves or shape any sort of understanding of ourselves as lesbians." Schools, youth groups, and other institutions deprive girls of information regarding sexuality in general, and alternatives to heterosexuality in particular. A lesbian quoted in the Romania report says that as a teenager she had no idea that other lesbians even existed. As the reports from India, South Africa, and many other countries make clear, the isolation that comes from this socially imposed silence can lead to drug and alcohol abuse, depression, and suicide. Thus the denial of the right to free expression often takes place long before the point of direct government repression. Through school curricula, social policies, and other means, governments foster conditions in which expressions of lesbian existence are dangerous or impossible.

Freedom of association.[17] One way in which governments directly violate lesbians' right to freedom of association is by carrying out raids on lesbian bars, which are often the only spaces in which lesbians can gather. In a 1987 raid on a lesbian bar in Lima, Peru, police arrested approximately 70 women. The raid was staged in cooperation with a local television station, which caught the women on camera as they left the bar one by one and aired the footage on the national news. As a result, many women lost their jobs, and some were reported to have been beaten by their families. The women were forced to leave the police station after curfew and at least two were raped on their way home.[18] The Argentina report contained here documents a more recent police raid of a lesbian bar in Buenos Aires.

As in the case of freedom of expression, we must look beyond these clear-cut examples of direct state action to consider the wider socioeconomic and cultural forces that deny lesbians the right to freedom of association. Lesbian bars exist in many places, but report after report documents the ways in which lesbians lack access to public space. Several reports mention that while gay men gather in bars, parks, and other kinds of commercial and public spaces, lesbians remain isolated, and most lesbian socializing takes place in small groups in private homes. Like other women, lesbians lack the financial means and the freedom of movement to sustain commercial establishments. Many live with their families, and as unmarried women they are subject to the control of parents and other family members. As the report from Japan notes, a large number of lesbians are in heterosexual marriages, and are unable to maintain any contact with other lesbians. The restrictions imposed on women's freedom, combined with widespread homophobia, greatly impedes the ability of lesbians to associate with one another, whether for social purposes or to organize to demand their rights.

Equal protection and nondiscrimination.[19] Despite the recent UN Human Rights Committee decision, laws criminalizing same-sex sexual relations continue to exist in countries around the world. The reports from Romania, Nicaragua, India, and elsewhere discuss the effects these laws can have on lesbians. Even in places without explicitly discriminatory legislation, broadly worded laws prohibiting acts against "public decency" or "public morality" are selectively enforced against sexual minorities. For instance, the Mexico report describes the case of two women who were cited under such a regulation for kissing one another in a car. Such laws have also been used to censor lesbian and gay publications and to prevent lesbian and gay marches and events.

Constitutional guarantees of equal protection and nondiscrimination are rarely interpreted to apply to sexual minorities, and lesbians who face discrimination in housing, health care, or employment have no legal recourse outside of the handful of countries that have specifically outlawed discrimination on the basis of sexual orientation. The United States report notes the frequent failure of police to investigate cases of anti-lesbian violence, and the reluctance of judges to impose harsh sentences on the perpetrators of such crimes. As the Nicaragua report points out, "Those who are defined by law as criminals have little reason to believe that the justice system will protect them." The Uruguay and Colombia reports describe the discriminatory treatment that lesbians receive within prisons.

Although anti-discrimination laws represent promising new developments, many obstacles stand between such laws and their enforcement. The Brazil report notes that not a single legal challenge has been brought under Brazilian anti-discrimination laws, because few people are willing to publicly reveal their homosexuality. The Philippines report documents the case of Elizabeth Lim and Evangeline Castronuevo, two lesbians who were dismissed from their jobs at a human rights organization in the Philippines and are currently mounting the first lesbian legal challenge in Asia. What is unprecedented about their case is not that they were fired from their jobs because of their sexual orientation but that they dared to speak out about it. While our attention rightly focuses on important legal challenges such as this one, we must also consider the myriad other cases that never come to light and the economic, social, and cultural forces which keep women from challenging such discrimination.

The right to family.[20] Compulsory marriage is a theme brought out most strongly in the India report, but echoed in many others. As the Brazil report notes, without the ability to support themselves financially, many women are unable to determine their most basic life choices.

Combined with the strong emphasis placed on heterosexual marriage in most societies, financial dependence means that few women can choose to remain unmarried. While the right to family protects the right *not* to form a family, the Serbia report and others demonstrate that single women are subject to discrimination in many spheres of life and that the social pressure to marry remains extreme in many countries.

At the same time, lesbian partnerships are not recognized by law outside of a few countries. The Norway report shows that even countries that provide legal recognition of same-sex partnerships often deny such couples the right to adopt children. In Germany and several other countries, this discrimination can extend to policies barring lesbians from availing themselves of donor insemination services in order to give birth to children of their own. Even when such policies are not in place, many hospitals and individual doctors refuse such services to lesbian clients. Numerous reports document the frequency with which lesbian mothers are denied custody of their children. In all but a few countries, immigration laws which allow families to be reunited refuse to recognize same-sex partnerships.

The right to work.[21] Employers, often with state approval, discriminate against lesbians (and in many cases, against all unmarried women) in all aspects of work—hiring, dismissal, promotion, training, and opportunities and conditions of the workplace. In most countries, the majority of lesbians remain "in the closet" (i.e., not revealing that they are lesbians) at their jobs, and with good reason. Reports from the Philippines and Argentina, among other countries, give examples of the consequences that women face on the job when they are known to be lesbians.

The right to health.[22] As reports from Serbia, Brazil, South Africa, Mexico and elsewhere make clear, few lesbians feel able to reveal their sexual orientation to their health care providers, and few providers are trained to be sensitive to the needs of lesbians. Because of this, lesbians avoid seeking medical care, often waiting until problems become acute and failing to obtain routine care. Those who lie about their sexual orientation are sometimes misdiagnosed. Those who do reveal that they are lesbians are often humiliated, mistreated, or told to seek psychiatric care. As is clear from the discussion of psychiatric incarceration, lesbians can expect little assistance from mental health professionals. Many avoid seeking care because they legitimately fear that psychiatrists and others will try to "treat" them for being lesbians rather than providing counseling for the real problems they may face.

The right to education.[23] As the Serbia report illustrates, girls who fail to conform to socially imposed gender roles or who openly identify themselves as lesbians are often denied access to education because of the discrimination they experience within educational institutions. Young lesbians are also subject to extreme forms of verbal and physical harassment from other students, and this harassment often goes unchecked by teachers and other authorities. The clearest example of this can be found in the Brazil report, which notes the case of a 19-year-old student barred from school "for her own safety" after other students threatened to physically assault her for having kissed her girlfriend.

The right to asylum and refugee status.[24] Although a number of countries have begun to grant refugee status to women and men fleeing persecution based on sexual orientation, many other countries have yet to grant a single lesbian or gay asylum claim.[25] For lesbians, the obstacles go beyond discriminatory policies; even in countries which have recognized such claims, the majority of those granted refugee status have been gay men. Lesbians, as women, often lack the freedom of movement and economic resources that would enable them to flee, and are thus less likely to leave home in the first place. If they do manage to escape, the abuses they have suffered (such as forced marriage) are often more difficult to document as persecution than are anti-sodomy laws and other forms of direct state persecution.

This list, while by no means exhaustive, provides an indication of the breadth of human rights violations that lesbians experience. Without recognition of these abuses, the human rights movement cannot begin to address the full range of gender-based persecution, nor the full range of violations based on sexual orientation.

METHODOLOGY

This project was initiated and coordinated by the International Gay and Lesbian Human Rights Commission (IGLHRC) in partnership with regional coordinators in Africa, Asia and the Pacific, Western Europe, Eastern Europe, Latin America and the Caribbean, and North America. These regional coordinators located authors from each of the countries represented here; in all, activists and researchers from approximately 60 different countries were approached, of whom about half were ultimately able to submit reports.

Each author received guidelines from IGLHRC (revised, in one region, by the regional coordinators) which suggested a set of issues that the reports might wish to address, including discriminatory laws, child custody, lesbian organizing, and anti-lesbian violence. Authors were encouraged to write about whatever issues were most important in their country. Each report was read by several advisors; IGLHRC staff and volunteers helped to supplement and verify the information that the authors provided.

Certain aspects of these reports represent notable advancements over prior reporting on lesbian human rights. With the exception of the India report, all were written by people who were raised in the countries in question, and all of the reports were written by people who currently reside in those countries. These factors, while significant, should not distract from consideration of the fact that this volume does not in any way constitute a definitive global survey. Among the countries that are not represented are some where lesbian organizing is well established, as well as many others (most notably from Africa and the Middle East) where lesbian organizations do not exist. The selection of countries represented here should not be taken as an indication of the countries that are the "worst" for lesbians or the "best." The kinds of issues that lesbians face vary significantly, but there is no country in the world in which women are entirely free to determine how and with whom they live their lives.

While this volume as a whole is not a definitive statement about the conditions of lesbians globally, neither are the individual country reports definitive statements about lesbians in the particular countries in question. A few authors preface their reports by stating that the scope of their analysis is limited by race, class, geography, and other factors. This qualification should be kept in mind in reading all of the reports contained here. Some focus on the legal situation, some on the media, some on historical background; this variation has as much to do with the authors as it does with the conditions in a particular country.

This book would not have been possible without the work that has gone before it. Many individuals and organizations are currently engaged in researching various issues relating to lesbians, and in the years to come this volume will likely be joined by others that will greatly increase our understanding.

For some countries, however, these reports represent a first attempt to describe the conditions under which lesbians live. Several authors make reference to the almost complete lack of documentation on human rights violations against lesbians, and the need for further research. In an early draft of the Uruguay report, the author explained, "We are not resigned to this situation: quite the contrary! The preparation of this report brought me into contact with many lesbians who expressed great hopes that something might come out of it. Since this is the first such report, we decided to present actual cases without naming the individuals involved. Something which was said to me again and again while compiling this report was: do not break the contact begun here."

WHAT'S IN A NAME?

These reports were written in response to the invisibility of lesbians in most existing human rights reporting, and for this reason they primarily discuss human rights violations based on sexual orientation. This approach has the benefit of focusing attention on issues too often silenced in other fora. However, it has also forced authors to forego more detailed discussions of the broader contexts which inform their reports.

There are undoubtedly women in every part of the world who have intimate and sexual relationships with women. To use the term lesbian to describe them, however, is grossly inadequate. At best, it serves as highly imperfect shorthand for a range of identities and practices too varied to sum up in any word or set of words. At worst, the exclusive use of this term runs the risk of suggesting that diverse histories and contexts can be understood through a single set of assumptions.

As the Hong Kong report notes, the idea that sexual acts create sexual identities is not universal. The construction of sexuality varies not only *among* but also *within* regions, countries, and communities. In India, some women choose to organize politically as single women, and others as lesbians. In Hong Kong, the group Queer Sisters is seeking to redefine lesbian issues to include all women who challenge dominant constructions of gender or sexuality. These vital discussions are taking place in many different places around the world.

The use of the term lesbian here reflects the chosen terminology of most of the country reports and of the documents that have come out of several different regions in preparation for the World Conference on Women. The reports that follow, written by women from a diverse range of locations—both geographic and theoretical—do not utilize one definition of their subject matter. Some authors focus on issues affecting gay men as well as lesbians, and some have explicitly included bisexual women in their discussions. Others discuss human rights violations against transsexuals. Several note that laws used against lesbians are the same laws used against sex workers. The Serbia report uses the terminology "lesbians, single women, and women not attached to men" to emphasize that the problems lesbians face sometimes spring less from their relationships with women than from the absence of a male partner.

Even the reports which use only the term *lesbian* demonstrate the impossibility of confining the subject matter within the neat lines that such a term suggests. For instance, compulsory marriage, while it is sometimes used by parents specifically to put an end to lesbian relationships, is also imposed on many girls and women regardless of sexual orientation, and the policing of same-sex relationships cannot be seen in isolation from the policing of relationships which cross lines of race, class, or religion. More than anything else, these reports discuss the control that societies and governments seek to exert over women's sexuality.

CREATING A BROAD SEXUAL RIGHTS AGENDA

While these reports speak of human rights abuses, they are also testament to the lesbian organizing that is flourishing in many parts of the world despite political, economic, and psychological obstacles. Lesbian activists have organized groups, newsletters, events, hotlines, and many other services and programs. Three Asian Lesbian Network conferences have taken place since 1990. Latin American and Caribbean lesbians have been holding regional conferences since 1986. The annual conferences of the International Lesbian and Gay Association and the conferences of the International Lesbian Information Service have brought activists in contact with one another and fostered international networking.

The courageous and groundbreaking work of lesbian activists, however, has yet to be recognized by many women's organizations and human rights organizations. At the World Conference on Population and Development (Cairo, 1994), sexual rights emerged as a central focus of the NGO agenda, and important gains in the realm of sexual rights were made in Beijing: in its final form, the Platform for Action recognizes that "The human rights of women include their right to have control over and decide freely and responsibly on matters related to their sexuality, including sexual and reproductive health, free of coercion, discrimination and violence." As in other areas of feminist struggle, however, the movement for sexual rights often leaves "controversial" issues such as sexual orientation and gender identity at the margins.

The reports contained here present stark evidence of the need for a broad sexual rights movement that addresses the human rights of all women—including lesbians, bisexual women, transgendered women, and other sexual minorities. Unless human rights organizations and women's organizations recognize these issues as their own, they will continue to be complicit in the silence that enables human rights violations against lesbians and other sexual minorities to occur.

NOTES

1 The text of these declarations appear as Appendices B-E.

2 The text of the petition and a list of organizational endorsements appears as Appendix A.

3 As a result of NGO recommendations and proposals by government delegates, the term "sexual orientation" appears in paragraphs 2 (a) and 145 of the ECE Regional Platform for Action (E/ECE/RW/HLM/L.3/Rev.2) and in paragraphs 48, 180 (b), and 226 (alternative text) of the Draft Platform for

Action (A/CONF.177/L.1).

4 The International Lesbian and Gay Association, established in 1978, is a federation of over 300 lesbian and gay organizations in 50 different countries, with an administrative office in Belgium. The International Lesbian Information Service, also established in 1978, is an international network of lesbian activists currently based in the Netherlands. The International Gay and Lesbian Human Rights Commission, established by U.S. and Soviet activists in 1991, is a U.S.-based non-governmental organization with offices in San Francisco.

5 For a more detailed account of international lesbian and gay activism, see Nicole LaViolette and Sandra Whitworth, "No Safe Haven: Sexuality as a Universal Human Right and Gay and Lesbian Activism in International Politics," *Millennium: Journal of International Studies*, Vol.23, No. 3 (1994), pp. 563-88.

6 *Nicholas Toonen v. Australia*, U.N. GAOR, Hum. Rts. Comm., 15th Sess., Case No. 488/1992, U.N. Doc. CCPR/c/50/D/488/1992 (Apr. 4, 1994).

7 These countries include Germany, Canada, the Netherlands, the United States, Australia, Belgium, Sweden, and Finland.

8 See Amnesty International, *Breaking the Silence: Human Rights Violations Based on Sexual Orientation* (NY: Amnesty International-USA, 1994).

9 Charlotte Bunch, "Transforming Human Rights from a Feminist Perspective." Julie Peters and Andrea Wolper, eds., *Women's Rights, Human Rights: International Feminist Perspectives*. New York: Routledge, 1995, pp. 11-17.

10 For instance, in the case of Irene Petropoulu, editor of a Greek gay and lesbian magazine, who was sentenced to five months' imprisonment for a comment published in her magazine, or Sharon Bottoms, who was denied custody of her son by a United States court because she was a lesbian.

11 Many laws, such as Section 377 of the Indian Penal Code, prohibit "acts against nature," a term which specifies neither gender nor sexual orientation; however, in practice these laws have generally been enforced only against male homosexual acts.

12 Article 3 of the Universal Declaration of Human Rights (UDHR) states that "Everyone has the right to life, liberty, and the security of person."

13 U.S. Department of Health and Human Services, "Report of the Secretary's Task Force on Youth Suicide," 1989.

14 Article 5 of the UDHR states that "No one shall be subjected to torture or to cruel, inhuman or degrading treatment or punishment."

15 Julie Dorf and Gloria Careaga Pérez, "Discrimination and the Tolerance of Difference: International Lesbian Human Rights." Julie Peters and Andrea Wolper, eds., *Women's Rights, Human Rights: International Feminist Perspectives*. New York: Routledge, 1995, pp. 324-34.

16 Article 19 of the UDHR states that "Everyone has the right to freedom of opinion and expression; this right includes freedom to hold opinions without interference and to seek, receive, and impart information and ideas

through any media and regardless of frontiers."

17 Article 20 of the UDHR states that "Everyone has the right to freedom of peaceful assembly and association."

18 Julie Dorf and Gloria Careaga Pérez, op. cit., p. 327; James Wilets, "International Human Rights Law and Sexual Orientation," *Hastings International and Comparative Law Review* Vol. 18, No. 1 (Fall 1994), p. 46.

19 Article 2 of the International Covenant on Civil and Political Rights (ICCPR) states: "Each State Party to the present Covenant undertakes to respect and to ensure to all individuals within its jurisdiction the rights recognized in the present Covenant, without distinction of any kind, such as race, colour, sex, language, religion, political or other opinion, national or social origin, property, birth or other status." Article 26 provides that "All persons are equal before the law and are entitled without any discrimination to the equal protection of the law. In this respect, the law shall prohibit any discrimination and guarantee to all persons equal and effective protection against discrimination on any grounds, such as race, colour, sex, language, religion, political or other opinion, national or social origin, property, birth or other status."

20 Article 23 of the ICCPR states that "The right of men and women of marriageable age to marry and to found a family shall be recognized. . . . No marriage shall be entered into without the free and full consent of the intending spouses."

21 Article 23 of the UDHR states that "Everyone has the right to work, to free choice of employment, to just and favorable conditions of work and to protection against unemployment."

22 Article 12 of the International Covenant on Economic, Social, and Cultural Rights (ICESCR) recognizes "the right of everyone to the enjoyment of the highest attainable standard of physical and mental health."

23 Article 13 of the ICESCR recognizes the right to education, and states that "education shall be directed to the full development of the human personality and the sense of its dignity, and shall strengthen the respect for human rights and fundamental freedoms."

24 The 1951 U.N. Convention Relating to the Status of Refugees and the 1967 U.N. Protocol Relating to the Status of Refugees define a refugee as someone who "owing to a well-founded fear of being persecuted for reasons of race, religion, nationality, membership of a particular social group or political opinion is outside the country of his nationality and is unable or, owing to such fear, is unwilling to avail himself of the protection of that country."

25 Even in Canada, which has been among the most progressive countries on this issue, at least one claim was denied to a gay man on the grounds that homosexuals are members of an "asocial group" and thus not entitled to protection under the Universal Declaration of Human Rights. See Nicole LaViolette and Sandra Whitworth, op. cit., p. 583.

Recommendations

The Universal Declaration of Human Rights recognizes the "inherent dignity and...the equal and inalienable rights of all members of the human family." The central principle of non-discrimination ensures that no one shall be excluded from the full enjoyment of human rights by virtue of characteristics of identity or status.

Based on the demands put forth by lesbians in various regions in the preparations for the World Conference on Women, and the reports contained here, the International Gay and Lesbian Human Rights Commission presents these demands to the United Nations:

- Investigate patterns of murder and gross violations of human rights perpetrated against women on the basis of their sexual orientation or marital status.

- Solicit specific information about the status of sexual minorities in country reports submitted to all human rights monitoring bodies.

We call on governments to:

- Take penal actions and pursue other sanctions against any individual or group, including police officers, prison guards, and other workers in the criminal justice system, who subjects lesbians to discrimination, harassment, torture or ill-treatment, including rape and sexual abuse, because of their sexual orientation.

- Recognize forced psychiatric incarceration, drugging, and electroshock of lesbians as forms of torture in violation of international law, and prosecute the perpetrators of such acts. Revise medical definitions of lesbianism and homosexuality in accordance with World Health Organization (WHO) guidelines which state that homosexuality is not a "sexual abnormality" or disease.

- Promulgate laws to protect citizens from discrimination on the basis of sexual orientation or marital status in all realms of life, including employment, housing, health care, and education.

- Repeal all laws and change all policies that discriminate on the basis of sexual orientation or marital status or which are used disproportionately against sexual minorities, including laws that penalize same-sex sexual relations or the promotion of homosexuality.

- Afford lesbian partnerships full protection of the law in the areas of pension and inheritance rights, taxation and social security, custody rights, adoption rights, access to donor insemination, and all other areas in which discriminatory policies and practices currently exist.

- Revise laws, policies and administrative practices regarding refugees and migrants to ensure lesbians equal treatment with regard to freedom of movement, immigration, and asylum, including the right not to be returned to a place of persecution.

- Ratify the Convention on the Elimination of All Forms of Discrimination Against Women and all other international instruments for the protection of human rights. In submitting reports to the appropriate international and regional treaty-monitoring bodies, include information on the ability of lesbians and other sexual minorities to enjoy the relevant rights and freedoms; steps being taken at the national and local levels to remove obstacles to their full enjoyment of these rights and freedoms; and provisions for their protection.

- Recognize that widespread societal prejudice severely constrains the ability of lesbians to participate in civic and political life, and take steps to counter such prejudice with human rights education that emphasizes the need to protect the human rights of all persons, including lesbians.

- Ensure that all sex education and health care materials, campaigns, and services include information relating to lesbians and their needs.

We call on non-governmental organizations to:

- Work in coalition with existing lesbian organizations to promote and protect the human rights of all persons regardless of sexual orientation.

- Promote awareness among non-governmental organizations of the barriers that lesbians face in participating in public life. Promote human rights education that raises awareness regarding the human rights of all people regardless of sexual orientation.

- Institute policies prohibiting discrimination based on sexual orientation in all aspects of the organization's work, including employment practices.

- Incorporate freedom of sexual choice into all programs relating to sexual and reproductive rights.

Country Reports

Argentina

● ● ● ● ● ● ● ● ● ●

Alejandra Sarda

A ttitudes towards lesbianism in Argentinian society are in transition. Argentina has suffered the effects of various military dictatorships, the most recent of which (1976-1984) was especially bloody and devastated the country economically. In recent years, democracy and the respect for diversity are values that have come to be accepted and defended by a large part of the population. This attitude has created conditions under which lesbian groups have been able to develop significantly in the last eight years.

Nevertheless, strong prejudices remain, and authoritarianism is deeply rooted in society. In many sectors violence is still the only response to those perceived as different. The hierarchy of the Catholic Church launches frequent attacks against lesbians and gay men.[1] However, society has for the most part not responded to the church's urgings to discriminate, in part because the church has been discredited by its collaboration with the dictatorships and its silence on human rights violations.

The socioeconomic situation plays an important role in creating conditions in which lesbians can become visible and demand their civil rights. Historically, Argentinian society has tended to become more intolerant toward marginalized groups during economic crises. In such times, the solidarity of dominant groups in society is strengthened at the cost of tolerance toward minorities of any sort. Argentina is currently facing such a crisis, and it remains to be seen if it will create a backlash against lesbians.

LEGAL SITUATION

In 1994 lesbian and gay groups lobbied Parliament intensely to amend the existing anti-discrimination legislation so that it would prohibit discrimination based on sexual orientation.[2] The Human Rights Commission of the Chamber of Deputies passed the proposal, but deliberation by the entire Chamber was interrupted by the national elections, which took place in May of this year. The new Parliament began its work in July, and activists are continuing to lobby so that this proposal will be discussed formally in the Chamber of Deputies.

> *On April 15, 1995, the police raided Boicot (a lesbian disco) and arrested 10 of the women there.*

Although homosexual acts are not criminalized under Argentinian law, there are two legal means by which police are able to arrest lesbians, gay men, and transvestites. The Law of Investigation of Antecedents allows police to arrest anyone and take her or him to police headquarters in order to check the person's police record. This law was modified in 1988 to shorten the number of hours the police can hold a suspect (the period was changed from 48 hours to 10), and to grant those detained the right to make one telephone call.[3]

The other means of control which the police can employ are the "Police Edicts," which are Federal Police regulations. These regulations allow the police to make arrests as long as they follow the Law of Investigation of Antecedents. The infraction under which lesbians are most commonly arrested is defined in Article 2 of the chapter entitled "Scandal," promulgated in 1949 as "incitement to commit a carnal act in the public street." This is the same charge under which sex workers are arrested. Any sign of affection between women in a public place can be cited under this charge, and if the police determine someone is guilty of contravening their regulations they can arrest and hold that person for 30 days. It is important to emphasize that these edicts drawn up by the Federal Police without any sort of legislative process. Since these are police regulations and not laws their application is left completely to the discretion of the police themselves. The judicial authorities are not involved unless the arrested person initiates some special procedure.

The Argentinian police have a long history of authoritarianism and violent repression. Police brutality (sometimes resulting in death), the rape of women in custody, psychological mistreatment—all of these abuses are common. The 10-hour limit on detention and the suspect's right to make a telephone call exist on paper but are often not respected. Lesbians who are arrested in bars or on the street are frequently subjected to verbal abuse or intimate body searches by male police officers. Another common practice is extortion. The police threaten to reveal to employers or to family members that someone was arrested in a lesbian bar. Lack of information about their rights together with the intense fear which the Argentinian police inspire in the majority of the population leads lesbians to comply with police orders without questioning them.

On April 15, 1995, the police raided Boicot (a lesbian disco) and arrested 10 of the women there. Mirta Molinari, a lesbian activist who was present on the occasion, reports that the police chose very carefully those they arrested. They chose the youngest and those who seemed to have the least economic resources. One reason for singling out the younger women is that it is illegal for people under 18 years of age to be present in nightclubs, and if any of the women were under age the police could close the establishment. (In this case, all were of legal age.) More importantly, the police presumed, as they often do, that the younger and apparently poorer women would be less informed and more easily intimidated.

The women were held for three hours and were subjected to verbal abuse. The police made fun of them and threatened to reveal their names and the fact that they were lesbians to the press. Some were told that there was still time for them to "change their ways" and get married and have children. The owners of the disco contacted Monica Santino, a lesbian activist, who put pressure on the police to see that they did not hold the women longer than was permitted by law. In the following days, the Frente de Lesbianas de Buenos Aires (Lesbian Front of Buenos Aires) launched a campaign in the bars to inform women of their rights and tell them what they should do if they were arrested. They also gave them the telephone number of a lawyer who has agreed to provide her services free of charge. In the event of future arrests, the Frente has set up a network of contacts to organize large and peaceful demonstrations to pressure the police into freeing the people arrested.

Another frequent practice in which the police engage is to discourage lesbians from going into bars or discos. They stand in front of these establishments and ask for identification or forbid women from "blocking the street."

DE FACTO DISCRIMINATION

The majority of acts of discrimination in Argentina take place outside of the legal framework. The following are two cases of anti-lesbian discrimination in the workplace. In 1993, C.M. was fired from her job as a primary school teacher after she had appeared in the news media as a lesbian. She had been a teacher for more than 20 years and was transferred to "administrative tasks" in another state agency. To date, she has not been allowed to return to teaching. Even though she has the support of colleagues in her new position, she cannot do the work for which she is trained, and which is her vocation, for the simple reason that she is a lesbian.

In another case, in December 1994, a teacher was accused of being a lesbian by one of her colleagues. The accuser had love letters the teacher had written to her. Although the teacher had worked in the school for 12 years, the directors of the school made her undergo a psychological examination. The examiners said she was unfit to be a teacher because of her "psychosexual immaturity." The teacher brought her case to the media, and an intense public debate ensued. Because of the pressure brought to bear by lesbian and gay groups as well as the publicity generated by the public debate, the accused was transferred to another school.[4]

As in the case of the arrests, the majority of lesbians who are the target of discrimination keep quiet, either out of shame or fear of the consequences, making it difficult to keep track of these acts of discrimination or to respond to them.

With regard to lesbian mothers who are seeking divorce, it is common for their husbands to force them into an out-of-court settlement with regard to the custody of children. To date, there have been no publicized court cases regarding custody for lesbian mothers. Most lawyers advise them to come to some sort of agreement with their former husbands since they have little chance of gaining anything by going to court. These agreements usually involve severe economic disadvantages for the mothers as well as leaving the possibility of seeing their children entirely to the discretion of their ex-husbands. Ana, who obtained a divorce in 1980, is one example of what can happen to lesbian mothers in these circumstances. She was forced to leave her home and all the community property accumulated during 12 years of marriage without any right of compensation. For more than five years her husband would not allow her to see her two children. Only when her children became adults and had decided on their own to reestablish contact with her did she see them again.

ECONOMIC ASPECTS OF DISCRIMINATION

Argentinian lesbians are part of an economic system in which women earn only 53% of what men earn. Unemployment is at 25%, and 22% of poor households in the country (30.6% in Buenos Aires) are headed by women. (Lesbians who live alone or in couples, with or without children, fit into this statistical category). The conditions for lesbians of middle, lower middle, or lower socioeconomic classes are particularly difficult. Many lesbians are obliged to live with their families for years because they do not have the economic resources to live alone. In these cases many choose to hide their lesbianism, and they live in constant fear of being discovered. Others are more open and are obliged to live with daily rejection and scorn on the part of their families. In middle and upper class families there is economic discrimination against lesbians; they are often denied their right of inheritance and are not offered the same economic assistance given to heterosexual members of the family.

LESBIAN ACTIVISM

Currently, there are five lesbian groups in Buenos Aires and three mixed groups with lesbian members.[5] Four lesbian activists appear with a certain frequency in the broadcast media, helping to increase the visibility of lesbians within society.

One of the lesbian groups, Las Lunas y las Otras (The Moons and the Others), has just rented a space in which to house a lesbian center. Since 1990, Las Lunas have been organizing an annual lesbian conference in Buenos Aires; approximately 100 women take part in its workshops and cultural activities. Last year, another group organized a "Day for Lesbian Art" open to the community. Lesbian artists presented their work. This event will be repeated again this year.

In addition, in the Faculty of Philosophy and Letters at the University of Buenos Aires, the Department of Human Rights hosts a seminar on lesbianism directed by lesbian activists. Lesbian activists also take part in the Encuentros Nacionales de Mujeres (National Women's Meetings). These meetings take place each year and from 8,000 to 10,000 women from diverse backgrounds and from all over the country take part. Lesbian workshops have been included in the official program of these meetings for the past three years. They are a very important point of contact with the women's movement and also an occasion to promote positive images of lesbians.

NOTES

1 Monseñor Quarracino has suggested that all lesbians and gay men should live together in a ghetto and called the community a "dirty stain on the nation's face." Claudia Selser, "A Quarracino que lo perdone Dios," *Página 12*, 30 August 1994. See also Claudia Selser, "La mancha del cardenal," *Página 12*, 23 August 1994.

2 Law No. 23,592, 1988.

3 Law No. 23,950, 1991. In reality this kind of check can be done in a matter of minutes using police computers.

4 Claudia Selser, "No te comerás las uñas: Dejan cesante a una maestra lesbiana," *Página 12*, 14 December 1994, and "'Me siento un trapo de piso': reincorporan a la maestra homosexual," *Página 12*, 15 December 1994.

5 The lesbian groups are convocatoria Lesbiana (Lesbian Call), Escrita en el Cuerpo-Archivo y Biblioteca Lésbica (Written on the Body-Lesbian Archive and Library), Frente de Lesbianas de Buenos Aires (Lesbian Front of Buenos Aires), Grupo de Madres Lesbianas (Lesbian Mothers Group), and Las Lunas y las Otras (The Moons and the Others). The mixed groups are Comunidad Homosexual Argentina (CHA-Argentinian Homosexual Community), Iglesia de la Comunidad Metropolitana (Metropolitan Community Church), and Sociedad de Integración Gay-Lésbica Argentina (Argentinian Society for Gay and Lesbian Integration).

ABOUT THE AUTHOR

Alejandra Sarda is a leo who was born in the year of the rat and is trying to survive her contradictions. She is a lesbian activist and is currently writing a book based on the lifestories of lesbians in Buenos Aires.

Austria

• • • • • • •

Barbara Fröhlich

BRIEF HISTORICAL OVERVIEW

In 1768, Austrian Empress Maria Theresia enacted the *Constitutio Criminalis Theresiana*, which provided, in paragraph 74, the death penalty for homosexual activities. The convict should, according to that paragraph "be exterminated from the earth by burning to death." Under Joseph II, who succeeded Maria Theresia, the penal codes were revised. The Austrian Code of 1787 distinguished between criminal and political felonies, and homosexuality fell within the range of the latter: "Somebody who disparages humanity to such extent as to decay in carnal desire with the same sex, is guilty of a political crime." Under this code, homosexuality was punished with imprisonment, forced labor, and flogging.

In 1803 this penal law was replaced with a new code in which "illicit practices against nature" were punishable with imprisonment for six months to one year. Section 129 of the Austrian code of 1852 increased the penalty for such "crimes" to imprisonment for one to five years, a sentence which could be extended to 20 years according to the severity of the case.

After the seizure of power by the Nazis (1933 in Germany, 1938 in Austria), so-called "Rosa Listen" (pink lists) of known gay men were drawn up. Many of these men were imprisoned in concentration camps, where they were identified with a "Rosa Winkel" (pink triangle). The persecution of lesbians was somewhat different. Along with sex workers, they were arrested under charges of demoralization of the troops, asocial behavior, and criminality. Many were kept in brothels or psychiatric hospitals. Others went directly to the concentration camps where they wore not the "Rosa Winkel" but the "Schwartzen Winkel" (black triangle) identifying them, together with sex workers, as asocial.

Article 221 prohibits both the establishment of lesbian and gay organizations and membership in such organizations.

LEGAL REFORM

The situation of lesbians in Austria after World War II was generally that of social repression and isolation. Though there were some attempts to organize groups, few spoke out publicly until the late 1960s. In 1971, Section 129, which criminalized homosexual acts, was repealed. However, protests from conservative circles and the church led to the adoption of four new articles which place restrictions on lesbians and gay men in their public and private lives:

• Article 209 dictates a higher age of consent for gay male sex. Men over the age of 19 are not allowed to be sexually active with men under the age of 18. (The age of consent for heterosexuals and lesbians is 14).

• Article 210 (which has since been repealed) prohibited male prostitution.

• Article 220 prohibits production and distribution of any material which presents homosexuality in a positive way.

• Article 221 prohibits both the establishment of lesbian and gay organizations and membership in such organizations.

Lesbian and gay organizations have formed despite these restrictive laws. In 1980, the first national lesbian meeting took place and since 1983, lesbians have met annually. While Articles 220 and 221 are rarely enforced directly to imprison lesbians or gay men, they do have several secondary effects. For example, in September 1990, Article 220 was used against two publications put out by Homosexuelle Initiative (HOSI), a Vienna-based lesbian and gay organization. The provincial court in Vienna seized the HOSI publications *Tabu* and *Lambda News*. *Lambda News* was seized by the authorities because of the following sentences: "From our own experiences we know that for young lesbians and gays, growing up believing they are the only ones with this 'problem' can be a very tough time. Isolation and weariness with life are often the result. Contact with kindred persons can help a lot." According to the judge, these sentences were promoting homosexuality and therefore in violation of Article 220.

Another example of the use of these provisions came in 1988. At the unveiling of a memorial to concentration camps victims, lesbian and gay activists wanted to draw attention to the lack of information and public awareness about homosexual concentration camp victims. A peaceful demonstration was held in Vienna with a banner bearing the words "1000e homosexuelle KZ Opfer warten auf ihre Rehabilitierung" ("Thousands of homosexuals are waiting for compensation"). The police violently interfered and confiscated the banner. The Constitutional Court ruled that "the carrying and prominent display of the banner—in itself an attempt to disturb the commemoration ceremony—warranted the action of the police in order to protect the event from interference." The court reminded members of HOSI that they could not claim to be exercising their right to free speech because Article 220 prohibited the promotion of homosexuality.

In another instance of censorship, lesbian activists met with a series of obstacles in their attempts to display a poster with the slogan "Lesbians exist always and everywhere." The conflict started in 1988 on

International Women's Day. Viennese lesbians and feminists wanted to draw attention to the situation of women through slogans displayed in public advertising spaces and commissioned an advertising firm to put up posters on trams. While 14 posters with the slogans "Power makes women powerful" and "The present time is feminist or it doesn't exist" were displayed on trams throughout Vienna for a whole month, the posters with the slogan "Lesbians exist always and everywhere" were not put on the trams. The advertising firm justified its refusal to carry out this part of the contract by citing national policy and public morals. Despite Article 220, a group of lesbians sued the advertising firm and won the suit. The advertising firm appealed the judgment, but in January 1990, the appellate court upheld the ruling. Although this judgment represented a triumph for lesbians in Austria, the posters were never seen by the public. The Viennese Traffic Management refused to display the slogan on the grounds that it would not be fair to female passengers, since, it argued, those reading the signs might assume that all the women on the train were lesbians.

SOCIAL POLICY

In terms of Austrian social policies, lesbians are subsumed under the category of "single women," regardless of the fact that many lesbians have long-term partners. The fact that their partnerships with other women are not acknowledged puts lesbians at a disadvantage under the Austrian legal system. For instance, Austrian fiscal law considers lesbians "single women," and lesbian couples are not granted the reduction in income tax that is granted to heterosexual married couples. The same situation can be found in the health insurance system: lesbians cannot be insured with their partners.

Under inheritance law, a lesbian's long-term partner does not exist. After the death of a partner, many lesbians suffer a loss that is often unacknowledged and at the same time may be confronted by a family claiming ownership of the couple's joint possessions. Lesbians also have no legal means to enter the tenancy contract of their deceased partner and are often forced to leave the apartment that they have paid for together. In the case of the paid caretaking leave for close relatives, although the phrasing is gender-neutral ("the person with whom the employee lives in a partnership"), there is still no paid leave for lesbians to care for their partners.

LESBIAN LIFE TODAY

HOSI Vienna, the oldest lesbian and gay organization in Austria, was founded in 1979 by gay men; in 1981, a lesbian group began meeting weekly in the HOSI center. In recent years a remarkable variety of groups have developed within the lesbian and gay community, including Homosexuelle und Kirche (Homosexuals and the Church), Judische Homosexuelle (Jewish Homosexuals), Rechtsgruppe (Legal Advice Group), and Lesben uber 30, (Lesbians over 30). However, there are still relatively few specifically lesbian groups in Austria. Many lesbians work within feminist organizations or within mixed lesbian and gay groups. While there are many places for gay men in Vienna, there are only a handful of places for lesbians to meet, and even fewer gathering places outside of Vienna.

Since the collapse of the communist regimes in Eastern Europe, Austrian society has becoming increasingly conservative. In all aspects of social and political life, xenophobia, homophobia, and anti-Semitism have once again become widely acceptable. The level of tolerance for verbal and even physical attacks on minority groups has become significantly higher. In these circumstances, the presence of discriminatory laws such as Article 220 becomes increasingly threatening to the human rights of lesbians.

ABOUT THE AUTHOR

Barbara Fröhlich is an activist with HOSI-Vienna, which was founded in 1979 and is the oldest lesbian and gay association in Austria.

Brazil

● ● ● ● ● ●

Míriam Martinho

Brazilian lesbians are subject to the same socio-economic conditions that impact all women in the country. Although they comprise 35% of the paid work force, Brazilian women continue to earn, on average, less than half the salary that men make for the same type of work; Black women earn half of what white women earn. This socioeconomic system makes it very difficult for most Brazilian women to take part in the decision-making processes that affect their lives. Under these circumstances, it is particularly difficult for Brazilian women to live openly as lesbians.

ATTITUDES WITHIN THE FAMILY

The majority of Brazilian lesbians hide their sexual orientation from their families and invent fictitious relationships or even marry in order to avoid the rejection of parents and relatives. Even when they are able to hide their lesbianism, many women experience tremendous stress resulting from the constant fear of being discovered or from the conflicts inherent in living a lie.

Um Outro Olhar (Another Perspective), a lesbian documentation center based in São Paolo, has received reports of lesbians being expelled from their homes or subjected to physical or emotional abuse when their families discover that they are lesbians. While it is illegal to disinherit a child, many parents disinherit their lesbian daughters, and many lesbians do not assert their rights because they are not aware of the law or are reluctant to publicly declare their lesbianism.

Many Brazilians still consider lesbianism a disease. Until they reach the age of 18, girls can be subjected to psychological treatments and behavior-modifying shock therapy without any legal recourse. Although homosexuality ceased to be classified by the Brazilian medical profession as a sexual deviation or psychological disturbance in 1985,[1] shock therapy, as well as prescribing tranquilizers, is still practiced as a "cure for lesbianism".

The discrimination and stigma that Brazilian lesbians experience can cause feelings of marginalization, anxiety, and isolation. If these feelings lead to alcoholism, depression, or (particularly among adolescents) suicide attempts, lesbians encounter little help from the psychiatric profession. Mental health professionals often try to convince lesbians to change their sexual orientation, worsening the situation rather than providing relief.

HEALTH ISSUES

The majority of gynecologists work under the assumption that every woman is sexually active with men. Women who openly declare that they are lesbians run the risk of being sent to a professional psychiatrist even if they are suffering from nothing more than a routine infection.[2] As a result, many lesbians forego routine examinations or lie to their doctors, which can sometimes result in incorrect diagnoses.

WORK

The majority of Brazilian lesbians lead a double life at work, engaging in fictitious relationships or arranged marriages as a survival strategy in the professional world. Sexual orientation can be a fundamental factor in both hiring and promotion in many fields, and psychological tests are sometimes administered to detect homosexuality in job candidates.[3]

With rare exceptions, the discovery of a woman's lesbianism leads to dismissal. In these situations, employers rarely cite their sexual orientation as the cause. This, combined with the unwillingness of most lesbians to speak out publicly, makes such cases extremely difficult to challenge.

THE LAW

Sexual relations between women are not prohibited by Brazilian law. There exist, however, a number of laws that can be used against lesbians:

1) Violent sexual assault (Article 214 of the Penal Code): "To coerce someone, using violence or serious threat, to practice or allow that a libidinous act with him/her distinct from a carnal union be practiced. Carnal union is understood here as heterosexual intercourse." Sentence: two to seven years in prison.
2) Sexual assault by fraudulent means (Article 216 of the Penal Code): "To induce an innocent woman by means of fraud, to practice or allow that a libidinous act distinct from a carnal union be practiced with her." Sentence: one to two years in prison, in the case where a victim is over age 18; from two to four years if the victim is under 18.
3) Corrupting a minor (Article 218 of the Penal Code): "Corrupting or facilitating the corruption of a person older than 14 and under 18 years of age, practicing libidinous acts with her or coercing her to practice them or witness them." Sentence: one to four years in prison.
4) Abduction (Articles 219-222 of the Penal Code) "To abduct an innocent woman using violence, serious threat, or fraud for libidinous aims." Sentence: two to four years in prison. If the woman in question is 14 to 21 years old, her family can allege that an abduction has occurred regardless of whether the woman acted under her own free will. Sentence: one to three years.
5) Obscene Act (Article 233) "The practice of an obscene act in a place that is public or openly exposed to the public." Sentence: three months to one year.

All of these statutes are subject to misuse and selective enforcement by police and other officials. Parents wishing to break up their daughter's lesbian relationship can accuse their daughter's lover of assault, abduction, or corrupting a minor, even when the relationship is consensual. Article 233, which outlaws "obscene acts," is often used by police against same-sex couples in situations which would never be considered criminal for heterosexual couples (for instance, kissing in public).

ANTI-DISCRIMINATION LEGISLATION

As a result of the struggles of the gay and lesbian movement in Brazil, some Brazilian cities and states have passed anti-discrimination laws. In large cities such as São Paulo, Rio de Janeiro, and Salvador, it is illegal to discriminate on the basis of sexual orientation. While these laws are of great symbolic importance, they do not penalize those who discriminate, which makes enforcement difficult. Furthermore, such laws are of limited use in the face of persistent prejudices in Brazilian society. There has not yet been a chance to test their application, because no one has been willing to risk the publicity that such a situation would entail.

Despite this legislation, many government and corporate policies continue to be discriminatory. Since the concept of a couple still remains restricted to a heterosexual pair, lesbians do not receive the same benefits—such as health care and pensions—that they would if they were married to men. When one member of a lesbian couple dies, the family of the deceased woman often attempts, and in general obtains, possession of the common property of the couple, because lesbian partnerships are not recognized by law.

In the realm of child custody, the courts often discriminate openly against lesbians. Lesbians who have children from previous marriages run the risk of losing custody of their children if their sexual orientation is revealed. Many lesbian mothers live with the constant fear of losing custody and are thus vulnerable to blackmail or extortion from their ex-husbands.

VIOLENCE

Lesbians encounter violence within and outside the family. Grupo Gay da Bahia (Gay Group of Bahia) has reported a number of cases in which women have been murdered for being lesbians. In 1991, 29-year-old Alice Dias do Amaral was brutally murdered by her lover's husband when he discovered that his wife was having a lesbian affair; newspaper coverage of the murder was inflammatory, with a front page picture in a Rio tabloid proclaiming that a "sapatão" ("big shoe," a derogatory term for lesbian) had been murdered.[4] In another case, Ana, a 23-year-old woman, was shot to death by her nephew in 1982 when she said that she was a lesbian.[5] In 1983, two lovers, Rita da Silva and Marly, were beaten and killed by Marly's relatives.[6] This violence must be viewed within the context of violence directed against all women, which in Brazil reaches alarming levels.

EDUCATION

Schools are, in general, inhospitable institutions for young lesbians. The educational system can help foster prejudices against lesbians by failing to provide information about alternatives to heterosexuality and perpetuating the heterosexual nuclear family as the only "natural" model. School administrators often stand by while intolerant classmates subject lesbian students to humiliation, mockery, and physical harassment.

In recent years, there have been two known cases in which young lesbians were expelled from school for being open about their sexual ori-

---

In large cities such as São Paulo, Rio de Janeiro, and Salvador, it is illegal to discriminate on the basis of sexual orientation.

---

entation. In 1993, a 19-year-old student at a branch of the Miguel Couto School in Rio kissed her girlfriend in front of the school and was booed and pelted with cans by other students as a result. The next day, when the student, Claudia, returned to attend class, she was informed by the directors of Miguel Couto that her enrollment had been canceled as a way to "protect her." Claudia, who herself feared future harassment, suggested a transfer to another branch of the school, but the directors denied her request. "She wasn't expelled. The directors concluded that her situation would become unbearable, and her physical well-being threatened," said Carlos Pavan, coordinator of the school.[7] In a 1994 case, a young North American lesbian who was studying in São Paulo through the Rotary Club Exchange Program was returned to her country of origin under the pretext of bad behavior.[8] In both cases, despite all evidence to the contrary, school administrators refused to admit that the students' sexual orientation was the reason for dismissal. As with cases of employment discrimination, discrimination within the educational system is difficult to prove, and most young women who face such discrimination remain silent about it out of fear and shame.

MEDIA

The media have often perpetuated stereotypes of lesbians and gay men, when they mention them at all. In recent years, however, this has begun to change. The print media are broaching the issue of homosexuality with increasing frequency, and many articles are written from a perspective of tolerance and acceptance. Nevertheless, the media still offer a public forum for those who wish to promote stereotypes and prejudices, such as religious authorities and mental health professionals. One can see in the media the striking contrasts that characterize Brazilian attitudes toward homosexuality: on one hand, the newspaper with the largest circulation in the country (*Folha de São Paulo*) sponsors a commercial on television which openly defends the acceptance of homosexuality. On the other hand, on a television channel owned by evangelists (TV Record in São Paulo), ministers preach the eradication of lesbianism by means of faith.[9]

POLITICAL PARTICIPATION

No woman has ever run for elected office in Brazil as an openly lesbian candidate. Research carried out on Brazilian public opinion has revealed that voters would not vote for a gay or lesbian candidate. However, some Brazilian politicians are becoming more supportive of lesbian and gay rights, as they discover that gay men and lesbians vote and are a growing political presence. Progressive individuals in various parties have begun to carry on the fight for human rights for gay men and lesbians by proposing anti-discrimination laws, by including gay and lesbian issues in their campaign platforms, and by supporting lesbian and gay organizations.[10] In general, however, political parties seek to avoid broaching such a controversial issue; even if individual politicians may be sympathetic to lesbian and gay concerns, they are wary of alienating conservative voters.

Within the party system, activism by gays and lesbians remains restricted to the Partido dos Trabalhadores (PT, Workers' Party), in which a small group of committed lesbian and gay members introduced the issue of freedom of sexual orientation into the platform of their candidate for presidency in 1994.[11] At the present time, the federal representative of the state of São Paulo, Marta Suplicy (PT), is considering the possibility of proposing an amendment to the Brazilian constitution to prohibit discrimination on the basis of sexual orientation. She is also considering legislation to recognize same-sex civil unions with the aim of guaranteeing social benefits and inheritance rights.

LESBIAN ORGANIZATIONS IN BRAZIL

Lesbian activism in Brazil began in 1979, when women started participating in the group Somos (We Are), Brazil's first gay and lesbian organization in Brazil. By 1980, however, the women's group within Somos became autonomous. It renamed itself Grupo Lésbico-Feminista (LF, Lesbian Feminist Group) and began to work primarily within the feminist movement.

LF disbanded in mid-1981, and several remaining members founded Grupo Ação Lésbica Feminista (GALF, Lesbian Feminist Action Group) which carried on the fight for lesbian human rights in Brazil until it disbanded at the end of 1990. During its years of existence, GALF produced 12 editions of the bulletin *Chanacomchana*. It also participated in international lesbian conferences, such as the Eighth Conference of the International Lesbian Information Service in Geneva in 1986, and the first meeting of Latin American and Caribbean feminist lesbians in Mexico the following year. The willingness of GALF member Rosely Roth to speak out publicly led to increased lesbian visibility on Brazilian radio and television programs at the national level in the mid-1980s.

In 1990, members of the disbanded GALF founded Um Outro Olhar information network. Um Outro Olhar collects and disseminates information about lesbianism, homosexuality in general, and feminism as a means of raising consciousness about lesbians and attaining the full rights of citizenship. Several other lesbian groups are now in existence in Brazil: Afins (Desire) in Santos; Coletivo de Feministas Lésbicas (Lesbian Feminist Collective), Deusa Terra (Earth Goddess) and Estação Mulher (Women's Season) in São Paulo; Colectivo de Lésbicas (Lesbian Collective) in Rio; and Grupo Lésbico da Bahia (Lesbian Group of Bahia) in Salvador.

These groups focus on both the women's movement and the national and international gay and lesbian movement. Lesbian activism in mixed lesbian and gay groups, such as Dignidade (Dignity) in Parana and Estruturacão Structure in Brasilia, has also begun to flourish.

CONCLUSION

From this brief overview of the condition of Brazilian lesbians, it can be seen that prejudice still greatly affects the life of many women in the country, depriving them of the basic rights of citizenship. In the large urban centers, there are at least some meeting places, such as bars and clubs, where lesbians can congregate and socialize. Far from the large cities, however, lesbians have few options. For lesbians in the interior of the country there is only the choice between a life lived in secrecy, with little emotional or sexual gratification, or the violence that can result from openly declaring that one is a lesbian.

NOTES

1 February 9, 1985, homosexuality ceased to be considered a sexual deviation or psychological disturbance in Brazil. The decision was recognized worldwide by World Health Organization on 1 January 1993.

2 Granado, Luiza, "Vivenciando nossa lesbianidade: saúde mental e gynecológica," *Um Outro Olhar* (São Paulo), No. 21, January-March 1994, p. 21.

3 "Empresas só aceitam homossexual que 'não dá banderia' na entrevista," *Folha de Sao Paulo*, 19 January 1992.

4 "Marido traído matou sapatão com 5 tiros," O POVO (Rio de Janeiro) 30 January 1991, p. 1.

5 Boletim do Grupo Gay da Bahia, N.27, March 1993. Information provided by Luiz Mott.

6 Boletim do Grupo Gay da Bahia, N.27, March 1993. Information provided by Luiz Mott.

7 "Manifestão Gay reprimida por estudantes," Folha de São Paulo, 13 January 1994.

8 "Intercambio 'devolve' americana," Folha de São Paulo, 8 May 1994

9 "Sem ética, programas de religião vendem a salvação como producto," Folha de São Paulo, 5 June 1993.

10 For example, the law proposed by Alderman Italo Cardoso, Worker's Party (PT), which would require information on real estate to be released to all prospective buyers regardless of race, sex, marital status, color, age, appearance, or sexual orientation.

11 On April 12, 1994, Luiz Inácio Lula da Silva, a well-known Brazilian politician and presidential candidate, declared to the church that he was not going to defend the rights to benefits of gay and lesbian couples. Members of the Gay and Lesbian Group of the Worker's Party sent out a bulletin on May 21, 1994, in which they declared that at a national meeting of the party homosexual rights were included in the party's program. "Lula se reúne com presidente da CNBB e diz que reconhecimento dos direitos de homossexuais também não sera tratado," Folha de São Paulo, 13 April 1994.

ABOUT THE AUTHOR

Míriam Martinho is co-founder of the first lesbian groups in Brazil: Grupo Lésbico-Feminista (1978-89), Grupo Acão Lésbica Feminista (1989-90) and Rede de Informação Um Outro Olhar (1990 to the present). She was the editor of the lesbian publication Chanacomchana (Woman to Woman) in the 1980s and currently publishes the lesbian magazine Um Outro Olhar (Another Perspective).

Britain

● ● ● ● ● ● ●

Anya Palmer

L esbian sex has never been illegal under British law. This leads
some to believe that lesbians, unlike gay men, do not face discrimination. This is, however, far from true. Legally, lesbians are
still denied basic civil rights and socially, discrimination and harassment
are still widespread.

DISCRIMINATION

Lesbians are not protected by law from discrimination or harassment
on the grounds of their sexuality. It is legal, and common practice, for
employers to provide pension schemes and other benefits to the partners
of heterosexual staff and to deny these benefits to the partners of lesbians and gay men. While there are comprehensive laws in existence
prohibiting discrimination on the grounds of sex and race, and legislation currently in progress that will make it unlawful to discriminate on
the grounds of disability, no legislation prohibiting discrimination on
the basis of sexual orientation has even been considered as a serious possibility.

There can be no doubt that legislation is needed. A 1993 survey of 800 lesbians published by Stonewall, a national lesbian and gay advocacy group, found that 8% of respondents believed that they had been dismissed from a position and 48% had been harassed because of their sexuality. Sixty-eight percent said they conceal their sexuality from some or all of those they work with. Only 10% said they had never concealed their sexuality at work.[1]

Government ministers have said on occasion that they deplore discrimination of any kind, but the government's own record as an employer suggests otherwise. It is government policy not to employ lesbians and gay men in the armed forces. The ban is actively enforced. Special investigation personnel are employed for the specific purpose of rooting out lesbians and gay men. Dozens of lesbians are dismissed every year, losing their careers and their pension rights. Lesbians are more likely to be thrown out than gay men: while women comprise only 10% of the armed forces, lesbians account for 26% of the discharges.[2]

> Karen Greig joined the Navy at 18 and did not at that age think of herself as a lesbian. During her 7 years in the Navy she never had a relationship with a colleague. Her one relationship was with a civilian woman off base. Karen's sexuality only became an issue after she told her commanding officer she had been raped by a fellow naval rating [enlisted man]. Some months later it was put to her that the reason she was "not coping well with the rape" was that she was a lesbian. When she eventually "confessed" to being a lesbian, she was interrogated for 10 hours over a period of 3 days. She was asked for names of other lesbians and asked for intimate details of her sexual relationships. Her room and all her personal possessions were searched and her address book and letters were taken as "evidence". She was then discharged for being a lesbian. At no point did the Navy offer Karen any counseling for the rape and following her discharge she had a nervous breakdown.[3]

This policy is currently being challenged by an application for judicial review and if that fails it will be challenged under European law in the European Court of Human Rights.

RELATIONSHIPS

Lesbian couples are not entitled to marry, nor are their relationships recognized on par with heterosexual domestic partnerships. Many lesbians are not interested in marrying, but the complete lack of recognition of same-sex couples causes many problems. For example, a great many lesbian couples face financial discrimination in pension schemes. They, or their employers on their behalf, pay the same contributions as everyone else, yet lesbians' partners receive no benefits if their partner dies first, whereas heterosexual partners receive a widow/er's pension for life.

Another example of legal discrimination is in the realm of immigration law. As immigration policy is applied in practice, heterosexuals can bring their spouse or common-law partner to live in Britain. Lesbians whose partners come from outside the European Community have no such right. Asked in May 1994 how he could justify such a policy, the then immigration minister, Charles Wardle, could only respond that "English law does not afford any legal status to homosexual relationships. Immigration practice in relation to homosexuals reflects this general position. It would be illogical to try to construct an immigration policy which did not accord with the general position."[4]

PARENTING

There are tens of thousands of lesbian mothers in Britain. Many, probably most, have children before they come out as lesbians, but an increasing number of lesbians are choosing to have children of their own, some by donor insemination, others through adoption or foster care. Lesbians wishing to adopt face legal barriers. Under the Adoption Act of 1976, only couples who are married are permitted to adopt, effectively ruling out unmarried or same-sex couples. In practice, however, it is possible for single people to adopt, and since the law regards all lesbians as unmarried, a few lesbians have been able to adopt in this way. However, there are only a very small number of children available for adoption each year and clear preference is given to married heterosexual couples.

Foster parenting is subject to different rules. In Scotland, regulations prohibit foster parenting by single people or unmarried couples. In England, Wales, and Northern Ireland, there is no legal bar, but lesbians wishing to be foster parents still face political and social barriers. It is up to each child-care charity or local authority to make its own policy on who may be foster parents. There is little to prevent local authorities or charities from adopting a policy which discriminates against lesbians and gay men, and in practice many do.

For example, in 1994 it was revealed that the Children's Society, one of the biggest child-care charities, had adopted a policy of refusing applications to be foster parents from lesbians or gay men. When lesbian and gay campaigners argued that this contravened government guidelines on foster parenting,[5] which say "it would be wrong arbitrarily to exclude any particular group of people from consideration,"[6] the Society replied that as a charity (rather than a local authority) it was exempt from those guidelines.

In recent years a number of local authorities have adopted nondiscrimination policies, but many lesbians and gay men applying to be foster parents in these areas find that in practice they go through long and thorough application procedures and eventually receive approval, but still don't have children placed with them. Even sympathetic local authorities are hesitant about such placements because if such a policy or placement becomes known to the media, the agency can find itself under intense media pressure to back down—a situation that is detrimental to both the child and the caregivers.

When lesbians do succeed in foster parenting it is often because they are willing to take on children who have problems such as a severe disability requiring extra attention and care or children who have been abused in the past and are traumatized as a result. Somehow with these children it has been possible to overcome the usual objections to lesbian caregivers, perhaps because such children are "hard to place" as most heterosexual couples don't want them, and the view taken is that any foster home is better for the child than remaining in the care of the state. This practice perpetuates two harmful prejudices: that children with disabilities are second-class citizens and that lesbian and gay foster parents are second-class caregivers. The success of these placements has had no impact on the general prejudice that lesbians are unfit to be parents, and healthy children, particularly those available for adoption, are still therefore "reserved" for "normal" married couples.

The extent of this prejudice is seen in sharp relief when one considers that there are currently 39,000 children in local authority care in

England and Wales. The majority of these children would rather be in foster care, but, according to the government, there is a shortage of suitable foster parents. Lesbians would provide an ideal pool of potential caregivers if the system did not discriminate against them. As things stand, it is much easier for a lesbian to have a child of her own than to become a foster parent, and that is what increasing numbers of lesbians are doing. It is the children left unwanted in children's homes who lose out.

PROMOTING HETEROSEXUALITY

A law passed in 1988, commonly known as Section 28, makes it unlawful for local authorities to "promote" homosexuality or to promote "the teaching…of the acceptability of homosexuality as a pretended family relationship." This law, which was the subject of a massive protest campaign by lesbians and gay men, has not led to a single court case, but it has undoubtedly had an effect on funding for arts and social initiatives aimed at lesbians and gay men. The law continues to have an arbitrary and uncertain effect. While many groups and projects have been relatively unaffected, some local authorities have withdrawn or refused funding for fear of breaching Section 28 and others have used Section 28 as an excuse. For example, the York Lesbian Line, an advice and counseling service, was asked to contribute to a display at the York Public Library to commemorate International Women's Week. Their contribution included an article from a national lesbian and gay newspaper about "coming out" and a magazine article on homosexuality. The local government decided that this part of the exhibit was illegal under Section 28 and had it removed from the library.

Section 28 also has immense symbolic importance as it clearly implies that homosexuality is not acceptable and that lesbian and gay relationships are not real family relationships. For the children of lesbian mothers this means the law says theirs is not a real family relationship, and if the school teaches otherwise then the local authority may be held accountable. Very little research has been done on the effect of this law, but its symbolic meaning is indisputable: it reinforces the government's view that lesbians and gay men are second-class citizens.

EDUCATION

The needs of young lesbians are still ignored by most schools. In 1993 Stonewall carried out a national survey of lesbians and gay men's experience of sex education. Three hundred lesbians responded. Two hundred and thirty-six, or 78%, had received sex education in school, but of those only 12 (5%) said that lesbianism had even been mentioned, and 11 of them said that the coverage of lesbianism was poor or very poor. Only one said the coverage was good.

One lesbian respondent in her twenties commented:

> Having tried to commit suicide twice under the age of 16, it breaks my heart to think there are those going through the education system right now, feeling alienated, confused and at odds with what they're fed as "the norm". It has to change. It's wrong. It hurts. Homosexuality just "is", it cannot be "encouraged". I will do anything to help change these ridiculous pathetic laws.[8]

The lack of good education in this area affects not only young lesbians and gays, but all children, fostering intolerance and prejudice and perpetuating discrimination.

VIOLENCE

Stonewall's most recent survey was on lesbian and gay men's experience of homophobic violence and harassment. Six hundred and thirty-

---

"I have moved 5 times in 2 years due to harassment."

---

five lesbians responded. According to the study's findings, 28% had experienced homophobic harassment at least once in the last five years. This included vandalism, graffiti about them, hate mail, threats, and blackmail. Thirty-one percent had experienced homophobic violence at

least once in the last five years. This included being beaten up; being
hit, punched, or kicked; having objects thrown at them; being assaulted
with a weapon; and other kinds of violence.

Two of the hundreds of personal stories received illustrate the problems many lesbians experience:

Sarah:

> I live in Eccles which isn't so bad, but I used to live on Salford
> Precinct which is quite rough. When I came home from work I
> used to get verbally and physically abused by gangs. My girlfriend
> stood up to them and we had a fight with these lads. We were
> both injured and so was a passer-by, a woman of 60 walking her
> dog. We reported it to the police and it went to court. We won
> the case, but it could have easily gone the other way. He even
> called my girlfriend a slag in court.
>
> We have since been called names and spat at and the police did
> nothing. We had to move in the end. We got an emergency move
> from the housing on harassment grounds. But it is a shame we had
> to move because of these small-minded people. We daren't even
> go shopping there for fear of more of the same.

Jane:

> I was married to a violent man for nearly 10 years. We split up and
> eventually divorced. I got involved with a woman and she moved
> in with me and my four children. My ex-husband found out and
> all hell let loose. I had to go to welfare courts to fight for custody
> of my kids as my husband said they were being perverted and they
> weren't safe. I was appalled by the welfare officer who told me to
> stand up and guarantee that my kids wouldn't turn out gay. It took
> months of pressure, stress and heartache but I won.
>
> I have moved 5 times in 2 years due to harassment and I have
> been very badly treated by the council. We have been shot at.
> Had dog dirt smeared up our front door and windows, even
> thrown through the windows. We've had eggs thrown at us, a lit
> candle posted through our door, a wall kicked down at the front of
> our house. Our cat was stabbed in the throat, dog had fat poured
> over him so we had to get rid of him. If we went out of the house
> we were verbally abused and stoned. Sex objects [were] posted
> through our door.
>
> I took photos and contacted the police but nothing was done

even though I knew one particular family who was involved but couldn't prove it. I saw local councilors who did nothing. I had letters put in the paper, still nothing. Now I have been moved by the council as an emergency as I had my windows smashed in, the council in the area I was living just wanted me out. I am not the problem, they are. I am the victim.

Fear of violence and harassment contributes to the continued invisibility of lesbians in society. Twenty-five percent of respondents said they never kiss or hold hands with their partner in public, and another 55% said they sometimes avoid doing so in order to avoid homophobic violence and harassment. As delineated in the UN Declaration on the Elimination of Violence Against Women (Articles 2 and 4), governments have a responsibility to end abuses even when they take place in the family and community. The police are slowly beginning to take homophobic violence more seriously, but the problem is that they can only tackle the symptoms, not the root of the problem. The root causes of violence are socially sanctioned discrimination against lesbians and gay men. As long as the government allows lesbians to be dismissed from their jobs without redress, as long as it continues to dismiss them from the armed forces, as long as it defines homosexuality as something that is not to be promoted (and implicitly, heterosexuality as something that is to be promoted), violence and harassment will continue to exist.

NOTES

1 Anya Palmer, "Less Equal than Others: A survey of lesbians and gay men at work," Stonewall, 1993.

2 Angela Mason, "Uniform Sexism," *Diva*, June 1994, p. 8.

3 *Ibid*.

4 *Hansard*, 4 May 1994, p. 825.

5 The government guidelines are binding on local authorities. They are not binding on charity agencies but are influential nonetheless.

6 The Children Act 1989: Guidance and Regulations, Volume 3: Family Placements, Section 3.14, H.M.S.O. 1991.

7 Section 28 of the Local Government Act of 1988: "(1) A Local Authority

shall not (a) intentionally promote homosexuality or publish material with the intention of promoting homosexuality; (b) promote the teaching in any maintained school of the acceptability of homosexuality as a pretended family relationship."

8 "Arrested Development," Stonewall survey on the age of consent and sex education, Stonewall, 1994.

ABOUT THE AUTHOR

Anya Palmer is deputy director of Stonewall, an organization which campaigns for equal rights for lesbians, gay men, and bisexuals in the United Kingdom. She is author of "Less Equal Than Others," a national survey of workplace discrimination.

Canada

● ● ● ● ● ●

Cynthia Petersen

PROTECTION AGAINST DISCRIMINATION

Canadian Charter of Rights and Freedoms

The Canadian Charter of Rights and Freedoms is part of the Canadian Constitution. Subsection 15(1) of the Charter provides as follows:

> Every individual is equal before and under the law and has the
> right to the equal protection and equal benefit of the law without
> discrimination and, in particular, without discrimination based on
> race, national or ethnic origin, colour, religion, sex, age or mental
> or physical disability.

In 1989, the Supreme Court of Canada ruled that the list of prohibited grounds of discrimination in Section 15(1) is not exhaustive and that analogous grounds of discrimination are implicitly prohibited by the Charter.[1] Subsequently, lower courts consistently ruled that "sexual orientation" is an analogous ground of discrimination because lesbians and gay men constitute a discrete and insular minority whose members have historically suffered social and political disadvantage.[2] The Supreme Court of Canada has yet to rule on whether sexual orientation constitutes an analogous ground of discrimination for the purposes of Section 15(1), but it will do so in a decision that is anticipated in the near future.[3] Most legal scholars believe that the Supreme Court will find in favor of lesbians and gay men on this issue, thus confirming that sexual orientation discrimination is prohibited by the Charter.[4]

The Charter does not apply to private relations, but it is nevertheless a very useful tool because it can be used to challenge the constitutional validity of legislation and of government actions. The Charter has been used successfully to advance lesbian rights in Canada. For example, it was used by Michelle Douglas to challenge the Canadian military's anti-gay policy; as a result, lesbians (and gay men) are now entitled to equal participation and equal treatment in the armed forces.[5]

It should be noted, however, that many courts have interpreted the implicit Charter prohibition against sexual orientation discrimination in a manner that restricts the scope of Section 15(1) and fails to prohibit discrimination against same-sex couples.[6] The Supreme Court of Canada will address this issue in an imminently forthcoming decision.[7]

Human Rights Statutes

Every province and territory in Canada has a human rights law that prohibits discrimination on the basis of enumerated grounds such as religion, race, sex, and disability. The Canadian federal government has a human rights law that similarly prohibits discrimination in areas of federal jurisdiction (e.g. interprovincial transportation, telecommunications, banking). These laws prohibit discrimination in employment and education and in the provision of services. Many of them prohibit sexual and racial harassment, in addition to various forms of discrimination, but none prohibits harassment on the basis of sexual orientation. Most provinces and territories have recently amended their human rights laws to include sexual orientation in their respective lists of prohibited grounds of discrimination,[8] but Alberta, Prince Edward Island, Newfoundland, and the Northwest Territories have refused to do so. The Canadian federal government has also failed to amend its law, despite repeated promises to do so over the past decade.

The failure to amend the federal human rights law has more symbolic than substantive weight, since the Ontario Court of Appeal ruled in 1992 that the government's failure to prohibit sexual orientation discrimination in the Canadian Human Rights Act (CHRA) violates the Charter equality rights of lesbians and gay men.[9] Thus the Canadian Human Rights Commission was ordered by the court to treat the CHRA as though sexual orientation were included among the prohibited grounds of discrimination. Similarly, in 1994, the Alberta Court of Queen's Bench ruled that the Alberta Individual's Rights Protection Act must be read as though it contains a prohibition against sexual orientation discrimination.[10] The latter decision is currently being appealed by the Alberta provincial government.

Human rights laws that are meant to protect lesbians are not always effective.

Despite widespread legislative protection against sexual orientation discrimination, anti-lesbian discrimination and harassment remains prevalent in Canada and the human rights laws that are meant to protect lesbians are not always effective. In particular, prohibitions against sexual orientation discrimination have been narrowly interpreted to deny protection to same-sex couples who suffer discrimination as a result of a failure to recognize and respect their relationships.[11]

RELATIONSHIP RECOGNITION

Provincial and Federal Legislation

There are hundreds of federal and provincial laws that define the term "spouse" in an exclusively heterosexual manner. Many of these laws confer economic and social benefits upon spouses. Unmarried cohabiting heterosexual couples are included in many, but not all, of these laws. Same-sex couples are excluded from all of these laws. The consequences of their exclusion are severe. For example, lesbian partners are not entitled to succession rights in any province in Canada (i.e., they cannot inherit their partner's property if the partner dies intestate). Similarly, lesbians cannot sponsor their foreign-born partners for the purpose of immigration to Canada.[12]

Lesbians and gay men have begun to challenge the constitutional validity of heterosexist definitions of the term "spouse." Only one such case has been successful, and it was a lower court decision that has subsequently been criticized by a higher court.[13] The Supreme Court of Canada will soon render a decision that will establish an important precedent for same-sex spousal cases involving Charter equality arguments.[14] A gay male couple is challenging the constitutional validity of the Old Age Security Act, which confers a spousal allowance on the opposite-sex spouses of elderly pensioners, provided that certain eligibility criteria are met. The younger of the two gay men qualified for the spousal allowance, but for the fact that he was of the same sex as his partner. When he was denied the allowance, the couple initiated a lawsuit. Their case has been winding its way through the Canadian court system for almost a decade. The decision of the Supreme Court of Canada is anticipated in 1995. The Court will address whether the Charter prohibits discrimination on the basis of sexual orientation, whether the Act discriminates on the basis of sexual orientation, and whether such discrimination (if it exists) is justifiable under the Charter.[15]

Employment Benefits

While very little progress has been made at the legislative level, lesbians and gay men have acquired significant recognition of their relationships in employment contexts. This has largely been due to the bargaining efforts of labor unions. Although many employers and insurers continue to exclude same-sex partners from plans that extend employment benefits to married and unmarried heterosexual spouses, many employers have recently extended their benefits plans to the same-sex partners of their employees. These include some municipal and provincial governments, some universities, some banks, and some large corporations, in addition to smaller employers. The employment benefits that are extended to same-sex partners include such things as insurance for dental care and extended health care. Employers who wish to extend survivor pension benefits to same-sex spouses have encountered difficulty because Canadian law requires the deregistration of any pension plan that extends spousal benefits to same-sex partners (registered pension plans enjoy preferential treatment under federal tax law); the constitutional validity of this aspect of the Income Tax Act is currently being challenged.[16]

FAMILY LAW

Relationship Breakdown—Property and Support Issues

Since same-sex spouses are not recognized in any provincial family law legislation, there are no laws to govern the dissolution of lesbian relationships. For lesbian couples, property division and spousal support are not mandated by law. There is, however, a common law doctrine that has been used by lesbians (and gay men) to acquire an equitable interest in property legally owned by their spouses.[17] This doctrine requires that the claimant demonstrate that she made a significant contribution (financial or otherwise) to the acquisition, maintenance, repair and/or improvement of the property in question, such that the property-owning spouse would be unjustly enriched if she were permitted to benefit from the contributions of the non-owning spouse. The non-owning spouse, if successful, can obtain an equitable interest in the property by way of constructive trust; the size of her interest will be proportional to her contributions to the property. Although the doctrine of constructive trust is useful, it does not amount to a guaranteed equal division of property (such as the law mandates for married spouses).

Although unmarried heterosexuals are covered by provincial spousal support legislation (provided that they meet a minimum period of cohabitation requirement), cohabiting same-sex couples are not entitled to support upon the dissolution of their relationships. There is a lesbian in Ontario who is currently challenging the constitutional validity of that province's family law legislation because it does not permit her to seek support from her ex-partner.[18]

The issue of child support is more complicated than that of spousal support because the provincial laws are somewhat ambiguous. Provincial laws clearly stipulate that every parent has an obligation to provide support to their needy children. In some provinces, the term "parent" is defined broadly, such that courts have imposed support obligations on men who, during the course of a relationship with a woman, demonstrate a settled intention to treat her child as a child of their family. Such support obligations have sometimes been imposed notwithstanding that the child's biological father already provides support for the child. A similar obligation could be imposed on a lesbian who has demonstrated a settled intention to treat a partner's child as a child of her family. This is particularly true since the Supreme Court of Canada has stipulated that child support is the child's right, not the custodial parent's right,[19] thus the sex and/or sexual orientation of the child's parents should not deprive the child of their right. However, each province's law is worded differently, which could give rise to differing interpretations. In the only reported case involving a child support claim by a lesbian mother, the judge ruled that it was not possible under the British Columbia family law legislation to seek child support payments from an ex-partner of the same-sex.[20]

Lesbians are not prohibited from entering into cohabitation agreements and/or separation agreements in order to resolve their support and property issues, but their contracts are not legally recognized as "domestic contracts." In some provinces, domestic contracts can be registered with provincial courts and the support provisions contained therein can be enforced as though they were contained in a court order (i.e., the payor's paycheck can be garnished if necessary). Lesbians who have signed a domestic contract can resort to the standard enforcement procedures that are available to anyone who enters into a valid contract, but they cannot benefit from the family law legislation enacted to facilitate the enforcement of support orders.

Child Custody and Visitation

Canadian courts have ruled that lesbianism is not a bar to custody and some lesbians have, indeed, obtained custody of their children, despite the heterosexist objections of the children's biological fathers. However, the judges' reasoning in those cases clearly reveals concern for the child's "normal" (read: hetero) sexual development. Thus a lesbian mother's chances of obtaining custody increase dramatically if she is closeted (i.e., if she is "discreet" about her sexuality, if the neighbors do not know that she is a lesbian, if she does not live with a same-sex lover, if she does not belong to lesbian organizations, if she is not "militant" about her sexuality, etc.).[21] Lesbians who are active members of lesbian communities or who are very open about their sexuality risk losing custody of their children to heterosexual fathers.[22]

As between lesbian ex-partners, the issues of custody and visitation have not yet been litigated in Canada. The few cases that have been initiated have been settled out of court. Custody provisions in family law legislation differ somewhat between provinces, but all provisions are supposed to be interpreted in accordance with the "best interests of the child." It should therefore be possible for non-biological lesbian mothers to obtain visitation rights or custody rights after the dissolution of a same-sex relationship, but given the court's discretion in interpreting what constitutes the child's "best interests," it is impossible to predict how such cases will be decided. In Ontario, one legal practitioner has successfully obtained joint custody orders for lesbian and gay couples who co-parent; these orders would presumably survive the dissolution of the parents' relationship.[23]

Adoption and Foster Parenting Rights

Individual lesbians are legally permitted to adopt children and to act as foster parents, but some lesbians have experienced heterosexism from children's aid workers and consequently, have not had children placed in their custody or care. The degree of heterosexism appears to vary considerably from region to region.

Lesbian couples cannot adopt children together, since provincial laws recognize the existence of only one father and one mother for every child.[24] A lesbian couple who want to adopt a child must therefore choose which one of them will assume the legally recognized role of mother. The unrecognized mother has no legal rights or obligations vis-à-vis the child, even if she is a de facto parent. The same problem arises when a lesbian wishes to adopt the biological child of her same-sex partner; provincial laws do not permit second parent adoption. In Ontario, a lesbian is currently challenging the constitutional validity of the provincial legislation that prohibits her from adopting her partner's children.[25]

In Ontario, some lesbian and gay male couples have obtained joint custody orders, which provide the non-biological parent with significant
legal rights (e.g., the right to make health care decisions in a medical
emergency and the right to accompany the child across international
borders).[26] These joint custody orders are useful but they do not amount
to full legal recognition of the non-biological parent (e.g., the child will
not inherit the property of the non-biological parent who dies intestate).

Donor Insemination and Sperm Donors' Rights

Lesbians are legally entitled to equal access to insemination services
in any province that has a human rights law that prohibits discrimination on the basis of sexual orientation.[27] Some lesbians have nevertheless suffered discrimination from doctors and hospitals that have anti-
lesbian policies. Currently, a couple in British Columbia is bringing a
human rights complaint against a Vancouver doctor who refused to provide them with frozen sperm from his private sperm bank because they
are lesbians.[28]

Many lesbians who conceive children through alternative insemination do so without seeking the assistance of medical doctors. Private
arrangements are common, with either anonymous or known sperm
donors. Frequently, agreements are signed with the sperm donor regarding support and visitation issues. The substance of the agreements varies
depending on whether the parties want the sperm donor to be involved
in some capacity in the child's life. Although such agreements are
becoming common, they have yet to be tested in court; there are not yet
any reported cases involving the validity and/or interpretation of such
agreements.

Same-Sex Marriage

Same-sex marriage is not permitted in Canada. Currently, two gay
men who were refused a license to marry in the province of Ontario are
challenging the constitutional validity of the common law principle
that prohibits same-sex marriage.[29] They lost at trial and their case will
be heard by the Ontario Court of Appeal in 1995. The case will likely
end up before the Supreme Court of Canada before the end of this century; a victory in the case could permit lesbians and gay men to marry

anywhere in Canada (since the validity of marriage falls within federal jurisdiction).

IMMIGRATION LAW

Refugees

In several cases, the Canadian Immigration and Refugee Board has granted refugee status to gay male immigrants because they have suffered persecution on the basis of their sexual orientation in their countries of origin.[30] At least one lesbian has similarly been granted refugee status.[31] These decisions have been made on a case-by-case basis and are not reported in a consistent fashion, thus it is difficult to compile accurate statistics. Some claimants have been denied refugee status in spite of their claims of persecution on the basis of their sexual orientation.[32]

Spousal Sponsorship

Same-sex partners are not recognized by federal immigration law. Consequently, lesbians are not permitted to sponsor their partners for the purpose of immigration to Canada.[33] Some foreign lesbians whose partners live in Canada have successfully obtained permission to immigrate based on compassionate grounds, but these cases have been decided on an ad hoc basis and have depended on the discretion of individual immigration officers. Permission to immigrate has occasionally been granted in the form of a ministerial permit, including one case in which the lesbian couple had initiated a law suit;[34] this suggests that the federal government was trying to avoid a Charter challenge to its immigration legislation. The current Minister of Immigration (Sergio Marchi) recently announced that he will no longer issue ministerial permits to lesbians and gay men who are seeking to immigrate to Canada in order to be reunited with their partners.[35]

CRIMINAL LAW

Sodomy

Lesbian sexual activity is not prohibited by the Canadian Criminal Code.

Censorship

The obscenity provision of the Criminal Code has historically been enforced in a manner that discriminates against lesbians and gay men. Lesbian and gay materials have been targeted by the police in anti-pornography raids; lesbian and gay bookstores and publishers have consequently been subjected to numerous criminal prosecutions.[36]

In 1992, the Supreme Court of Canada ruled that the criminal obscenity provision constituted a justifiable limit on freedom of expression.[37] The Court clarified the manner in which the provision should be interpreted, specifying that obscene materials are censored, not because they offend public morals, but rather because they are perceived to be harmful (particularly to women). Some feminists hailed the Supreme Court's decision as a victory since it defined obscenity in terms of the harm that it causes to women's pursuit of equality. Many lesbians, however, did not welcome the Supreme Court's decision; they suspected that the new harms-based approach to obscenity would not alter the conduct of the police forces that are entrusted with the enforcement of the Criminal Code. In fact, the first obscenity charge after the Supreme Court decision was laid against a lesbian and gay bookstore for carrying a lesbian magazine.[38]

Canadian customs officials have the power of prior restraint, which means that they can prevent materials from crossing the border if they believe that the materials violate the obscenity provision in the Criminal Code. This power has frequently been used to delay and seize multiple shipments of materials destined for lesbian and gay bookstores in Canada.[39] Little Sisters, a lesbian and gay bookstore in Vancouver, British Columbia, is currently challenging the constitutional validity of the powers bestowed upon Canada customs officials, alleging that the powers have been (ab)used to harass lesbian and gay bookstores and publishers.[40] The trial in the Little Sisters case ended in December 1994; a decision is expected in 1995.

Hate Propaganda and Hate Crimes

There is a provision in the Criminal Code that prohibits some forms of hate propaganda, but it does not proscribe hate propaganda directed at lesbians and gay men. Attempts to amend the provision in order to include anti-lesbian and anti-gay propaganda have consistently failed.

Lesbians and gay men in Canada are frequently the victims of hate-motivated crimes, including murderous assaults.[41] Currently, the federal government is considering an amendment to the Criminal Code that would enhance the penalties imposed on persons convicted of hate-motivated crimes. The proposed amendment includes hate crimes motivated by the victim's sexual orientation. The inclusion of anti-lesbian and anti-gay offenses in the proposed sentencing bill has generated a lot of controversy and is opposed by some vocal members of the federal government.

POSTSCRIPT

In May 1995, an Ontario provincial court judge ruled that the province's law on second-parent adoption was unconstitutional. As a result, four lesbian mothers were permitted to adopt their partner's biological children. Also in May 1995, the Supreme Court of Canada released its decision in the *Egan* case (discussed above). The Court ruled unanimously that sexual orientation is an analogous ground of discrimination under Section 15 of the Charter. Five judges ruled that the denial of a spousal pension to same-sex partners constitutes discrimination on the basis of sexual orientation and that the Old Age Security Act therefore violates Section 15 of the Charter. Only four judges ruled that the law was not discriminatory. The gay male couple nevertheless lost their case because one of the five judges who held that the law was discriminatory ruled that the discrimination was justified under Section 1 of the Charter.

NOTES

I thank Jan Cheney for her research assistance. This paper was completed on February 1, 1995. For information on subsequent legal developments, I can be contacted at: Sack Goldblatt Mitchell, 20 Dundas Street West, Suite 1130, Toronto, Ontario, M5G 2G8, Canada.

1 *Andrews v. Law Society of B.C.*, [1989] 1 S.C.R. 143.

2 See, for example, *Veysey v. Correctional Services of Canada*, (1990) 1 F.C. 321; *Brown v. B.C.* (Minister of Health) (1990), 42 B.C.L.R. (2d) 294 (B.C.S.C.); *Knodel v. B.C.* (Medical Services Commission), (1991) 58 B.C.L.R. (2d) 356 (S.C.); *Douglas v. Canada*, [1992] 58 F.T.R. 147; Haig v. Canada (1992), 9 O.R. (3d) 495 (C.A.); *Layland v. Ontario*, [1993] 14 O.R.

(3d) 658 (Div. Ct.); and *Vriend v. Alberta*, [1994] 152 A.R. 1 (Q.B.).

3 *Egan v. Canada* (1991), 87 D.L.R. (4th) 320 (F.C.T.D.), aff'd [1993] 3 F.C. 401 (C.A.). This case was appealed to the Supreme Court of Canada; oral arguments were made on November 1, 1994 and a decision is anticipated in 1995. See text accompanying notes 15 and 16, *infra*.

4 The Canadian federal government has, however, adopted the position that Section 15(1) of the Charter prohibits sexual orientation discrimination in only limited circumstances. See the Factum of the Attorney General of Canada in *Layland, supra* note 2, and the Factum of the Attorney General of Canada submitted to the Supreme Court of Canada in *Egan*, supra note 3 (on file with the author).

5 *Douglas, supra* note 3.

6 See *Egan, supra* note 4 and *Layland, supra* note 3. There are three cases in which Section 15(1) of the Charter was held to protect gay couples against discrimination: *Knodel, supra* note 2, *Leshner v. Ontario* (1992), 16 C.H.R.R. D/184 (Ont. Bd. Inq.), and *Clinton v. Ontario Blue Cross* (1993), 18 C.H.R.R. D/377 (Ont. Bd. Inq.). *Clinton* was reversed on appeal, [1994] O.J. No.903 (Gen. Div.) (QL). *Knodel* was not appealed, but it was criticized by the Federal Court of Appeal in *Egan*. *Leshner* was also not appealed, but it is only a Commission decision and therefore carries little weight as a legal precedent. See also text accompanying note 12, *infra*.

7 *Egan, supra* note 3. See also text accompanying notes 15 and 16, *infra*.

8 See, for example, An Act to Amend the Saskatchewan Human Rights Code, S.S. 1993, c.61, Sections 4, 5(1), 6(1)(2), 7(1), 8, 9, 10(1), 11(1)(2)(3)(4), 12, 13, 14, 15, and 18.

9 *Haig, supra* note 3.

10 *Vriend, supra* note 3.

11 See *Vogel v. Manitoba* (1992), 16 C.H.R.R. D/233 (Man. Bd. Adj.), aff'd, [1992] 90 D.L.R. (4th) 84 (Man. Q.B.).

12 See text accompanying notes 34-36, *infra*.

13 *Knodel, supra* note 3.

14 See *Egan, supra* note 4.

15 Section 1 of the Charter permits the imposition of "reasonable limits" on constitutional rights if the limits are "demonstrably justifiable in a free and democratic society."

16 *CUPE v. Canada*, Court File No. 79885\94, Ontario Court General Division.

17 See, for example, *Anderson v. Luoma* (1986), 50 R.F.L. (2d) 127 (B.C.S.C.).

18 See *M. v. H.* (1993), 15 O.R. (3d) 721 (Gen. Div.) and *M. v. H.* (1994), 20 O.R. (3d) 70 (Gen. Div.).

19 *Richardson v. Richardson*, [1987] 1 S.C.R. 857.

20 See *Anderson, supra* note 18.

21 See, for example, *Re Barkley and Barkley* (1980), 28 O.R. (2d) 136 (Prov. Ct.) and N v. N., [1992] B.C.J. No.1507 (S.C.) (QL).

22 See *Case v. Case* (1974), 18 R.F.L. 132 (Sask.Q.B.).

23 See Nicole Laviolette, "Family affair: providing joint custody for same-sex parents" *Capital XTRA* (27 January 1995): 13. The practitioner, Philip McAdam, can be reached at: 67 Daly Avenue, Suite 1000, Ottawa, Ontario, K1N 6E3, Canada.

24 See Stephanie Small, "Gays beat adoption hurdle," *Ottawa Citizen*, 22 May 1993, p. C1.

25 See Bruce DeMara, "New style activists in gay rights fight," *Toronto Star*, 3 January 1995, p. A14.

26 See note 24, *supra*.

27 See text accompanying note 9, *supra*.

28 See Richard Banner, "Lesbians refused AI," *Angles*, August 1993, p. 1.

29 See *Layland, supra*, note 3.

30 See Estanislao Oziewicz, "Homosexual granted status as refugee," *Globe and Mail*, 11 January 1992, p. A1, and Bruce Demara, "Gay Refugee Allowed to go Free," *Toronto Star*, 25 January 1995, p. A20.

31 She was a 27-year-old woman from Costa Rica who had been active in lesbian organizations. Her life had been threatened, her home had been vandalized, and she and her partner had been arrested and physically and sexually assaulted by police. She obtained refugee status in Canada in 1994. This information was obtained from her lawyer, Noël Saint-Pierre, who has represented numerous gay and lesbian clients in proceedings before the Immigration and Refugee Board. Information on the particulars of his client's cases can be obtained from him at: 917 est, avenue du Mont-Royal, Montréal, Québec, H2J 1X3, Canada.

32 See Eleanor Brown, "Gay man sent back to Brazil; stories of persecution can't be believed, immigration board rules," *XTRA* (Toronto), 15 October 1993. p. 1. See also note 32, *supra*.

33 See "Growing Old Together," brief of the Lesbian and Gay Immigration Task-Force to the Minister of Immigration, May 1992 (on file with the author).

34 See Rob Hughes, "Love across borders: Immigration of same-sex partners," *Outcomes* (1993), p. 32 (conference proceedings from the Outrights Conference held in Vancouver in October 1992).

35 "Marchi Buckles," Capital *XTRA*, 27 January 1995. p. 10.

36 See Chris Bearchell, "Gender Bender: Cut That Out!" *This Magazine*, January-February 1993, p. 36.

37 *R. v. Butler* (1992), 70 C.C.C. (3d) 129 (S.C.C.). See also note 16, *supra*.

38 *R. v. Scythes*, [1993] O.J. No.537 (Ont. Ct. Prov. Div.).

39 *Glad Day Bookstore v. Canada*, [1992] O.J. No.1466 (Gen. Div.).

40 Catherine Creede, "Lesbian Erotica Caught in Porn Net," *Herizons*, Winter 1993, p. 9.

41 See Cynthia Petersen, "A Queer Response to Bashing: Legislating Against Hate," 16:2 *Queen's Law Journal* 237, (1991).

ABOUT THE AUTHOR

Cynthia Petersen is a professor of law at the University of Ottawa who specializes in the area of lesbian and gay legal issues. She has been actively involved in lesbian and gay rights litigation and is currently on leave from the university to practice labor law at Sack Goldblatt Mitchell in Toronto.

Colombia

● ● ● ● ● ● ● ● ●

There are currently no lesbian organizations in Colombia. A lesbian group called Las Brujas (The Witches) sought to establish a presence in the feminist movement in the city of Medellin in the mid-1980s. However, the group is no longer active, and while informal lesbian social groups exist in various cities in Colombia, they are in no way public or politically active. This invisibility is evidence of the first and most undeniable form of discrimination: lesbians are not able to establish a public, visible community. The invisibility of lesbians is evident in the law, in the women's movement, and in many spheres of Colombian society.

THE LAW

Although the Constitution of Colombia does not explicitly recognize sexual choice as a fundamental right, Article 16 states that all citizens of Colombia have the right to "personal and family intimacy," and the right to develop their own personality.

The legal status of domestic partnerships was recognized in 1990, giving long-term unmarried couples the same conjugal and inheritance rights as married couples.[1] However, this law defines such couples as consisting of a man and a woman, and thus excludes same-sex couples, echoing Article 42 of the constitution, which defines "family" in a similar way. This distinction has far-reaching effects. For instance, if a lesbian dies, her female partner has no right to receive the benefits that the law provides for surviving heterosexual partners.

A recent case illustrates the difficulties that lesbians face in the Colombian legal system. In Colombian prisons, heterosexual inmates (whether married or not) are allowed intimate visits with their partners. In September 1994, Martha Lucia Alvares, an inmate in La Badea prison in Pereira, requested permission to receive such a visit from her female lover. Her lover received initial clearance from the Prosecutor's office, but prison administrators refused to comply, and the case went before a judge. The judge expressed the opinion that the denial of conjugal visits violated her rights under the Colombian Constitution, but would not rule on the case because there was no written evidence that prison administrators had violated her rights.[2] The case was appealed to Superior Court, which declined to hear it, and in June 1995, the Constitutional Court also declined, thus exhausting all possibilities for appeal within Colombia. Alvarez, who formed a human rights group within the prison, was harassed by prison authorities and denied visitors of any sort; many of the women who were active in the group have been moved to other facilities.

SEXISM WITHIN THE GAY COMMUNITY

In Colombia, the term "homosexual" has a fundamentally masculine frame of reference. Colombian society denies women the exercise of sexuality for pleasure. Even in gay publications, both the text and the illustrations are profoundly sexist. Lesbianism is generally invisible in the mainstream press and in the gay press as well.

With few lesbian and gay organizations and widespread prejudice within Colombian society, bars are the only public spaces in which lesbians and gay men are able to socialize. In Bogota there are over 50 bar that gay men patronize. Few, however, have significant numbers of women patrons. Several of the gay bars actually exclude lesbians; gay men in such establishments often openly express their disdain for women. In general, if any problems arise between men and women in gay bars, it is the women who are forced to leave. Thus, lesbians are denied access to the only public place in which they can gather. This forces women to retreat to more private venues, further diminishing their possibilities for establishing a community or organizing politically.

The Colombian Association of Lesbians and Homosexuals was founded in July 1994. Although the Association's policy stresses the equal participation of men and women, the organization is predominantly male, and the needs of lesbians have on the whole been marginalized. Some of the lesbians who have been involved are currently holding meetings with a view toward establishing a lesbian organization.

DISCRIMINATION

Discrimination against lesbians in Colombia is part and parcel of the general discrimination against women in a male-dominated society. Unfortunately, this bias against lesbians can be found even among

---

Inside the women's movement, lesbian existence is no longer denied, but neither is it fully acknowledged.

---

women who think of themselves as the defenders of women's rights and opportunities. Inside the women's movement, lesbian existence is no longer denied, but neither is it fully acknowledged. Although there is currently a great deal of discussion regarding sexual rights, emphasis is for the most part on reproductive rights and lesbian issues remain on the margins.

Interviews conducted with a number of lesbians revealed a range of responses that women have encountered when they acknowledge their lesbianism to others. Some women reported that friends, particularly those who have been involved with the women's movement, responded with support, respect, and acceptance. However, many of the women interviewed reported physical and psychological aggression from male family members, constant interrogation, and acceptance only on the condition that their sexual orientation was never mentioned or revealed to other members of the family. Some women report having been thrown out of the house by their family.

Out of fear of such reactions, the majority of lesbians lead a double life and avoid the few places that lesbians are known to congregate. They remain isolated, invisible to society and to each other. This invisibility means that the concerns of lesbians—their health, education, economic situation, and so forth—are ignored in public life. Under these conditions, it is very difficult for lesbians even to form organizations which would allow them to support and help one another.

NOTES

1 Law 54 of 1990.
2 Letter from Blanca Delia Díaz Saray, Director of the Women's Prison, to Martha Lucia Alvarez Giraldo, 5 February 1995, on file with the author and the International Gay and Lesbian Human Rights Commission.

ABOUT THE AUTHOR

Elsa Rondón is an activist in the Colombian feminist movement and is involved in organizing a lesbian group in Bogota.

Estonia

● ● ● ● ● ● ●

Lilian Kotter

There is no historical evidence concerning the presence of lesbians or lesbian groups in Estonia before World War. II. Neither female nor male homosexuality was punishable; the article outlawing male sodomy was introduced to Estonia directly from the penal code of the Russian Federation immediately after the Soviet occupation in 1940.[1] While lesbians were not specifically named in the law, this did not mean that they were free to express their sexuality. Few people of any sort were able to live their private lives freely. Sexual liberation, even for heterosexuals, was regarded as something which promoted individuality and was considered threatening to a totalitarian society.

At the end of the 1980s, thanks to the opening up of Soviet society, the silence around questions of sexuality—including homosexuality—was broken, and women identifying themselves as lesbians had new opportunities to organize. Although lesbian and gay life was still largely invisible, discussions about homosexuality have helped shift popular attitudes towards tolerance. The economic difficulties of making the step from totalitarianism to a market economy and civil society have been more "vital" problems than homosexuality. However, many Estonians understand the concerns of lesbians and gay men because they can

see the parallels to the repression that all Estonians experienced during
the years of Soviet occupation.

SOCIAL CLIMATE

Compared to neighboring Latvia and Lithuania, Estonia is relatively
tolerant of sexual minorities. The first study of attitudes toward homosexuality in Estonia, carried out in 1990,[2] found diverse opinions among
Estonian students. Approximately one half of the people questioned in
the survey expressed the view that homosexuality was either a disease or
an abnormal form of sexuality. However, the majority objected to the
isolation of lesbians and gay men from society. One third of the respondents said that they considered homosexuals to be normal people who
have been unjustly deprived of human rights. Approximately one fourth
of respondents expressed outright condemnation of homosexuality. Attitudes toward lesbians were generally less hostile than attitudes toward
gay men. It should be taken into account that the attitudes expressed
were merely theoretical, since only a few of the respondents reported
having had any direct contact with people they knew to be lesbian or
gay.

Most material on homosexuality published in the last five or six years
in Estonia has been relatively positive. There have been a few homophobic attacks but they are usually followed by protests. In May 1990, a
conference entitled "Sexual Minorities and Society in 20th Century
Europe," the first of its kind in Eastern Europe, was held in Tallinn, the
capital of Estonia. The conference and its subject received positive and
encouraging press coverage.

LESBIAN ORGANIZING

During the conference, Estonian lesbians met for the first time with a
group of lesbians from another country (Finland). The Estonian Lesbian
Union was established at this meeting; it was the first such organization
to be formed in the Baltics. Through an interview in an independent
newspaper and an interview with the chairwoman of the Estonian Lesbian Union on Estonian television at peak viewing time the group's formation was given prominent coverage.

The ELU has never had its own office space, which has greatly limited its activities. Nevertheless, for nearly five years the ELU has arranged lesbian and mixed (lesbian and gay) parties as well as some fundraising events. Recently, the ELU has arranged sports activities for lesbians. Advertisements about certain events as well as information about the ELU's telephone hotline have been published in newspapers, which has kept the ELU visible in the local media. Members of the ELU have often been interviewed by the local press, and the information leaflet for lesbians started by the ELU is developing into an information bulletin.

In December 1992, a regular lesbian hotline was started, operating twice a week on Thursdays and Saturdays for three hours at a time. The organization also maintains a modest library consisting of books, periodicals, conference papers, educational materials, and information about lesbian and gay groups in other countries.

Since March 1993, the ELU has been an officially recognized Estonian non-governmental organization. As of March 1995 the ELU has a

***

While the ELU represents a significant step forward in forming a lesbian community, many lesbians remain isolated.

***

mailing list of nearly 200 lesbians and bisexual women, who are of diverse ages, occupations, and educational backgrounds. Transgendered people in Estonia also contact the ELU and take part in events. Although there is no mixed organization for lesbians and gay men, this has not prevented actual collaboration.

While the ELU represents a significant step forward in forming a lesbian community, many lesbians remain isolated. Lesbians in Tallinn have few public places in which to socialize. In April 1993, a mainly female bar opened in the center of the city, but it unfortunately closed after only six months. Lesbians living in small towns have even fewer options for coming into contact with other lesbians.

PARENTING

Since the end of the last century the number of single women in Estonia has been remarkably high, and no great social pressures exist for women to get married. It is possible for a single woman to adopt a child if she has a regular income and is able to provide for a child's needs; it is also possible for single women to undergo donor insemination.

In a 1993 divorce case in Tallinn, a man sought custody of his two children on the grounds that his ex-wife was a lesbian and lived with her female partner. The lawyer objected, indicating that the law does not mention lesbians and therefore provided no justification for refusing the wife custody of her children. The mother retained custody of the children and is raising them with her companion.

DISCRIMINATION

There has been no government harassment of activists in the 1990s and no problems with registering lesbian groups or publications. Some years ago there were attacks on a lesbian household in the countryside, but such cases are infrequent.

There are only a few reported cases of employment discrimination, but this reflects the fact that few lesbians are open about their sexual orientation rather than indicating a positive situation for lesbians in the workplace. The majority of lesbians do not reveal their sexuality at work; they may suffer only minimal discrimination as single women, but as outspoken lesbians they would likely encounter negative consequences.

As this example illustrates, Estonian lesbians are able to live their lives in a climate of relative tolerance but only within certain limits. There is little stigma attached to being a single women, and many lesbians can thus live their lives without constant pressure to get married. However, Estonian lesbians still have a long way to go in building a strong, visible community.

NOTES

1 Russian Penal Code, Art. 121: "Sexual relations between men [man lying with man] shall be punishable by incarceration for a period of up to five years." Quoted in Masha Gessen, *The Rights of Lesbians and Gay Men in the Russian Federation*. San Francisco: International Gay and Lesbian Human Rights Commission, 1994, p. 9.

2 Ivika Nogel, "How Homosexuality Is Regarded among Students in Current Estonia," *Sexual Minorities and Society: the Changing Attitudes Toward Homosexuality in 20th Century Europe. Papers presented at the International Conference in Tallinn May 28-30, 1990. Udo Parikas and Teet Veispak, eds. papers on the History of Sexuality, No. 1 Tallinn: Institute of History, pp. 115-121.*

ABOUT THE AUTHOR

Lilian Kotter, 39, is a veteran of the Estonian lesbian and gay movement. She was one of the founders of the Estonian Lesbian Union in 1990. She is the chairwoman of the ELU and coordinator of the ILGA Phare/Tacis Lesbian and Gay Anti-Discrimination Project in Estonia.

Germany

● ● ● ● ● ● ● ● ●

Alexandra Duda and Maren Wuch

Although Germany has an increasingly vibrant lesbian subculture, lesbians remain targets of physical violence as well as more subtle forms of unfair treatment, including ignorance of lesbians' specific needs by state agencies and other service providers. Discrimination against lesbians is often ignored or tolerated in ways that human rights violations against other groups in society are not. For example, Steffen Heitmann, who campaigned for the post of the Federal President of Germany in 1994, once wrote: "Despite all of the openness regarding homosexuals one must not forget that the genetic code of people is heterosexual and that homosexuals will always remain a minority and hence must accept the resulting disadvantages."[1] While Mr. Heitmann's remarks about foreigners and the German Nazi past were widely criticized in public, this remark was never condemned or even noticed outside the lesbian and gay community.

In recent years the German media seem to have "discovered" lesbians. Talk-shows, newspapers and magazines often touch on lesbianism. However, in most cases the subject is treated in a sensational way.

Reports are often biased and show lesbians as polygamous, exotic, sexualized objects. Lesbians are also rarely represented on their own, but rather together with gay men. While there are many similarities and areas of cooperation between lesbians and gay men, this approach fails to consider that in addition to homophobia, lesbians encounter further difficulties because they are women living in a male-dominated society.

Such visibility has not greatly reduced the societal pressures on individual lesbians to remain "in the closet," and the socialization of girls leaves little room for considering alternatives to heterosexuality. Girls who come out to their parents are often subjected to emotional and financial pressures to conform to heterosexual norms of marriage and childbearing.

LAW

In Germany, consensual sexual relations between women have never been prohibited by law.[2] This may be because women's sexuality in and of itself was not taken seriously, and thus lesbianism was never perceived as being as "threatening" as male homosexuality. There are no federal laws in Germany prohibiting discrimination on the basis of sexual orientation, but the Brandenburg Constitution, applicable only in Brandenburg, does provide such protection within the state.

Many lesbian and gay organizations lobbied for the inclusion of prohibitions against sexual orientation discrimination in the federal constitution when it was amended in 1994. However, while these efforts received support from many Social Democrats and members of the Green Party, the conservative Christlich-Demokratische Union/Christlich-Soziale Union (CDU/CSU) argued that such a paragraph would "dilute the constitution" and that "sexual orientation" is not defined and could include forms of sexuality such as "pedophilia and excessive sadomasochistic acts."[3]

PARTNERSHIP

There is no legal recognition in German law for lesbian partnerships. In August 1992, 200 lesbians and gay men who tried to "marry" were rejected by local marriage license bureaus, which cited a 1966 Constitutional Court decision defining marriage as a "relationship between a man and a woman."[4] The case law of lower courts varies from support of same-sex marriage to complete rejection of it. Test cases were brought to the Constitutional Court. While interpreting the right to marry as an exclusive right for heterosexual couples, the court suggested that Parliament adopt legislation recognizing non-married couples.

Same-sex partners do not have many of the rights and privileges that married heterosexuals have, such as social security benefits and reduced income and inheritance tax. Nor do they have rights that have been recognized for non-married heterosexuals, such as the right of the surviving partner to retain possession of an apartment in the event of that one member of the couple dies. In the course of amending the federal constitution, a proposal was introduced to expand the protection of marriage to long term partnerships. It failed due to the opposition of the CDU/CSU, which stated that it "respects non-marriage cohabitations but rejects their legal equalization with marriage."[5]

If lesbian mothers manage to retain custody, their female partners have no rights whatsoever with regard to the children.

CHILDREN

Under current adoption regulations, married couples and single people are permitted to adopt children. Lesbians are not able to adopt children as a couple, and it is virtually impossible for lesbians to adopt children even as single women if their sexual orientation is known.[6] Donor insemination is available only to married women, and lesbians who want to have children are forced to find doctors abroad. Lesbian mothers are often denied custody rights by the courts on the grounds that their lifestyle is "immoral." In a 1988 case that removed a 10-year-old boy from the custody of his mother and her female partner, the psychological report ordered by the court recommended that the father receive sole custody so that the boy would be in a better position to develop his sexuality and his male identity. Another court decision in 1988 stated that it would be "irresponsible to let a child of school age be brought up by a homosexual couple."[7] If lesbian mothers manage to retain custody, their female partners have no rights whatsoever with regard to the children.

CHURCH

Religious institutions are an important employer for people working in the field of social services. Catholic institutions are free to discriminate against their lesbian employees in that they may discharge them if they do not observe the morals and norms of the church. As a result, to work in such institutions lesbians must remain silent about their identity.

The Evangelical Church has initiated a dialogue in the last several years on the subject of homosexuality and has stated publicly that lesbians and gay men should be more fully integrated into communities and that prejudices should be broken down. Openly lesbian pastors are, for the most part, tolerated. However, even though the relationship between the church and openly lesbian women is slowly improving, lesbians are still not treated equally. For example, the partners of lesbian pastors may still not live in church-sponsored housing, while the spouses of heterosexual pastors can.

For the past fifteen years an ecumenical group of lesbians and gays called Homosexuelle und Kirche (HuK, Homosexuals and the Church) has sought to break down prejudices within the church. In addition, there is a group in Berlin called Lesben und Kirche (LuK, Lesbians and the Church) which is open to all lesbians, whether ordained or not, and Maria und Martha (MuM, Maria and Martha), a network of lesbians employed by the church. The Catholic Church has vocally opposed such groups. When HuK held a service to celebrate their fifteenth anniversary in May 1995, a spokesperson for the Archdiocese of Cologne responded that the organization violated basic principles of Catholicism and thus had no place in the church.[8]

ASYLUM

In 1988, the German Federal Court of Justice recognized persecution on the basis of sexual orientation as a valid ground, under certain circumstances, for granting refugee status. This pronouncement by the German Federal Court has the virtual effect of law, but is also subject to interpretation. Those who apply for asylum must substantiate that homosexuality is a driving component of their personality and identity. Should there be doubt as to the irreversibility of an applicant's sexual orientation, a psychological evaluation may be obtained.[9]

The Federal Administrative Court has determined that asylum based on sexual orientation may be granted if the applicant is threatened in her country of origin by severe and unbearable penalties not acceptable from the viewpoint of German law. Discriminatory laws in the country of origin are not sufficient proof, nor is the threat of death. Before a decision on the application is made, the court seeks to obtain information on the country in question, and the applicant must establish that homosexuality is equated with possessing dissident political opinions. If the persecution is by non-state agents, the applicant must demonstrate that the government denies protection to the affected persons. The decisions regarding asylum for lesbians and gay men have been inconsistent. A deciding factor in such cases is how much tolerance a particular court has for matters relating to homosexuality.[10]

VIOLENCE AGAINST LESBIANS

Violence by right-wing extremists has increased in Germany in recent years, and lesbians have been a target for their aggression. Consequently, the more lesbians become visible, the more they are threatened. Still, such violence frequently goes unreported. Many victims fear that reporting such an incident would result in their having to publicly reveal their lesbianism.

LESBIAN INSTITUTIONS

Lesbian institutions in large and medium-sized cities have undergone considerable development in the last 10 years. In addition to an ever-growing bar and disco culture, whose main goals are mostly commercial, many cities have increasing numbers of meeting places with social, political, or cultural purposes. These venues are run mostly in cooperation with heterosexual women or gay men. The last five years has brought greater specialization among lesbian groups and associations. Lesbian sport leagues have formed, as well as dance clubs, choirs, theater, rock groups, and much more. Counseling services sensitive to the needs of lesbians have also become increasingly available. Many groups have been founded in order to give voice to specific interests and needs within and outside the lesbian world, bringing together groups of deaf lesbians, Afro-German lesbians, lesbians with children, lesbians over 40, lesbian businesswomen, and many others. In 1987 the Lesbenring, a nationwide association of lesbian groups, was established. However, this subculture is limited to urban areas, and lesbians in villages and rural areas remain isolated from one another.

NOTES

1 *Tageszeitung*, October 1993.

2 From the late 19th century until 1969, male homosexual relations were criminalized. In 1969, the total ban was replaced by Article 175, which established a higher age of consent for sex between two men (18) than for sex between two women (14) or between a woman and a man (14). In 1994, Art. 175 was superseded by Art. 182, which set an equal age of consent (16) for hetero- and homosexual relations.

3 Letter to Alexandra Duda from Susanne Rahardt-Vahldieck, CDU/CSU Member of Parliament, 26 March 1993.

4 BverfGE 10,59/66.

5 *Frankfurter Allgemeine Zeitung*, 12 October 1994, p. 9.

6 Article 174 of the Civil Code, cited in Kees Waaldijk, *Tip of an Iceberg: Anti-Lesbian and Anti-Gay Discrimination in Europe, 1980-1990* (December, 1991 draft). Utrecht: Interfacultaire Werkgroep Homostudies, Rijksuniversiteit te Utrecht, 1991, p. 24.

7 Both cases cited in Waaldijk, *Tip of an Iceberg*, p. 41.

8 *Kölner Stadtanzeiger*, 30 May 1995.

9 For example, in the case of an Iranian lesbian who applied for asylum, a gynecologist provided expert testimony stating that her lesbianism was irreversible.

10 *Homosexualität als politischer Asylgrund?* Berlin: Referat für gleichgeschlechtliche Lebensweisen. Pamphlet No. 11, Summer 1994.

ABOUT THE AUTHORS

Alexandra Duda, 25, has been working with the Lesbian and Gay Liberation Front—Cologne and the International Lesbian and Gay Association (ILGA) for four years, focusing on human rights issues for gays and lesbians in Europe and lobbying European institutions.

Maren Wuch, 30, has been an ILGA activist for six years, partly as a member of the Action Secretariat. Her main interests are human rights and cultural issues.

Hong Kong

● ● ● ● ● ● ● ● ● ●

Anson Mak, Ken Hui, Joanne Poon, and Mary Ann King

The cultural, historical and socio-political differences between Hong Kong and the West leads to a very different reality for lesbian and bisexual women. Sexuality, in a western sense, has not been highlighted in Chinese "his"tory. There is not much emphasis on the concept of sexual identities, but rather on sexual behavior. This makes it hard to mobilize lesbian and bisexual women for a socio-political movement or even to organize around issues of human rights and women's sexuality.

By looking at some aspects of the early stages of the lesbian and gay movement in Hong Kong, we can see some of the dynamics of the situation of lesbian and bisexual women and their current issues.

DECRIMINALIZATION

Homosexual acts in private places, between consenting male adults age 21 and above, were successfully decriminalized in Hong Kong in 1990-91. Buggery, gross indecency, and charges of nuisance and injustice have since then been abolished. In many respects, this legal reform is inadequate. Love motels are not considered private places, and the age of consent for sex between gay men (21) is higher than that for heterosexuals (18). Further, these changes decriminalized homosexuality, but did nothing to protect against discrimination based on sexual orientation. Finally, throughout the entire process, lesbianism was marginalized and treated as if it were nonexistent. Yet the significance of the legal reform should not be diminished, according to Julian Chan, the activist behind the lobbying process.

Chan recalls the period of the '70s-'80s as a time when homosexuality was a social taboo and gay meeting places were often raided by the police. Social bias linked homosexuality with decadence, perversion, immorality, deviance, and caucasian dominance. Incidents such as the suicide of an expatriate British gay officer, the homicide of a local gay businessmen, and the discovery of a substantial gay population in the civil service made decriminalization a public issue. It took until 1988 to get decriminalization on the legislative agenda, and public opinion was divided on the issue. The Tiananmen Square massacre in Beijing in June 1989 increased turmoil in the public mind and diverted attention from the issue, but by 1990-91 the decriminalization bill was finally passed due to the strength of human rights arguments.

Acknowledging human rights and privacy as aspects of homosexuality is one step toward gradual social acceptance. In the wake of decriminalization the lesbian, bisexual, and gay community has been more expressive. Apart from the social scene—gay pubs, saunas, discos and karaoke—the activist arena has seen the growth of lesbian and gay advocacy and social clubs, such as the Hong Kong 10% Club and Horizons.

Lesbians have been empowered by the formation of lesbian subgroups within these groups. Critics have argued from the beginning that the battle for decriminalization has totally neglected lesbians. To be sure, the British legal system (Hong Kong remains a British territory until 1997) is patriarchal in its historical construction, and decriminalization is merely a remedy to mitigate injustice in laws concerning buggery and gross indecency; lesbianism has never been forbidden because it has been understood to be "nonexistent" as a legal problem. Yet even so, the spill-over effect of decriminalization can still provide the basis for lesbian organizing to take off.

QUEER ORGANIZATIONS

There were no groups specifically for lesbians or bisexual women in Hong Kong until 1994. This may give some indication of the male dominance in the "gay" liberation movement. The Hong Kong 10% Club, Horizons, and the Satsanga are the only three mixed lesbian and gay groups in Hong Kong. Horizons has a lesbian subgroup, but it does not amount to much since very few women attended their functions. The other two groups want to have equal participation of lesbians and gay men, and therefore have not instituted special lesbian subgroups. However, there was a lack of awareness among the group's members of the special needs of women within this patriarchal society, and therefore lesbian activities organized by these groups have not really been successful.

Then came the XX Gathering (started in mid 1994), primarily made up of dissatisfied women members of the Hong Kong 10% Club and Horizons. It began as a nonpolitical all-women's gathering held each month, and soon turned into a specifically lesbian and bisexual gathering, where lesbian and bisexual women's issues were discussed. This new group was greeted warmly by women in the community and now has an attendance of 30 to 90 people every month.

Queer Sisters was established in early 1995. It is the very first group in Hong Kong to directly address queer women's sexuality and politics (that is, issues that concern not only lesbians but all women who challenge heterosexism, including bisexual women, transgendered women, and women who are single by choice). This new group plans to deal with social and political issues, providing referral services for legal, medical, and other needs. These activities will hopefully lead to campaigns to educate the public about queer women's issues. The group's first task, however, is to conduct a queer women's survey, the first ever in Hong Kong, and the results of this survey will be presented at the United Nations Fourth World Conference on Women and the Third Asian Lesbian Network conference, which will take place in Taiwan in August 1995.

WOMEN'S/FEMINIST GROUPS

Hong Kong's women's groups and feminist groups are heterosexual and family-oriented. Lesbianism and women's sexuality more generally have not been part of their agenda. According to Rose Wu, the founder of the Hong Kong Women's Christian Council, the only aspects of sexuality that women's groups deal with are sexual violence and the representation of women in the media. Sexuality and sexual orientation are not issues considered at their meetings. Their main focus has been on women's equality and such issues as child care, sexual abuse, and maternity leave, and they have not really been aware of the fact that lesbian and bisexual women constitute a minority within a minority.

"There are mutual benefits for the solidarity of both groups."
— Rose Wu, Hong Kong Women's Christian Council

Although the most radical feminist group in Hong Kong—the Hong Kong Association for the Advancement of Feminism—held a couple of "meet the lesbians" workshops with the Hong Kong 10% Club in 1991-92, nearly all cooperation came to a halt later. The Hong Kong Women's Christian Council (HKWCC) is, at the present time, the only group that views women's sexuality positively and cooperates with lesbian, gay, and queer groups. During the consultation period for the Basic Law (which will govern Hong Kong after 1997), the HKWCC took the lead in suggesting "sexual orientation" in the law for women's rights, and alliance with lesbian and gay groups became the council's policy thereafter. HKWCC has co-presented religious and feminist workshops with the Hong Kong 10% Club since 1994, and the organization started to work in cooperation with the newly established Queer Sisters beginning in 1995. "There are mutual benefits for the solidarity of both groups," says Rose Wu. "The experiences were new and important for us as we can re-read and re-think the Bible and our religious beliefs with them. To side with marginalized people is Christianity."

MEDIA

There are no magazines or newspapers by or for lesbian and bisexual women, and no mainstream media that creates a strong positive attitude toward lesbian, bisexual, and gay issues. Only a few TV programs and radio programs offer positive views of lesbian, bisexual, and gay issues or visibility for lesbian and bisexual women. Radio Television Hong Kong had one radio production focusing on these issues, but it lasted only four months. The first positive radio program dealing with lesbians and gays to appear on Commercial Radio II began in 1992, but it too lasted only a few months.

There are no mainstream movies dealing positively with lesbians. Lesbianism—or, more accurately, sex between women—mainly appears in pornographic films such as *The Wife's Lover*. Lesbians in other films such as *He and She* and *He's a Woman, She's a Man* all turn straight in the end. In the mainstream press, magazines such as *East Week, Next Magazine, Easy Finder, Oriental Sunday*—all of which have very wide circulation—sometimes contain feature articles on lesbians which appear to be done by reporters who take a voyeuristic point of view and don't really discuss lesbian issues.

As a result, people concerned with lesbian and bisexual women's issues have tried a number of different strategies. Some have gotten into the mass media themselves by writing articles, taking the power of interpretation back into their own hands instead of being manipulated by the heterosexism of the well-known vehicles of the press. They usually write in more liberal and open newspapers (*Hong Kong Economic Times, Hong Kong Economic Journal*, and *Ming Pao*) and magazines (*Marie Claire, Crossover Cultural Magazine, Elle*). Others have turned to alternative media and create independent space for the voices of lesbian and bisexual women—writing, for example, for the newsletters of lesbian and gay groups (Hong Kong 10% Club and Horizons) or feminist groups (Hong

Kong Women's Christian Council). There are also two independent magazines; one (*Tung Chi Hau Long*) is a monthly press cutting summary of lesbian and gay issues, and the other (*Nufengliu*) is a bimonthly magazine about women's issues.

The Hong Kong Arts Centre has organized the Hong Kong Lesbian and Gay Film/Video Festival for five years. This year it has over 80 films and videos, including local productions. Categories such as When a Woman Loves a Woman, Bi-the-way, Labels Kings and Queens, and Big Girls Don't Cry are designed to explore different issues. This is a big event every year because people can see programs not purely for entertainment but also to get information about lesbian and bisexual women and their issues in other parts of the world.

Recently, books on lesbian bisexual and gay issues have begun to appear. *The Coming Out of Queers in Hong Kong*, edited by Anson Mak, Danial Kwong and Chou Wah Shan, was published in February 1995.[1] It contains separate chapters for lesbians and bisexuals, and it is the first book about local people "coming out" to be published in Chinese. Two other books published in 1995 are *Queer Theories* and *Queers' Theology*, both written by Chou Wah Shan. They are the first books in Chinese about western queer theories.

The resources and power of the alternative media are still limited, as the distribution network is small and the circulation ranges from a few hundred to somewhat under 3,000 copies in Hong Kong's population of six million. Women's issues are still overshadowed not only by heterosexual society, but by the patriarchal values which allow gay men to be perceived as the entire queer population and leave women out of the spotlight, particularly in the mass media.

THE EQUAL OPPORTUNITIES BILL

In 1994, Legislative Council member Anna Wu proposed the Equal Opportunities Bill, which would address nine types of discrimination and set up an independent Human Rights Commission as a statutory body to foster arbitration and settle disputes with tribunal power.

Under the proposed legislation, discrimination, harassment, and vilification on the basis of sexual orientation would be unlawful in employment, education, access to places and vehicle, provision of goods and services and facilities, accommodation, land registered clubs, and government programs.

Societal Reaction to the Bill

The bill has stirred up heated controversies. Many organizations support the bill in its entirety, including feminist groups, a support group called Movement Against Discrimination, lesbian and gay groups, such as Hong Kong 10% Club and Horizons, and activist trade unions. Some religious groups claim no objections per se to the bill, but nevertheless have reservations. Conservative and religious groups approve "the protection of basic human rights" but have expressed concern about the inclusion of an "influential minority culture." They have expressed reservations in particular on issues of homosexuality and bisexuality.

Hong Kong Monitor, a political concern group, holds the view that the society is not yet prepared for a comprehensive equal opportunities law, and that issues like same-sex marriage and tax allowances for queer couples similar to those afforded to married couples, should be subject to further public debate.

However, the most negative view has been expressed by a pro-China newspaper, *Wen Wei Po*, which stated in an editorial that the "Equal Opportunities Bill is an attempt to preserve the immoral and sick tradition of the expatriates, in particular the British." It claimed that homosexuality was "shameless perverted behavior" of the British and that it was ridiculous to allow homosexuals to seek damages if they were discriminated against by "normal people."[2]

The Legislative Council members, after two internal hearings of the bill, held the view that they could support protection against discrimination only on the grounds that are most commonly recognized, such as gender and disability. This view is generally supported by the business sector representatives and the Liberal Party (a middle of the road political party). Furthermore, the Governor has rejected the proposal for setting up an independent Human Rights Commission.

A Critique of the Bill

In spite of the "great leap" of equal opportunities awareness in Hong Kong fostered by the proposal of the bill, the bill itself is not free from flaws. Because of its failure to set up a Human Rights Commission, the effectiveness of the bill remains doubtful. The possibility of independent grievance procedures in settling disputes on issues of discrimination is, in the near future at least, effectively destroyed.

Moreover, lesbian and bisexual women's participation in discussions of sexuality has been absent from the debate on the bill. Feminist groups have dealt only with gender issues and not with sexuality. At the same time, the notes, statements, and examples quoted by the Equal Opportunities Bill proposal and the Hong Kong 10% Club cover only gay male cases. In so doing, they once again render lesbians invisible. Further, the situation of bisexuals is noted in the bill, but has not been highlighted in the campaigns by lesbian and gay groups to raise public awareness of equal opportunity for women of different sexual orientations.

The proposed protection of sexuality is not comprehensive. In the bill, "Sexuality means heterosexuality, homosexuality (including lesbianism) or bisexuality" only. Other voices, such as those of transsexuals, are erased, rendered invisible in the political context.

Finally, the amended version of the bill happens to group sexuality together with age and family responsibilities. Because it does not deal separately and specifically with issues like same-sex marriage; donor insemination of lesbians; adoption of children by lesbian, bisexual, and gay parents; and the tax and housing allowances that married heterosexuals receive, the bill does not encourage new policies that would generate positive and accurate attitudes toward lesbian and bisexual women.

The third hearing of the bill in the Legislative Council was scheduled to take place in July 1995.

CONCLUSION

In spite of the community's variety and vigor, lesbian and bisexual women in Hong Kong have never been the subject of discourse. Decriminalization, which had its roots in English notions of "buggery," did not directly address lesbian sexuality or well-being. The lesbian subgroups affiliated with a gay-dominated homosexual group (and subordinated to gay patriarchy) did not flourish. More recent independent women's/queer groups are either social groups that are "in the closet" or they are too small to be politically influential. Mass media has always been preoccupied with vulgar stereotyping and the issues of lesbian and bisexual women have often been the subject of ridicule rather than positive discussions about lesbianism as a sexual identity. Even the Equal Opportunities Bill, although undoubtedly progressive in its inclusion of sexual orientation, nevertheless treats lesbianism as a subcategory of homosexuality, rather than as a separate identity like bisexuality. One positive piece of news is that at least one academic institution, the University of Hong Kong (a state university), is in the process of putting forward its own code of sexual ethics that would protect anyone on the campus against discrimination on the basis of sexual identity. This suggests the possibility that guidelines on harassment can be implemented in a variety of institutions.

NOTES

1 Anson Mak, Danial Kwong and Chou Wah Shan, eds., *The Coming Out of Queers in Hong Kong* , (Hong Kong: Hong Kong Queer Culture, 1995).

2 *Wen Wei Po*, 28 October 1994.

ABOUT THE AUTHORS

Anson Mak, Ken Hui, Joanne Poon, and Mary Ann King are activists in Hong Kong.

India

• • • • •

Cath

Because of the tremendous silence which surrounds the issue of lesbianism, it is difficult to know where, when, and by whom the
human rights of lesbians living in India are being violated. Lesbian voices are not being heard, and as this report will illustrate, this
silence is in itself a human rights violation. Finding the space to talk
openly is rarely possible, and the fear of exposure is so great that very little meaningful discussion of lesbianism can take place.

This report is based on the following sources: collected articles and
news clippings in the Sakhi Lesbian Resource Center in New Delhi; letters from lesbians in different parts of India who have written to Sakhi;
personal accounts from lesbians who have contacted Sakhi; and conver-
sations with lesbians within and outside the women's movement. It is by
no means a complete picture of the situation, especially when it comes
to how class, caste, and geographic settings (i.e., rural versus urban)
affect the choices and experiences of lesbians in India. However, one
can say, most definitely, that the silence surrounding lesbianism affects
women in every sector of society. The heterosexualization of Indian culture and society denies all women the right to choose and freely live
their lives.

FAMILY PRESSURE

The family plays a significant role is prohibiting lesbianism. Most Indian women who do not marry are dependent upon the financial and social support of their families and are thus prevented from asserting their independence. Some middle-class women are exposed to alternative ways of living and have the financial means to attain them. Often, however, financial resources become meaningless in the face of the pressure they feel to remain with their families. Privacy, freedom of movement, and freedom of association all become difficult for lesbians living with parents and family.

Marriage is instilled in the minds of young girls as the focal point of a woman's life.

Most Indian lesbians have been pressured to marry by their families. Some find a way to resist; others get married as a result of being coerced or simply because they have not considered the alternatives. Marriage is instilled in the minds of young girls as the focal point of a woman's life. It is an expected duty, an unquestionable norm, and inescapable for the majority of Indian women. In certain castes, it is still considered a dishonor to the family if a girl is not married by the time her menses begin. Child marriages are still arranged, sometimes prior to the birth of the child.

The societal and familial pressures that force many lesbians into marriage contribute to the invisibility of lesbians in Indian society and culture. A statement that is made repeatedly is that "there are no lesbians in India." Such statements can be made because although some women have chosen to take the risks involved in living openly as lesbians, many others have been forced to assimilate into heterosexual norms, all the while recognizing their true sexuality and suppressing their feelings, often for years. Letters received by Sakhi illustrate the frequency with which this happens. Many of the letters are from lower middle-class women, in smaller towns and cities.

A woman from Lucknow writes:

> I am a 33-year-old married bi-sexual woman. Although I am a married woman...from my early adolescence I was very much attracted to people of my own sex but at that time this type of feelings could not be revealed to anyone, as I belonged to a very conservative family....[1]

A woman from Bangalore writes:

> I was attracted to boys but...five and a half years [ago] I met a girl. (She is from another city.) I took [an] instant liking for her and so did she. We fell in love and got involved emotionally and physically.
>
> Though madly in love I felt the society would never accept our relationship. So I decided it would be better if we split. I told her this and gave her [a] reason (that I was involved with a boy). She had depression for almost two years after this because she just could not accept it.
>
> I did try in [the] last two years to get involved with boys and finally have decided to get married to a boy who has proposed marriage to me....[The problem is that] I really feel that I am in deeply love with that girl and if you ask me what I want then I would want to spend my life with her [be]cause I feel happiest when I am with her....
>
> If I marry I will be making my parents happy but I will not be truly happy. If I decide to spend my life with her I will be the happiest person but I will make my parents unhappy.
>
> Please tell me what I should do....I am proud of this relationship and I do not feel guilt or inferior because I am a lesbian [be]cause this relationship gives me pleasure as much as any other relationship would give.[2]

The following letter appeared in *Trikone*, a South Asian lesbian and gay newsletter published in the United States:

....My mother thought I'd be better off married....How come there is no one else in Vellore who is lesbian? It did feel strange to be the only person to feel this way. Do you know of some one just to talk to? It felt very lonely and I was so crowded with my thoughts that I agreed to marriage. Perhaps it will work.[3]

Sakhi has been in contact with lesbians who have tried to leave home, been emotionally blackmailed and gone back, and with others who have struggled and succeeded in becoming independent from their families. A lesbian couple who came to Sakhi for support reported that their families had prohibited them from communicating with one another, and that one had been forced into marriage. One woman who contacted Sakhi said her family would kill her if they discovered her lesbianism. Sakhi has heard of few cases where parents are supportive.

Because of the consequences that many lesbians face if their sexuality is revealed to their family, they are especially vulnerable to blackmail and other forms of harassment. One woman who contacted Sakhi reported being terrorized by anonymous phone calls and letters threatening to expose her lesbian identity. Some letters contained pornographic images of lesbians and, purporting to be from Sakhi, tried to blackmail her to "Join our gay organisation." Her main fear was that her family would find out she was lesbian. One Sakhi member has received obscene telephone calls, including a death threat.

LAWS USED AGAINST LESBIANS

While the pressure to conform to heterosexual norms does not, in general, come directly from the state, legal pressure can in certain situations be brought to bear. Same-sex sexual relations are illegal under Section 377 of the Indian Penal Code:

OF UNNATURAL OFFENCES: Whoever voluntarily has carnal intercourse against the order of nature with any man, woman or animal shall be punished with imprisonment for life or imprisonment of either description for a term which may extend for ten years and shall be liable to fine.

When the law was instituted in India in the 1830s under British colonial rule, lesbian sexuality was not even conceived of as a threat, and the law was intended to apply to acts of sodomy and bestiality. Few have investigated the implication of the law for lesbians, as the sentences reported have all involved men. However, only those cases that come to the level of the higher court are recorded. Furthermore, as the "offense" is non-bailable, the "offender" may be arrested and languish in prison until such time as the case is decided, and the law can thus be used as a mechanism of coercion.

In 1990, a case was reported in which Section 377 was used against Lila Chadva and her lover, Tarunkumar, a female-to-male transsexual. The two had been lovers since 1985. In 1987, Tarunkumar underwent sex reassignment surgery, and in December 1989 the couple got married. However, Chadva's father petitioned the Gujarat High Court to annul the marriage on the grounds that it was a lesbian relationship and therefore illegal under Section 377. The writ petition contended that "Tarunkumar...possesses neither the male organ nor any natural mechanism of cohabitation, sexual intercourse, and procreation of children. Adoption of any unnatural mechanism does not create malehood and as such Tarunkumar is not a male."[4]

The marriage of Lila Chadva and Tarunkumar

The petition was accepted by the court. While the case subsequently disappeared from the public eye, the fact that the high court was willing to accept the petition demonstrates the coercive potential of the law. While this particular case involved a female-to-male transsexual, Sakhi is aware of other reports of the threatened usage of the law to break up relationships between women. Such cases are very difficult to document because, due to the stigmatization of lesbianism, many women are reluctant to admit publicly that such coercion has occurred.

Even when Section 377 is not directly enforced, the criminalization of lesbianism contributes indirectly to the abuses that lesbians endure. Beyond the barriers that all women face to securing state intervention when they are the victims of domestic violence, lesbians also must contend with the psychological impact of a law that defines them as criminal and abnormal. Anti-lesbian violence is almost never reported to the police, although Sakhi has received reports of battering, rape by male family members, and murder.[5]

LESBIAN MARRIAGES

As the examples above make clear, women who want to spend their lives together face many obstacles. However, a few courageous women, all from working-class backgrounds, have made the news in recent years for attempting to marry their women lovers. The most widely publicized case was that of 20-year-old Leela Namdeo and 29-year-old Urmila Shrivastava, two policewomen with the 23rd Battalion of the Special Armed Forces. The couple had undergone a Hindu marriage ceremony in December 1987 and were discharged from the force when news of the marriage spread. Their commander was quoted as saying "Urmila and Leela were sacked because their conduct was unbecoming of a police constable. It could lead to indiscipline and what is more, others could learn from their example too. It could lead to problems in the battalion too. They would want to sleep in the same bed, share food from the same plate and things like that which cannot be allowed."[6]

The two women appealed to the top authorities of the state police to reinstate them, but their requests were denied. The case attracted a great deal of media attention, and most of the coverage perpetuated common stereotypes. Urmila was portrayed as the "husband" and Leela as the "wife," and their relationship was explained to be the result of tragic, lonely lives. Faced with intense media scrutiny, the two women denied that they had any sexual relationship and explained that their close friendship was one of many such partnerships among the women in the barracks.[7]

Although Leela and Urmila's respective families condoned their marriage, other women who have attempted to marry each other have faced strong opposition. In the 1993 case of 18-year-old Vinoda Adwekar and her 21-year-old lover, Rekha Chaudhary, the respective families joined forces with the police and the marriage registrar to keep the couple apart. Four years after they had first met each other, the two women announced to their respective families that they were planning to get married. When their families expressed their opposition, the two fled to the nearby town of Chandrapur and submitted their application to the Registrar of Marriages. On the day that they were to present themselves to the Registrar, a crowd of hundreds gathered at the court. While Rekha was left waiting outside, Vinoda was brought

Gita Darji and Kishori Shah.

inside the building and subjected to arguments against the relationship from the Police Superintendent, the Registrar, and her family. As the papers reported, "It took three hours for [Police Superintendent] Karkhare to talk Vinoda out of it [but he succeeded], much to the relief of the parents of both the girls, district officials and the large gathering that waited eagerly for the judgment."[8] This case shows the lengths that officials, families, and communities will go to to stop two women from choosing to live their lives together.

LESBIAN SUICIDES

Another indication of the difficulties that lesbian couples face is the significant number of double suicides that are reported in the press. The most well-known case is that of Gita Darji and Kishori Shah, two nurses in their mid-twenties who lived in the small town of Meghraj in Gujarat. The two hanged themselves rather than allow Gita's marriage to separate them from one another. Love letters between them found after their deaths revealed that the man Gita had recently married abhorred their relationship and, with the help of Gita's brother, forced her to apply for a transfer to another town.

One researcher has pointed out the large number of such cases reported in newspapers in the southern state of Kerala. The reports demonstrate little understanding of the reasons that such suicides may occur and little sensitivity to the women themselves.[9] Those who seek to explain such suicides in the context of compulsory heterosexuality are silenced, as was the case when the researcher in question displayed articles on lesbian suicide at a recent conference on gender and sexuality in Kerala. An hour after he put the articles up for viewing they were removed.

PSYCHOLOGICAL IMPACT

These examples show the obstacles that lesbians encounter when they reveal their love for other women. However, those who remain silent also suffer consequences. An autonomous, unmarried woman in India is seen as an outsider. Within their families, schools, workplaces, and social groups, single women are told they are not "real women" and are asked when they will be married. For many lesbians, this means facing a daily struggle of being "different." Denying one's lesbianism to oneself and others, leading a double life, having to suppress one's true sexuality, constantly feeling on guard and afraid—these constraints take their toll in a number of different ways. Regardless of class and caste, the sense of isolation and the fear of being ostracized impacts all women who are lesbians. Isolation can lead to depression and to drug and alcohol use, and lesbians receive little assistance from mental health professionals. Within the psychiatric profession, homosexuality is widely viewed as a deviant sexual behavior. One woman psychologist has informed Sakhi that "curative" therapy is practiced, including aversion therapy. Although sensitive to lesbian and gay issues, she herself believes in the potential for some patients to "convert" to heterosexuality.[10]

INVISIBILITY

It is virtually impossible to find any literature, films, or art by, for, or about lesbians in India. While the last several years the issue of lesbianism has received increased media attention, most of the coverage echoes the general social attitudes that view lesbianism as a curiosity, an illness, or an abnormality.[11] Where representations of lesbians exist in popular culture, they are generally voyeuristic. In Indian films, which are filled with violence, rape, and macho culture, women's sexuality is expressed within only a very narrow range of acceptable roles and any non-stereotypical female characters, such as the tomboy in the film *Nadaan*, are eventually shown their "true" sexuality, by ending up in the arms of the hero. When lesbian characters do appear, such as in the depiction of a relationship between two women in Vijay Tendulkar's film *Subah*, they are portrayed as abnormal.

As opposed to the contemporary invisibility of lesbians, ironically, there exist rich histories of lesbian and other non-heterosexual sexualities in ancient Indian culture. If one looks, it is possible to find images and documentation of women-to-women bonding, feminine culture, and goddess traditions in temple sculptures, historical texts, miniature paintings, etc. In many temples, women in various sexual positions together indicates that, at one time, heterosexuality was perhaps only one of many diverse sexualities. Over the centuries, the images have been either destroyed, plastered over, or heterosexualized, thus creating the almost perfect denial of their existence. Similarly, modern translations of ancient texts, such as the Rig Veda, have been heterosexualized.

LESBIANS AND THE WOMEN'S MOVEMENT

Very little room exists within the women's movement for lesbians to comfortably reveal their sexual identity, and lesbians have only rarely been recognized as a marginalized group whose issues must be included in the work of women's organizations. Many lesbians working within the movement fear that if their sexual orientation becomes known they will be marginalized and shunned.

The women's movement has dealt with the politics of sexuality in various ways—under the banners of women's health, violence against women, reproductive health rights, and "single" women. Campaigning to raise the status of single women of poorer classes has meant focusing on those women who are not within the institution of marriage—widowed, divorced, or unmarried women. Creating spaces where these women can share their experiences and build a sense of self-worth in a society that looks down upon unmarried women has been an important contribution of the movement. Lesbian sexuality, however, is rarely mentioned. India's foremost feminist magazine, *Manushi*, has never carried any articles on lesbian experience. Even feminists who are themselves lesbians feel the necessity to censor themselves at women's conferences in India. They are critical to a degree of issues like the power of the family or marriage, yet remain careful not to talk of lesbianism as an alternative to the heterosexual norm.

Recently, some cracks have begun to appear in the wall of silence. The National Women's Conference in Calicut, 1991, saw the first-ever meeting among women who stand outside the institution of marriage. Many other women felt threatened by this group claiming space for themselves, some saying married women were in many ways "single" due to the loneliness they felt in their marriages. In January 1994, another women's conference took place in Tirupathi. This time, in a workshop on sexuality, many women spoke of their lesbian relationships, feelings, and experiences, and various discussions took place around the issue of lesbianism. The atmosphere was highly charged as women, many for the first time, exchanged stories and spoke of their pleasure and pain. Objections were raised by some of the women present, who deemed lesbianism as either immoral or abnormal. One particular group of women went to the extent of trying to pass a resolution at the conference stating that lesbianism should not be promoted as normal. Others tried to encourage women to shout slogans such as "down with lesbianism!" In the evening a lesbian-only meeting was held to continue the sharing, networking, and bonding without such interference or harassment.[12]

Another indication of change came when Vimla Farooqui, a leading member of the National Federation of Indian Women, made a public statement earlier this year calling for the Prime Minister to put a stop to a gay men's conference in Bombay. This opened up space for dialogue on the issue of lesbian and gay rights, and one feminist group in Delhi took action by writing to other women's groups for comments and support over the issue. Many positive letters were sent in opposition to Farooqui's statement, which demonstrates that there is potential within the movement for more discussion on lesbian rights in the future.

LESBIAN ORGANIZATIONS

Sakhi, the only openly lesbian organization in India, is based in New Delhi. Sakhi works to increase visibility of lesbians and lesbian culture within India, to provide a space for lesbians to identify with each other and counteract lesbophobia within India. The group was started in 1991 by four women who established a library of lesbian books and information and a post office box number to which lesbian women could write. The Sakhi address was publicized through the limited avenues that existed, such as the gay magazine Bombay Dost. Over the last two years, mail has increased to an average of seven letters a week, and both national and international networking with groups and individuals has been established.

NOTES

1 Letter to Sakhi, 1992.

2 Letter to Sakhi, 20 September 1993. Copy on file with the International Gay and Lesbian Human Rights Commission.

3 *Trikone*, April 1990.

4 *India Today*, 15 April 1990, p. 110.

5 For further reports of violence by family members, see "I am a lesbian. So what?" *Network*, January 1993, p. 22.

6 Manjeet Singh, "Urmila weds Leela, both get sacked," *Times of India*, n.d.

7 See "Love Between Two Women" *Eve's Weekly*, 19 March 1988; Married Policewomen May Be Reinstated," *Indian Express*, 27 February 1988; "Wed-

ded women cops to challenge sack," *Times of India*, n.d.

8 Shishtir Joshi, "The bold, beautiful and the damned," *Indian Express*, 18 April 1993.

9 Murali, "Till Death Do Us Part: An analysis of lesbian suicides in Kerala," *Trikone*, Vol. 10, No. 2 (April 1995), p. 7-8.

10 Conversation with the author, February 1995. The psychologist wishes to remain anonymous.

11 See, for instance, "Lesbians—their number is amazing" and "Ahmedabad shows the way for those who are gay," both in *Indian Express*, 13 September 1993.

12 Parvez Sharma, "Emerging from the Shadows," *Statesman*, 3 July 1994, p. 7.

ABOUT THE AUTHOR

Cath is an activist with the Sakhi Lesbian Resource Center, and lives in Delhi, which she considers her new home. She enjoys music, theater, and living life to the fullest.

Israel

● ● ● ● ●

Haya Shalom

When the first lesbian and gay organization in Israel was established in the city of Haifa in 1976, its founders were not even able to publicly identify the nature of the organization. The Israeli Interior Ministry refused approval for a name that explicitly stated "homosexuals and lesbians," and the organization was thus founded as the Society for the Protection of Personal Rights.

Several significant changes have occurred since that time. In 1988, the criminal code was amended to no longer prohibit male homosexual relations. In 1992, an amendment to the Equality in Employment Law made it illegal to discriminate on the basis of sexual orientation in hiring, promotion, dismissal, and several other aspects of employment. In 1993, an order from the Personnel Department of the Israeli Defence Forces lifted restrictions on the military service of lesbians and gay men, although commanding officers must still report lesbian and gay soldiers to the security unit and ensure that those soldiers undergo a security check.

Further, an important legal precedent was established last year regarding the recognition of same-sex partnerships. In November 1994, the Supreme Court ruled that a male partner of a male flight attendant employed by El-Al Airlines was entitled to benefits provided to partners of heterosexual flight attendants.[1] Another potentially significant case, which has been in both the Magistrate and District Courts since May 1993, concerns the same-sex partner of an army general who died during the course of his army service. The surviving partner is claiming eligibility for the rights of an army widow/er.[2]

In January 1995, following the legal precedent set in the El-Al case, two more cases were settled regarding Israel's largest universities. At the Hebrew University of Jerusalem, same-sex partners of university employees are now entitled to a waiver of tuition fees and use of university facilities. At Tel Aviv University, the same-sex partner of a faculty member won entitlement to rights of pension, flight tickets for a sabbatical, waiver of tuition, and use of university facilities.

This struggle for recognition of the legitimacy of same-sex partnerships is taking place in various other governmental and non-governmental settings. As of late 1994, Magen David Adom, the Israeli equivalent of the Red Cross, now provides blood insurance[3] for same-sex partners. The Ministry of the Interior has approved the use of the same last name by lesbian and gay couples. Currently in the legislative process is a bill that would award pension rights to the same-sex partners of civil servants. The Deputy Foreign Minister has declared that "the sexual orientation of candidates does not in itself prevent someone from being accepted to the foreign service,"[4] and directives have been issued from the Civil Service Commission stating that during the course of a job interview, "the candidate shall not be asked questions pertaining to sex, sexual orientation, personal status, or parenthood." Further, a committee for gay and lesbian rights was established by the Tel Aviv City Council in November 1994 specifically to address rights of sexual minorities. To begin with, the committee will focus on educating municipal workers employed in education and social welfare and raising funds for a lesbian and gay youth support group.

REMAINING PROBLEMS

While these gains are significant, many obstacles remain for lesbians. Progress has been made in Israel regarding legislation and public awareness, but public school education and the religious establishment still do not encourage any changes in the widespread stigmatization of homosexuality. Until social perceptions change radically, most lesbians and gay men will remain in the closet.

In the legal realm, an area in which lesbian and gay activists have made few inroads is the religious law that governs all matters of personal status. For Jews, marriage and divorce are carried out in accordance with the laws of the Bible, and any change in personal status can be written in an identification card or passport only after the proceedings of a rabbinical tribunal.[5] Women are not permitted to become members of rabbinical tribunals nor to serve as witnesses before them.

In matters of divorce, child custody, and child support, the impact of religious law on lesbians can be particularly acute. Every lesbian who seeks a divorce faces the threat that the rabbinical tribunals will use biblical injunctions against lewdness or homosexuality to rule in favor of the husband in matters of property and custody. Thus, women often

Until social perceptions change radically, most lesbians and gay men will remain "in the closet."

make concessions even before the court reaches its decisions. Women in this situation are vulnerable to demands by their husbands and ultimately feel compelled to accept conditions such as removal of their partners from the home as a condition for custody of the children. For instance, Sh., a Tel Aviv woman with three children, spent three years (1989-1992) trying to obtain custody and child support payments from her ex-husband. He finally agreed, but only after she promised never to bring her female partner into her home. She was forced to abide by this condition because she knew that her ex-husband could bring up her lesbianism in court.[6]

Even where exceptions can be seen in the influence of religious law, the sanctity of the heterosexual family is deeply ingrained in Israeli society, and social and economic systems work to support the family structure in order to foster and preserve the family unit. For instance, although Jewish law can pose obstacles for certain heterosexual partnerships, Israeli society generally recognizes the legitimacy of such partnerships even if the couple has not been married under biblical law.[7] In these common law marriages, defined as two people of the opposite sex living together as a couple and conducting a common household, civil law bestows upon the couple rights and responsibilities that are similar to those of a married couple. However, except for in the specific cases cited above, Israeli law does not accord this recognition or these rights to a couple of the same sex who live together in a common household. As one lesbian has written,

> My lover and I have been together for nearly nine years, but our relationship "doesn't count." When we bought a house together, it was in her name only, because she was eligible for a mortgage (the smaller one offered singles, instead of the heftier one offered married couples). As a new immigrant, she bought a car that I may not drive if she is not with me. If we were a heterosexual couple, I could drive it at any time. If she gets pregnant and has a child, I have less legal status than a one-night male pickup. We are not entitled to each other's hard-earned pensions in case of death. We cannot register with a sick fund as a couple, nor receive income tax deductions for one another.[8]

While most lesbian mothers in Israel have children from previous relationships with men, some lesbians are now considering becoming pregnant through donor insemination. However, every woman who requests donor insemination must meet various psychological and sociological criteria, and lesbians are excluded entirely. Professor Schenkar, head of the gynecology department of Hadassah Hospital in Jerusalem, has publicly expressed his opposition to inseminating a woman who is known to be a lesbian.[9]

LESBIAN ORGANIZING

The Society for the Protection of Personal Rights, founded in 1976 and made up of approximately 500 members, remains active in working to change the legal status of lesbians and gay men. Since 1977 it has been joined by CLAF (Community for Lesbian Feminists), which now has over 300 members. For the past five years, CLAF has published a periodical called *CLAF Hazak*.

Currently, these groups are focusing their efforts on recognizing same-sex partners as common law spouses. Such recognition would have repercussions in many areas, including pension, inheritance, and a variety of social benefits. The approach that activists are employing is to attempt to amend existing laws rather than to pass a comprehensive law that would recognize same-sex partnerships. The specific struggles underway include gaining the recognition of same-sex partners as parents of their partner's children in every respect; defining every type of harassment, exclusion, and discrimination based on sexual orientation as a criminal act prohibited by law; and obtaining the inclusion of sexual orientation in all relevant anti-discrimination laws. In the realm of family law, future efforts will be focused on changing the law so that a woman's sexual orientation cannot be used against her in divorce and custody battles.

NOTES

1 Case of Jonathan Danilowitz, November 1994.

2 Case of Adir Steiner, which began in the courts in May 1993.

3 Blood insurance entitles the family of blood donors to receive blood transfusions if they become sick or wounded.

4 Letter from Deputy Foreign Minister Yossi Beilin to Member of Knesset Yael Dayan, 2 August 1994.

5 Members of different religions are governed by their own religious courts in these matters.

6 Interview by the author with Sh. in January and June 1995.

7 In addition to not recognizing interfaith marriages, Jewish law also prohibits certain unions between Jews.

8 Liora Moriel, "From Shadow into Full Light," *Jerusalem Post*, 21 June 1994.

9 "Out Lesbians Are Not Entitled to Artificial Insemination," *Jerusalem*, June 1989.

ABOUT THE AUTHOR

Haya Shalom, 50, is a Sephardic lesbian feminist peace activist who was born in Jerusalem. She is the founder of Community of Lesbian Feminists (CLAF), co-founder of the Women and Peace Coalition, an organizer for Women in Black, and a member of the Board of Directors of Bat-Shalom (of Jerusalem Link), the feminist center for peace and social justice.

Japan

• • • • • •

Sachiko Ishino and Naeko Wakabayashi

LESBIAN ACTIVISM

The lesbian movement in Japan grew out of the women's liberation movement in the 1970s. In 1971, the first lesbian social group, Fresh Green Club, was formed. *Subarashii Onnatachi* (Wonderful Women), the first lesbian feminist magazine in Japan, began publication in 1976, and the establishment of many small groups and newsletters followed in its wake.

In 1985, the first lesbian overnight gathering took place near Tokyo and was attended by 60 Japanese and foreign lesbians. Later, these informal conferences came to be known as weekends, and since then weekends have been held three or four times a year, and approximately 100 women generally attend. They provide a rare opportunity for lesbians to discuss their concerns, participate in sports programs, and interact with other lesbians living in Japan. However, the lesbophobia in Japan is such that it is impossible for the group that organizes these gatherings to use its real name when renting space.

A major turning point for the lesbian movement came in 1987 with the release by a mainstream publisher of a book titled *Onna O Aisuru Onnatachi No Monogatari* (Story of Women Who Love Women). The book included personal life stories of lesbians in Japan and other countries, as well as information regarding existing organizations and bars, and its publication expanded the lesbian liberation movement in Japan considerably.

In the same year, a group of lesbians set up the first lesbian activist organization in Japan, Regumi Studio Tokyo, under the auspices of JOKI, a cooperative office for feminist groups. Regumi Studio established a monthly newsletter (*Regumi Tsushin*), a library of lesbian literature, support and discussion groups, and a telephone information and referral line. This helped to support isolated lesbians living in various parts of the country. The organization played an important role in extending the network of lesbians living in Japan by organizing overnight gatherings in various places in Japan and motivating rural lesbians to start newsletters and groups of their own.

In 1986, during the Eighth International Lesbian Conference in Geneva, Switzerland, lesbians from Thailand, India, Bangladesh, the United States, and Japan formed the Asian Lesbian Network (ALN). In 1990, the first ALN conference was held in Thailand. The second ALN Conference was held in Japan in May 1992 and was attended by approximately 170 lesbians. The conference contributed to the growth of the Japanese lesbian movement.

For the most part, the publications and activities of lesbian groups have taken place within the feminist movement. However, in 1992, *LABRYS*, a magazine that serves lesbians who are not part of the feminist movement, began publication. It includes features, reviews, and letters, and has has become very popular among many lesbians in their teens and twenties, as well as among bisexuals and transsexuals. The magazine provides a forwarding service for readers' letters, encouraging more communication among lesbians in Japan. Its readership has grown to 1,600 women, and it has significantly changed the lesbian community, adding to dialogue between women and fostering positive images of lesbians.

The lesbian movement gained new energy after the first Lesbian and Gay Parade was held in Tokyo in August 1994. More than 1,200 lesbians, gay men, and their friends joined the parade and walked from Shinjuku to Shibuya (two major shopping and entertainment areas) singing and dancing all the way. More than 80 reporters also attended, and many lesbians and gay men living in rural areas were encouraged by watching TV reports of the parade. Kokusai Bian Renmei (International Lesbians United), a group formed to take part in the parade, continued to plan activities afterwards, and is now the most active lesbian group in Japan. Most of the group's work has focused on increasing lesbian visibility in mainstream Japanese society. Its members monitor and respond to representations of lesbians in the media, organize cultural events, and perform street theater to call attention to important issues. In one such action, a group of women sang about dental dams[1] in front of a popular sex toy shop in Harajuku to bring attention to the fact that people still cannot purchase dental dams in Japan. During the event the women kissed each other in the street to show heterosexual bystanders that they are proud to be lesbians.

DISCRIMINATION

Japanese lesbians experience discrimination not only on the basis of their sexual orientation but also on the basis of their gender. The social and economic disparity between men and women that characterizes Japanese society as a whole can be seen as well within the lesbian and gay community. For example, in the biggest gay neighborhood in Tokyo, Shinjuku 2-chome, there are said to be 200 to 300 gay men's bars, discos, and shops, while there are fewer than 10 bars for lesbians. The lack of commercial establishments aimed at lesbians is not an indication that the lesbian population in Japan is small, but rather that lesbians do not have nearly as much disposable income. In general, women hold lower paying jobs than men and receive lower wages than men for the same work. In addition, lesbians, like all women, have much less freedom to socialize, particularly at night. Many unmarried women live with their parents, which greatly restricts their mobility. Furthermore, there is great pressure to marry in Japan (see below) and a significant number of lesbians are completely hidden about their sexuality and are married to men. While married men generally have considerable freedom to socialize in gay meeting places, married women can almost never consider such a thing.

Another example reflecting the social and economic disparity between gay men and lesbians is the difference in the circulation of lesbian and gay magazines. While there are currently at least five gay men's magazines in publication, ranging from pornography to political commentary, mass-market magazines about lesbians are limited to pornography geared toward heterosexual men. Magazines published by lesbians are not sold at general bookstores and circulate only through small existing networks. This disparity again reflects the fact that gay men have greater access to the resources necessary to launch such publications, as well as customers with more buying power.

One lesbian from Kyushu, in the southwestern part of Japan, lamented that in her home town women who remained single after 30 years of age would be labeled as "katawa" or deformed.

MARRIAGE

Japanese society attaches great importance to marriage, and those who remain unmarried have to contend with considerable social stigma. For anyone—male or female, homo- or heterosexual—remaining single can be an obstacle to promotions at work and to recognition by family and by society. For lesbians, however, refusing to marry can have drastic consequences, particularly for those living in small towns where women face greater discrimination in employment and can hardly find jobs to support themselves. Women often have no other choice than to marry. One lesbian from Kyushu, in the southwestern part of Japan, lamented at a recent lesbian gathering that in her home town women who

remained single after 30 years of age would be labeled as "katawa" or
deformed. (The term "katawa" is a derogatory term referring to a disabled person, and its use has been banned in the Japanese media.)

EMPLOYMENT

Discrimination based on sex is prohibited by Article 14 of the Constitution. However, discrimination against women in the workplace is
widespread, with few women attaining high-paying or powerful positions in any sector of the economy. Women are expected to conform to
traditional gender roles within the workplace. For instance, although by
law employees are guaranteed a total of 60 minutes a day for caring for
infants under one year of age, this has until very recently applied only to
women, reflecting the widespread assumption that raising children is
women's work. In the workplace, being public about one's lesbianism or
failing to conform to traditional female gender roles can lead to harassment and discrimination.

DISCRIMINATORY GOVERNMENT POLICIES

Many government policies relating to taxation and social benefits
discriminate on the basis of marital status. Married women are exempt
from taxes if their income is below one million yen (approximately
10,000 U.S. dollars). Further, they do not have to pay for health insurance or pensions, for they are considered to be dependents of their husbands. Official marriage registration forms have spaces in which names
of the husband and wife are written, but they do not specify the sex of
the "husband" or "wife." However, same-sex partnerships are not legally
recognized in any way under Japanese law, and lesbians are not entitled
to any benefits that their partners may receive through their employment, such as health insurance and pensions.

LESBIAN IMAGES IN THE MEDIA

In Japan, lesbians are often referred to by the pejorative term "lez,"
meaning "women who have sex with women" or "women who want to
be men." Lesbian-themed pornography made by and for heterosexual

men has had a great influence on popular perceptions of lesbians, and the mainstream media rarely seeks to counter these stereotypes with articles or reports showing the diversity and complexity of lesbian life.

For example, in 1981, a weekly magazine called *Shukan Bunshun* published a report about a lesbian social group, Fresh Green Club, which was celebrating its 10th anniversary. The report was accompanied by a pornographic photo that had nothing to do with the group, and the caption made fun of them with a pun referring to the three divine symbols of the Japanese Imperial throne, "three sacred treasures for them are fingers, tongue and lips." Another weekly magazine called *Shukan Sankei* reported in 1977 that a homicide occurred within a lesbian relationship. The article appeared in a series titled "Porno Memorandum of Daily Incidents," and reported a love relationship between two women with the sensational headline "Lez Pleasure: An Ordinary Wife Risked her Life." In another incident, a lesbian popular singer lost her career after her sexuality was disclosed by her enraged ex-lover in 1980 and widely covered in a sensational way in the media.

In the last five years, the media has begun to treat lesbians and gay men as a fashionable subject, and television and magazine coverage has been increasing. However, the approach of the media is still voyeuristic. One journalist went incognito into the lesbian community in Tokyo in order to write an expose of Alis, a disco which she expected to be a promiscuous sex party. The truth was just the opposite: Alis was a grassroots disco organized by a few lesbians. In order to research the article the reporter went into the disco, pretended to be a lesbian, and published the article without getting permission from anyone she spoke to or giving any notice beforehand.[2] Lesbian characters are also beginning to appear in television shows but they are generally portrayed as tragic characters who try to seduce pretty women and fail.

In May 1995, under the slogan "Hetero exploitation no more!! We are the people who tell the truth!!" several lesbian and bisexual journalists began to publish *Phryne*, a magazine for women-loving women. The magazine, which contains comics, fiction, interviews, and feature stories, is available at regular bookstores.

After years of building small communities in which to interact with one another, Japanese lesbians are beginning to make their voices heard. Through publications such as *Phryne* and actions of the sort that Kokusai Bian Renmei has begun to organize, lesbians are beginning to challenge the pervasive stereotypes that both promote discrimination against lesbians and reinforce the isolation and self-doubt that many lesbians experience.

NOTES

1 Dental dams are latex barriers that prevent the transmission of HIV during oral sex.
2 "Lez Party Sneak-In Report," *Josei Seven*, November 1993.

ABOUT THE AUTHORS

Sachiko Ishino is a photographer and a member of the editorial staff of the newly established lesbian magazine Phryne.

Naeko Wakabayashi has been involved in the women's movement and the lesbian movement since 1970 and is one of the founders of the Asian Lesbian Network—Nippon.

Jordan

● ● ● ● ● ● ●

Akhadar Assfar

Author's note: This statement was written to reflect my personal, individual perspective and not to speak on behalf of other lesbians in Jordan.

The difficulty in writing a report on lesbians in Jordan stems from the fact that we live our lives deprived of healthy and free chances, deprived of a forum in which we can express ourselves or shape any sort of understanding of ourselves as lesbians. There has been no research on lesbians in Jordan. There are no visible lesbian communities, no lesbian organizations, no services for lesbians. Even when we meet as friends and talk about our lives, we do not have a public language to describe ourselves. I may find myself talking with a "lesbian" (that is, a woman whose intimate relationships are with other women) but she may not wish to call herself a lesbian so our discussion cannot be established or developed into action—either on the personal level, to build self-esteem and a sense of community, or on a public level, to promote greater understanding of our existence and the problems that we face.

What is the reason for this invisibility, this absence of public discourse? Although Jordanian law contains no mention of the word *suhak* (lesbianism), widespread prejudice within Jordanian society is more

---

Widespread prejudice is more powerful than any legal prohibition.

---

powerful that any legal prohibition. Lesbians are afraid to be visible because they fear losing whatever freedom of movement they may have. Jordanian society is a closely knit, family- and religion-oriented one in which people know one another and there is little opportunity for anonymity. Even if a woman is financially independent, her family can still exert great control over her. The main support system is the family (rather than the legal or political system), but in the case of a lesbian who is open about her sexuality, the family itself may become the offender.

Although lesbians are unable to live their lives openly, small networks have been developing since the 1970s as part of the more general changes taking place for women. One of the most important of these changes has been women's increased access to higher education, in particular education abroad. The existing networks are limited to social groups that have no political form. Nevertheless, they provide a chance for lesbians to begin to discuss their issues. In the past five years, some individual lesbians have begun to network with lesbians from other countries within and outside the region. Contacts with two Arab-American groups, the Gay and Lesbian Arabic Society and the Arab Lesbian and Bisexual Women's Network, have been particularly important because their members share a similar cultural background.

Lesbians in Jordan are without a mention, without recognition, very marginalized.... YET WE EXIST.

Malaysia

● ● ● ● ● ● ● ●

Rais Nur

Author's note: This account is not by any means meant to be a country report of lesbian rights. It is at best an attempt to share some experiences of lesbians in Malaysia and is limited by many factors, including class, ethnicity, and geographical location.

It is not every day that lesbians get a mention in the Malaysian media. However, in December 1994, the headlines of a widely circulated daily in Malaysia read: "Mate accused of killing lesbian freed." According to the *Star* newspaper, "A factory worker accused of murdering her housemate who made lesbian advances at her was freed by a seven-man jury who accepted her claim of self-defence."[1]

In its three-day coverage, the *Star* reiterated typical public perceptions of lesbians: that they all look like and behave like men. The message was consistent with the mass media's portrayal of lesbians as unnatural and deviant.

LESBIANISM AND THE STATE IN MALAYSIA

The above-mentioned case coincided with a systematic campaign by the Malaysian government, with support from religious quarters, to condemn acts of homosexuality, abortion, and drug abuse, which they pointed to as causes of the disintegration of the Malaysian family. This campaign was presented under the rubric of upholding "Asian values," which, in the government's view, were in conflict with all of the acts in question.

Lesbianism is not outlawed in Malaysia. Section 377D of the criminal code prohibits "gross indecency," but this law is not known to have ever been enforced against lesbians. The Minor Offences Act of 1955, which prohibits acts that offend public morality, is often used against sex workers and transsexuals; it too, could conceivably be used against lesbians, but there are no known cases of this happening.

In 1994 there were two major assaults on Malaysian women, and in particular on young women. In September of that year, an article in the *New Straits Times* drew public attention to a group of teenage women—*boh sias* —who hung out in public places and engaged in casual sex with men. The article generated further coverage in several papers and brought a strong response from the government. The Women and Girls Protection Act of 1973, which permits the arrest and detention of young women who may be "exposed to moral danger" or who are "being used for the purpose of prostitution or any immoral purposes," was used to arbitrarily round up these young women (including those who frequented shopping malls) in the name of protecting them. Similarly, the Act was used in a case where the then Chief Minister of Malacca, Rahim Tamby Chik, was accused of being sexually involved with a 16-year-old girl. According to Malaysian law, this would be classified as statutory rape. However, despite acknowledging that there were "strong suspicions," the Attorney General announced that the case was dropped as there was insufficient evidence for it to be brought to the court.[2] Thus, while the Minister was not prosecuted, the 16-year-old was put under police custody and later sent to a rehabilitation center using the Women and Girls Protection Act.

The Women and Girls Protection Act, while it makes no mention of lesbians, shows the lengths to which the state will go to control women's sexuality. Another means of control is the Internal Security Act (ISA) which gives the State the right to detain anyone it perceives as being a threat to national security. Since its passage in 1960, this law has been used according to the whims of the state, and given the current emphasis on morality and "Asian values," it is quite possible that it could be used against sexual minorities if the need arises.

Although Malaysia has only briefly been a police state (when the Emergency was declared in 1969 and Parliament was suspended for several months), and has never been dominated by a strong presence of the military, fear of the law and authorities is enough to keep all citizens in check, especially those who know they are perceived as "morally deviant."

THE STATUS OF LESBIANS VERSUS GAY MEN

The AIDS epidemic has led to the rise of a visible gay organization, Pink Triangle (PT), that at least in the eyes of the Health Ministry is considered to be credible. Although PT opens its doors to lesbian participation, the organization is predominately male and the majority of its work is with gay men. In the face of this epidemic, the Malaysian government has reached out to all quarters to assist in curbing the spread of HIV and AIDS. Recognizing PT as one of the few organizations (if not the only one) working with the gay male community, the state seems to have "closed its eyes" for now on the homosexual element of the organization.[3] Such state recognition and opportunity for legitimacy, however, has not been extended to the lesbian population, which the government rarely acknowledges in any way.

Likewise, while gay spots and events in Kuala Lumpur draw crowds including the rich and famous, such a response is not experienced by the lesbian community. The only known lesbian space organized for the middle-class community in Kuala Lumpur was closed by the proprietors within a year of operations to make way for an even more exclusive space for upper middle-class lesbians.[4] The majority of lesbians in Kuala Lumpur have little access to public spaces in which they can be open about their sexual orientation.

Compared to the "progress" made by gay men, then, lesbians in Malaysia are far behind. The closest equivalent to Pink Triangle is a lesbian group which started in 1992. Although it does not identify publicly as a lesbian group, over the last few years it has become increasingly known among the local lesbian community, particularly among Chinese lesbians. The early days of the group's existence were spent grappling with direction and objectives, and its members have only recently begun to clarify their objectives of empowering lesbians and building community.

LESBIANISM AND THE WOMEN'S MOVEMENT

The women's movement in Malaysia consists of a spectrum of groups, from the ultra-conservatives to those more open-minded and liberal. None have come out in support of lesbian rights. While legal reform is not at the forefront for all women's groups, it is significant that calls to amend Article 8 of the Federal Constitution—which currently prohibits discrimination on the basis of religion, race, descent, or place of birth but not discrimination on the basis of sex—have gone unheeded.

The invisibility of lesbians in women's groups often depends on the group's openness to discussing women's sexuality more generally. While the more progressive groups appear to have no objections (in theory) to addressing issues related to sexuality, many women's groups are resistant to it. If the experience of a Kuala Lumpur-based women's group is any indication, efforts to mention sexuality, especially in a way which challenges norms, will not be tolerated even by some women's groups. As part of its work to raise young women's awareness about safe sex, the All Women's Action Society produced a booklet entitled *Lina's Dilemma: The story of a young woman and AIDS*. It was obtained by a local tabloid and for three days the paper ran articles pronouncing the booklet to be pornographic and saying that it promoted free sex because the booklet mentioned kissing, licking, and massaging and included a clinical diagram on how to use a condom.[5] Several women's groups came out in opposition to the booklet, saying that it was culturally insensitive.

Certainly, another reason for the invisibility of lesbians in Malaysia is that lesbians impose it on themselves for fear of public backlash if they are too outspoken. Here support by women's groups is essential; the absence of this support contributes to the ongoing invisibility of lesbians.

CONCLUSION

Although lesbians in Malaysia have much to do to create a safe environment, there are indications of change. For example, the formation of the lesbian group mentioned above would never have been conceivable 10 years ago. Even the exodus of lesbians to overseas countries, as witnessed in the '70s and '80s, has slowed in recent years. However, it remains to be seen who will dare to lead the fight for lesbian rights and how they will accomplish this enormous task.

NOTES

1 "Mate accused of killing lesbian freed," *Star*, 18 December 1994. See also "Lesbian tried to rape me: accused," *Star*, 15 December 1994.

2 *Star*, 22 October 1994.

3 Of course the state is not monolithic. Thus, in spite of some level of acceptance and tolerance, the gay community is still subjected to periodic attacks from other quarters of the state. An incident several years ago at a local gay bar saw hundreds of gay men rounded up and kept at the police station over night on the pretext of having their urine tested for drugs. More disturbing, however, was the presence of the press during the raid and the repercussions that followed after photos of the incident and references made to the gay bar were published the following day. See "Kelab gay di serbu: 263 orang ditahan" ("Gay club raided: 263 detained"), *Utusan Malaysia*, 4 October 1993; "Gay joint raided," *Sun*, 5 October 1993; "*Ramai kesal adanya kelab gay*" ("Many regret gay club exists"), *Utusan Malaysia*, 6 October 1993.

4 This decision seems to have backfired on the proprietors, as the number of women who turn up for the weekly "women only" nights is far lower than the number that turned up previously for the monthly "women only" nights.

5 "Risalah Biadab" ("Indecent booklet"), *Harian Metro*, 24 August 1994.

ABOUT THE AUTHOR

Rais Nur is a Malaysian lesbian feminist who works with different women's groups. She looks forward to the day when she does not have to use a pseudonym anymore.

Mexico

● ● ● ● ● ● ●

Gloria Careaga Pérez and Patria Jiménez

LESBIANS AND THE LAW

In Mexico, there are no laws or regulations that specifically prohibit same-sex sexual relations. Lesbianism is also not mentioned in any restrictions imposed on civil rights, and there are no laws against free speech and association by gay and lesbian groups. However, lesbians experience significant coercion and stigma within Mexican society, and their treatment within the legal system is reliant on the interpretation of those in charge of administering justice. Frequently, the homophobia of individual civil servants can result in lesbians being denied equal protection under the law.

For example, the Regulations for Police and Good Government mention "moral lapses" and "accepted customs" and these provisions have been used to impose fines or arrest lesbians who have been caught publicly kissing or embracing. A recent example involved two women who were kissing in a car. A police patrol approached, demanded an explanation, and gave them a citation on the grounds that what they were doing was deviant; they were threatened with being taken to the police station for "moral culpability." Even after the women accepted the citation, the officers continued the interrogation with prurient questions about the nature of the women's relationship. They were made to get into the police wagon separately and they were asked to pay a certain sum for their release.

In this particular case, the women noted the identity of all the officers involved in this attempted extortion and plan to file a complaint. However, few lesbians are willing to challenge such harassment because they fear the consequences of being public about their sexual orientation. Women who speak out as lesbians have limited chances of achieving prominent positions or even of keeping their jobs, and lesbians have no legal recourse in such cases because no anti-discrimination legislation exists to protect them. This makes lesbians vulnerable to wrongful arrest, extortion, and other forms of harassment. In addition, because of police bias, lesbians who are victims of crimes are often hesitant to report them, out of fear of facing moral disgrace when placing a complaint or making criminal allegations. At the same time, if a woman who commits a civil or criminal offense is known to be a lesbian, her sexual orientation is likely to be brought out in her trial.

DISCRIMINATION IN SOCIETY

Lesbians in Mexico suffer discrimination on two counts—as women and as lesbians. For this reason, few manage to attain prominent positions or develop their personal abilities. Any attempt to live freely and express one's sexual orientation requires a high degree of autonomy and emotional and economic independence, not only from one's family, but from society as well, and this autonomy is beyond the reach of many Mexican women.

In small towns, the state of isolation, loneliness, and lack of information can be overwhelming. Those who manage to live as couples generally have only a small nucleus of friends. El Clóset de Sor Juana, a lesbian-feminist group based in Mexico City, receives several letters each week from lesbians in need of information and emotional support. Many of these letters speak of social isolation and fear. Teresa, from Tabasco, writes: "Honestly, I would like to be free and open and not secretive as I am most of the time; unfortunately, out of fear I cannot do that here." Judith, from the State of Mexico, writes, "I have a big problem. I am 25 years old. I have just realized that I am a lesbian and I am very much afraid of coming out of the closet. I don't know any girls with whom I could live and share my life—something I cannot do with my family. They would prefer to see me dead."

In larger cities, there are more lesbian and gay meeting places, and the communities tend to be larger. Lesbian groups, while limited in number, offer at least a point of reference for many women seeking contact with other women in spaces other than bars and discos. Even so, however, social invisibility still leaves many lesbians, even in large cities, lacking information about their lives or the opportunities available to them. El Clóset de Sor Juana publishes a bulletin, *Las Virreinas* (The Vicereines) and has also produced a supplement, *Las Amantes de la Luna* (Lovers of the Moon) for the recently defunct gay magazine *Del Otro Lado* (From the Other Side). However, lesbian publications have minimal and often irregular circulation, so they do not as yet provide an effective vehicle for information.[1]

VISIBILITY

Lesbian images are denied or avoided in almost all forms of public life. Because of this, few women dare to declare publicly that they are lesbians, despite the fact that some hold prominent positions in political, intellectual, artistic, and sports circles. This silence contributes to the isolation and sense of powerlessness that many lesbians experience.

There are, however, a few significant exceptions to this silence, particularly within the artistic arena. Nancy Cárdenas, theatrical director, writer, and poet, was the first lesbian to argue for human rights for sexual minorities, initially from anonymity and later publicly. She approached lesbian, gay, and bisexual themes in her art, promoting social reflection on the subject.[2] Chavela Vargas, a performer of Mexican music, has earned worldwide fame while her lesbianism has not gone unperceived; the content and language of her songs are directed principally at women. Jesusa Rodriguez, writer, theatrical director, comedian, and feminist, has been a sharp political critic and a strong supporter of women's issues throughout her career. Her production *Concilio de amor* (Council of Love) gave rise to a great debate within Mexico on the church and sexuality, and she has been the subject of threats and violent attacks from conservative leaders and groups such as Pro-Vida (Pro-Life). She and her companion, the singer and composer Liliana Felipe, provide space for political and social discussion in their theater-bar El Hábito. Rosamaria Roffiel, writer, poet, and feminist, takes an active part in the lesbian and feminist movement.[3] Sabina Berman, writer, theatrical director, and poet, has won the National Theater Award four times.[4]

CULTURAL AND RELIGIOUS ATTITUDES

Mexican culture is deeply patriarchal. Women who do not fulfill the roles of mother and spouse—single mothers, prostitutes, lesbians—are seen as posing a threat to society. Women are educated from a young age to become wives and mothers; they are under pressure to marry and are subjected to frequent questioning from friends and family. The small number of lesbian support organizations and the social invisibility of les-

---

Women who do not fulfill the roles of mother and spouse are seen as posing a threat to society.

---

bians cause many women to live out their lives in isolation, without benefit of knowledge or personal acceptance, and many end up marrying. Family pressure is aggressive, sometimes even violent. When violence does occur, lesbians rarely seek redress from the authorities because of the culture's tradition of homophobia.

> I felt affection and desire for my girlfriends ever since I was young; I didn't know what was wrong with me. I thought it would pass when I got married. I tried never to be alone, to avoid temptation. When I learned that a group existed, I knew it was the place for me. Now, at the age of 40 and with two daughters, I am starting to live my own life.
> —Clara, a 40-year-old woman who has only recently come to terms with her sexuality[5]

When I first became attracted to other women, I told my parents; my father got extremely angry. Once he caught me with a girlfriend, and he beat me so hard I had to go to the hospital. When I got out of the hospital a male friend went with me to make a formal complaint, but we received no legal response. In high school, I had a girlfriend, but my family found out, and my father sent three guys to rape me, so I got married. I separated after a year. Now I have a son, and my family is still watching me.
—Dely, 25 years old[6]

Religion reinforces the culture's patriarchal ideology, promoting the image of the traditional family as the sacred ideal to which all respectable people must adhere. The Catholic Church has been outspoken in its condemnation of homosexuality. In 1991, when the 13th annual conference of the International Lesbian and Gay Association was scheduled to take place in Guadalajara, the church joined local authorities in a campaign of harassment and intimidation towards lesbians and gay men. The Mayor of the City, Gabriel Covarrubias Ibarra, stated to the daily newspaper *Metropoli*, "An event of this nature cannot be authorized in any way because neither our customs, nor history, nor education, nor religion, nor anything will permit it."[7] The mayor also stated that conference participants would not receive police protection in his city. Fearing violence, the organizers were forced to move the conference to another city.

LESBIAN FAMILIES

Recently, lesbian couples have begun considering the possibility of having children through donor insemination. Since it is a private service, donor insemination is available only to those with significant economic resources. Not only is it an expensive procedure, but few doctors are willing to assist lesbians with donor insemination, and lesbians have no legal recourse in such instances. Adoption laws stipulate numerous requirements even for heterosexual couples, such as legal marriage, economic solvency, emotional stability, moral authority, conjugal assistance, and ownership of community property, making it impossible for lesbians to adopt.

In the majority of cases, lesbian mothers have children from previous marriages. For these women, divorce and custody proceedings can be extremely difficult. Lesbians can be denied custody of their children if the judge deems them "morally unfit" on the basis of their sexual orientation. Even if they manage to hide their sexual orientation from the judge and retain custody of their children, their ex-husbands can blackmail them with the threat of having the children taken away. This puts lesbian mothers in a vulnerable position in divorce negotiations.

Lesbian mothers are also faced with another difficulty: if they are in a relationship with another woman, their partner has no legally recognized relationship with the child. Same-sex couples are not recognized in any way under Mexican law. Thus, the rights afforded to heterosexual married couples are denied to lesbians. These include not only the ability to obtain parental rights over a partner's children but also to bequeath or receive an inheritance, to recognize their partner in a public ceremony, to obtain loans for purchasing real estate as a couple, and to obtain medical and life insurance with legal recognition as a partner.

HEALTH AND SOCIAL SERVICES

The opportunity to speak openly to health care providers about sexual orientation rarely exists. Doctors are often highly conservative and do not consider sexual orientation in their diagnoses or treatment. A significant number of mental health professionals continue to claim that they are able to "cure" homosexuality. Homosexuals Anonymous, an organization supported by religious groups and Pro-Vida which expanded in the early 1990's but never managed to establish itself in Mexican society, takes a repressive stance, aiming to control homosexual urges through abstinence, and classifying homosexuality as an illness or a compulsive disorder. At the same time, however, a significant number of mental health professionals, and organizations such as the Consejo Nacional de Lucha contra el SIDA (National Council for the Struggle against AIDS) and various feminist and gay organizations not only acknowledge lesbians but have increasingly begun to diversify their efforts in order to fulfill the differing psychological, legal, recreational, and political needs of lesbians.

VIOLENCE

Lesbians are subject to various forms of verbal and physical harassment. Right-wing groups, especially anti-abortion groups such as Pro-Vida, have shown great intolerance towards lesbian existence and lesbian activism. Some lesbian activists, such as Guadalupe Lopez, founder of Grupo Patlatonalli, a Guadalajara lesbian group, have received telephone death threats. Lesbians have also been victims of aggression and neighborhood pressure regarding the establishment of assistance centers, suffering sexual harassment and requests by neighbors that the police investigate their activities. This harassment necessitates frequent changes of location, resulting in a lack of continuity in the work that such centers can perform. Frequently, in neighborhoods surrounding lesbian centers, members of the organization—and sometimes visitors— find their automobiles damaged or scratched, their windows broken, their mirrors and antennas stolen.

LESBIAN ACTIVISM

The lesbian movement began in 1977 with the founding of Lesbos, whose primary purpose was to organize lesbians and encourage consciousness raising. It survived for approximately three years. The years 1978 through 1987 can be considered the formative period of the movement, with a proliferation of groups such as OIKABETH, Oasis, Madres Lesbianas (Lesbian Mothers), Coordinadora de Lesbianas (Coordinator of Lesbians), Mulas (Mules), Gestación (Gestation), La Colectiva (The Collective), Seminario de Lesbianas Marxistas Leninistas (Seminar for Marxist-Leninist Lesbians), and Patlatonalli, a group which has managed to survive in the conservative city of Guadalajara since 1986 and to achieve recognition and prestige on both a national and international level. It is important to note that in the years 1987-90, the lesbian movement consisted of Patlatonalli, Oasis, and a few other shadow organizations, and yet maintained the tradition of organizing national meetings of lesbians, taking part in the annual march, assisting Latin American meetings, and becoming involved in international events. The Fourth National Lesbian Feminist Meeting took place in 1994. In 1994-95, El Clóset de Sor Juana held the office of Women's Secretariat within the International Lesbian and Gay Association. Several lesbian activists attended the final preparatory meeting for the UN Fourth World Conference on Women, and three had the opportunity to address governmental and non-governmental delegates. In 1982, the first openly lesbian candidates, Claudia Hinojosa and Patria Jiménez, ran for seats in the Federal Congress, and in 1991 Patria Jiménez was among the

Lesbian activist Patria Jiménez with a female member of the EZLN, April 1995.

10 political candidates nationwide who were fielded by the Coordinadora Feminista (Feminist Coordinator).

Lesbians have also been active in mixed lesbian and gay organizations, such as Lambda, El Movimiento de Liberación Homosexual (MLH), El Comite de Lesbianas y Homosexuales en Apoyo a Rosario Ibarra (CLHARI), El Comité Nacional de Lesbianas y Homosexuales (CONALH), Colectivo Sol, Círculo Cultural Gay, La Asamblea Lésbica Gay, El Foro Lésbica Gay, and La Semana Cultural Lésbico Gay. However, discrimination, disdain, and misogynistic attitudes within gay male organizations have led lesbians to keep their work separate and to collaborate only in certain specific activities, such as the Lesbian and Gay Pride march, which has been held annually in Mexico City since 1978.

While still relatively invisible within society as a whole, lesbians have gained a measure of visibility within social and political movements. Lesbians have become involved in many aspects of Mexican political life, participating in political campaigns and other activities undertaken in the struggle for democracy. Responding to an invitation from Subcomandante Marcos of the Ejército Zapatista de Liberación Nacional (Zapatista Army of National Liberation), lesbian and gay activists participated openly in the National Democratic Convention that began in Chiapas in September 1994 and presented the proposals of the lesbian and gay movement.

LESBIANS AND THE FEMINIST MOVEMENT

The lesbian movement has been tied to the feminist movement since its advent. Discussions regarding patriarchy, oppression, and sexuality within the feminist movement have led to various examinations of female sexuality, and lesbian participation in national feminist meetings has been extensive. After 10 years of lesbian efforts under the feminist banner, the demand for respect for the human rights for lesbians became one of three principal goals to which the feminist movement is dedicated.[8]

NOTES

1 Another significant publication is *Debate Feminista*, a review of the feminist movement that appears every six months; it is in great demand in all of Latin America. Since its beginning in 1990 it has discussed the theme of homosexuality in each of its issues. It is, however, a theoretical review with limited distribution.

2 In 1972, Nancy Cárdenas put on the first play with homosexual content in Mexico: *Los Chicos de la Banda* (The Boys in the Band). She went on to write, produce, direct, and act in three performances with lesbian content: a musical comedy based on the short story *Claudine a l'Ecole de Collette* (Claudine at the School of Collette); *The Bitter Tears of Petra Von Kant*, by W.R. Fassbinder; *El día que pisamos la luna* (The Day We Set Foot on the Moon), a work she wrote herself, which portrays the lives of four lesbians of varying ages. Just before her death in 1994, she completed *Cuaderno de amor y desamor* (A Notebook of Love and Disaffection), a book of erotic poetry about lesbian love.

3 Her writing is in the field of lesbian romance. Among her notable works are two books of poetry, *Todas mis amigas son poetas* (All My Friends Are Poets), and *Corramos libres ahora* (Let Us Run Free Now). Her first novel, *Amora* tells of the relationship of two women, their uncertainties and their passions.

4 Among her principal books are *Lunas* (Moons), a book of erotic lesbian love poetry; *Entre Villa y una mujer desnuda* (Between Villa and the Naked Woman), an enormously successful novel that describes the fantasies and secret agendas in male-female relations with superb irony; and *Un grano de arroz* (A Grain of Rice), a story about the relationship between two sisters.

5 Conversation in a workshop on couples organized by Gloria Careaga Pérez, El Clóset de Sor Juana, 1994.

6 Conversation in a workshop on lesbian identity organized by Gloria Careaga Pérez, El Clóset de Sor Juana, 1994.

7 Rex Wockner, "Mexican officials condemn international gay conference," *Outlines*, June 1990. See also Guadalupe Lopez and Martha Naulart, "En Guadalajara: gobernio heterosexista, sociedad plurisexual" ("In Guadalajara: a Heterosexist Government, a Plurisexual Society") *FEM* No. 106, October 1991; Carlos Rubio Rosell, "XIII Conferencia Anual de ILGA," *El Nacional*, 15 July 1991; Manuel Gonzales, "Carta pública de personalidades de la sociedad civil manifestando su preocupación por la intolerancia contra las legitimas libertades" ("Open Letter to Authorities on his Concern for Intolerance against Legitimate Freedoms"), *El Occidental*, 23 June 1991; Katherine Ellison, "Mexico's Gays, Lesbians Struggle to Organize," *San Jose Mercury News*, 23 June 1991; David Tuller and Dawn Garcia, "Gays Call Off Big Meeting in Mexico," *S.F. Chronicle*, 13 June 1991.

8 The other two goals are reproductive rights and the eradication of violence against women.

ABOUT THE AUTHORS

Gloria Careaga Pérez is a social psychologist and coordinator of the Programa de Estudios de Género at the Universidad Autónoma de Mexico. She is one of the founders of El Clóset de Sor Juana.

Patria Jiménez has been an activist in the lesbian and gay liberation movement since 1979. She is one of the coordinators of El Clóset de Sor Juana and one of the founders of the Convención Nacional de Mujeres.

Netherlands

● ● ● ● ● ● ● ● ● ● ●

Astrid Mattijssen, Mirjam Turksma and Ineke de Vries

Lesbians in the Netherlands no longer have to meet secretly in small back rooms. Cities such as Amsterdam offer plenty of opportunities for lesbians to socialize with one another and participate in public life. Lesbians living in small towns are more isolated, but the country is small enough that lesbian organizations and meeting places in urban areas are accessible to almost everyone. There are lesbian bars, discos, sports activities, movie festivals, exhibitions, book shops choirs, dancing schools, and so on.

With over 10,000 members, the Nederlandse Vereniging tot Integratie van Homoseksualiteit (NVIH COC, The Dutch Society for the Integration of Homosexuality) is the most important lesbian and gay organization in the Netherlands. There are, however, numerous other lesbian and gay organizations, including political, religious, trade union, athletic, and many other groups. Black Orchid, a national network of Black and immigrant lesbians, was recently established.

In Amsterdam, the center of gay life in the Netherlands, a monument commemorates homosexuals who died in the Second World War. It is an important recognition of the existence of lesbians and gay men, and of the fight that is being fought for equal rights and protection against discrimination on the basis of sexual orientation. Pink Saturday, a celebration of lesbian and gay pride that takes place each June, brings lesbians from all walks of life together. Every year the event is held in a different town in order to support the gay and lesbian movement outside Amsterdam.

ATTITUDES WITHIN SOCIETY

Generally speaking, Dutch society is open-minded about the existence of homosexuality as long as it remains relatively hidden. Lesbians are tolerated as long as they are not very outspoken about their sexuality or openly defiant of heterosexual norms. In this atmosphere of qualified tolerance, many lesbians do not feel the need to conceal their sexual orientation but are nevertheless hesitant to speak out publicly as lesbians for fear of damaging their careers. Many are reluctant to use their positions in politics, in trade unions, or in women's organizations to speak out on lesbian issues.

Government policies on issues concerning the elderly completely ignore the existence of lesbians.

Studies by the Lesbian and Gay Studies Department of the University of Utrecht have shown that young lesbians face particular difficulties in being open about their sexual orientation. In a survey of students ages 12 to 18, three out of five reported being afraid of being regarded as homosexual when associating with gay and lesbian classmates. Homosexuality is not often discussed in school curricula outside of an occasional mention in sex education classes.

Older lesbians are almost completely invisible. Most older lesbians grew up in a time when sexuality was not discussed, and many continue to be reluctant to talk about their sexual orientation. If two older women are living together they are seldom regarded as a couple, and government policies on issues concerning the elderly completely ignore the existence of lesbians. Older lesbians have few public meeting places, and many socialize only within a small circle of friends. These women often face very deep isolation when their partner dies.

While young lesbians, older lesbians, and others who are marginalized within the lesbian community may be particularly vulnerable to isolation and other psychological problems, most lesbians are affected in some way or another by the negative attitudes toward homosexuality that continue to exist in Dutch society. The SAD-Schorer Foundation and a number of other organizations and independent counselors specialize in providing support to lesbians on issues such as "coming out," acceptance, appreciation, identity and sexuality, anti-lesbian violence, and lesbian parenting.

THE WORKPLACE

Complaints at the Centrum Anti-discriminatie Homosexualiteit (Homosexual Anti-Discrimination Center) show that even in an atmosphere of increasing tolerance, lesbians and gay men still encounter a number of problems in the workplace. Studies have shown that a significant part of these problems has to do with company culture and with the way in which colleagues associate with each other. Homophobia can manifest itself in ordinary remarks and jokes as well as in explicit provocations from colleagues.[1]

Overt or covert discrimination in company policies is widespread. Many companies have equalized benefits for married couples and unmarried heterosexual couples but have explicitly excluded same-sex couples. Lesbian employees are frequently passed over for promotion or discriminated against in hiring.

LEGAL POSITION

Until 1971 the age of consent for lesbian sex was higher than that for heterosexual sex. From that time onward, the gay and lesbian movement fought for equal rights, focusing on a General Act on Equal Treatment (see below).

In 1983 the Dutch Constitution was amended, stating that all forms of discrimination were prohibited. Sexual orientation was not included as grounds for protection against discrimination. However, lesbians and gay men enjoy constitutional protection against discrimination according to a number of parliamentary documents and judicial interpretations that have placed sexual orientation in the purview of the first article of the Constitution.[2]

In 1992, existing articles on racial discrimination were augmented with the term "homosexual and heterosexual leanings." With this change, discrimination on the basis of sexual orientation became a criminal offense, along with the public expression of discriminatory remarks; participation in or support of acts of discrimination; and discrimination against lesbians or gay men in employment.

After a long battle, the General Act on Equal Treatment finally came into effect in 1994. This Act prohibits discrimination on the basis of sexual orientation in many areas of life. The first bill was proposed in 1981, and included homosexuality as grounds for protection against discrimination. Under a storm of protest, particularly from conservative religious groups, the bill was voted down, as were several other similar bills proposed in the 1980s. Finally, after more than fifteen years of debate, the bill was reintroduced and came into effect in September 1994.

The Act prohibits discrimination on the basis of religion, belief, political conviction, race, sex, heterosexual or homosexual orientation, or civil status in employment, housing, medical care, and the provision of goods and services. While the scope of the Act is quite broad, it includes an escape clause for religious institutions. Thus, a Christian school is allowed to make demands that the staff adhere to the institution's principles. However, such institutions are prohibited from making any distinction purely on the basis of the single fact of sexual orientation. The question of whether religious school are allowed to fire a teacher who openly states her lesbianism has yet to be determined in the courts. There are numerous reports of religious hospitals that refuse lesbians donor insemination services, but these have not yet been subject to legal challenges.

IMMIGRATION AND REFUGEE POLICIES

Under Dutch immigration law, no distinction is made between heterosexual and homosexual relationships, and non-Dutch partners of Dutch citizens can obtain Dutch citizenship. Lesbians and gay men who have fled persecution based on sexual orientation in other countries have also been granted political asylum in the Netherlands.

PARTNERSHIP

Outside of immigration law, same-sex couples receive little legal recognition. Same-sex couples are not permitted to be legally married. There are some churches in which lesbian and gay couples can be joined in matrimony, and several municipalities allow registration of same-sex couples. However, neither of these procedures grants any legal rights to the couple. In 1988, the Supreme Court ruled that prohibition of same-sex marriage is not in violation of international law. However, as a consequence of a campaign conducted by the gay newspaper *de Gay Krant* for the introduction of same-sex marriage, the government has proposed a bill enabling registration of lesbian and homosexual couples. This registration would grant full legal recognition to same-sex couples except in the realm of parenthood. Registered couples would not be able to adopt any children jointly, nor obtain joint parental authority over children they are raising jointly.

PARENTHOOD

At present, the female partner of a lesbian mother cannot acquire legal parenthood over a child that they are raising together. This means that the child cannot inherit from the co-mother or acquire her name or nationality. It also means that the co-mother has no parental authority regarding choice of schools, admission to a hospital, or any other such matter.

Under pressure of a number of legal challenges, the government has introduced a bill with regard to lesbian and gay parenthood. The bill would allow the partner of the legal parent to obtain joint parental authority and would give her the responsibility of financially supporting the child. This bill has already been criticized by the lesbian and gay movement and the women's movement because it still does not allow the co-mother to be a full legal parent. This would be an impediment for the child as well as for the co-mother in matters of inheritance, naming and nationality.

NOTES

1 Letty Bonfrere, Homosexualiteit en bedrijfscultuur, een onderzoek naar de bestrijding van discriminatie op grond van homosexualiteit in bedrijven (Den Haag: VUGA, 1992); Adrianne Dercksen, Vertrouwenspersonen en homosexualiteit in arbeidssituaties (Den Haag:VUGA, 1992).

2 Dutch Lower Chamber 1975-1976 13872, no 4. Schedules of Explanatory Memorandum, p. 87. The revised Dutch Constitution came into force in 1983. Homosexuality is not explicitly mentioned, but it states '...discrimination based on...sex or on any grounds whatsoever, shall not be permitted.'

ABOUT THE AUTHORS

Astrid Mattijssen is a lawyer and works at the Clara Wichmann Institute for Women and Law. She is a member of the Commission on Homosexuality and Law of NVIH COC.

Mirjam Turksma is a psychologist and coordinator of the gay and lesbian emancipation policy of the city of Amsterdam. She is on the board of NVIH COC.

Ineke de Vries is a sociologist and independent researcher/consultant who is a member of the International Commission of NVIH COC.

Nicaragua

● ● ● ● ● ● ● ● ● ●

María Bolt González

On June 11, 1992 the National Assembly of the Republic of
Nicaragua passed Law No. 150, "Law of Penal Code Reforms."
The law, which was subsequently ratified by Violeta Barrios de
Chamorro, contains the following provision:

> Article 204: Anyone who induces, promotes, propagandizes or
> practices in scandalous form sexual intercourse between persons
> of the same sex commits the crime of sodomy and shall incur one
> to three years' imprisonment.

Article 204 also criminalizes homosexual relations with a person
under one's responsibility, regardless of age or whether in private, as
"unlawful seduction," punishable by two to four years.

REACTION TO ARTICLE 204

In response to the passage of the amendment, lesbian and gay
activists, along with many allies within the progressive community,
launched a campaign "For a Sexuality Free from Prejudices." In June and
July 1992, the campaign presented a series of debates and film forums,

and more than 4,000 signatures were gathered and delivered to the President's office. The administration did not respond.

The Comisión en Pro del Orgullo Lésbico-Homosexual (Lesbian-Gay Pride Commission) then produced an analysis of Article 204 that was sent to the National Assembly in September 1992. The assembly also failed to respond. In a final step, in November of the same year, the Centro de Derechos Constitucionales (Center for Constitutional Rights) presented an appeal to the Supreme Court challenging the constitutionality of Article 204. The appeal cited numerous articles of the Nicaraguan Constitution, including the right to privacy, to freedom of expression and to non-discrimination before the law. After considerable delay, the court dismissed the appeal in March 1994.

The response to Article 204 has extended far beyond Nicaragua's borders. However, although letters of protest have arrived from countries around the world, the law continues to be on the books. There are

---

Those who are defined by law as criminals have little reason to believe that the justice system will protect them.

---

no known cases thus far of Article 204 being applied to lesbians. The article has been applied primarily to gay male sex workers and to prison inmates. While it has not, to date, been used against lesbians, its existence represents a clear infringement on the rights of lesbians in Nicaragua. Those who are defined by law as criminals have little reason to believe that the justice system will protect them.

LESBIAN ACTIVISM

Currently, no national lesbian organizations exist in Nicaragua. The lesbian feminist group Nosotras (We) was formed in 1992 by 30 lesbians, with a core group of 10, and remained active until mid-1994. Lesbians have been very involved in the fight against Article 204 and continue to be involved in many feminist organizations and mixed lesbian and gay organizations, such as Neconi, a lesbian and gay collective. The Xochiquetzal Foundation, an officially recognized non-governmanetal organization (NGO), is directed by two lesbian coordinators. The Foundation works to promote a nonsexist society and open-mindedness toward sexuality; it has programs to prevent sexually transmitted diseases and HIV/AIDS and publishes a quarterly magazine, *Fuera del Closet* (Out of the Closet), which discusses society's myths and prejudices related to sexuality and HIV/AIDS.

In 1988, Colectivo de Educadores Populares Sobre VIH/SIDA (CEP-SIDA, Collective of Popular Educators Concerned with HIV/AIDS) was formed. The group, made up of gay men and lesbians, started performing HIV/AIDS prevention work within the gay and lesbian community. CEP-SIDA was successful in achieving a working relationship with the Ministry of Health, but this relationship became tenuous after the Chamorro government was elected in 1990, and CEP-SIDA ceased operating in mid-1992.

In 1992, in reaction to Article 204, the first Gay and Lesbian Pride Day celebration was organized by the Comisión en Pro del Orgullo Lésbico-Homosexual. The media coverage was balanced and respectful, and for the week following the parade several newspapers carried interviews with lesbians and gay men. The parade has become an annual event. It takes place as part of an annual Day for a Sexuality Free from Prejudices, in which different NGOs and lesbian and gay groups take part.

LESBIANS AND THE FEMINIST MOVEMENT

Lesbians have attained the most recognition and visibility within feminist organizations. Lesbians work at both the leadership level and as participants in different groups, centers, institutions, and NGOs that work with and for women. Within these groups lesbians have been able to work with heterosexual women and gain acceptance and respect. In these groups, in contrast to society at large, lesbians are able to be open about their sexual orientation with relatively few consequences.

Various attempts have been made to call a meeting of Nicaraguan lesbian feminists who belong to different NGOs. Though there is interest, the meeting has not yet taken place. A new feminist group called La

Corriente (The Current), which has lesbian participation, has begun to organize Central American conferences and to publish a magazine.

LESBIAN LIFE

All women, by the mere fact of being women, are discriminated against in Nicaragua. If someone is lesbian, then she experiences double discrimination. This is intensified if the woman is poor and more so if she is Black or belongs to the Misquita or Suma indigenous groups.

It is extremely difficult to be public about one's lesbianism in Nicaragua. Women who are known to be lesbians face discrimination within their family, their neighborhood, and their workplace. Women who are fired from their jobs because they are lesbians cannot bring legal challenges; there are no laws prohibiting discrimination on the basis of sexual orientation, and regardless of the legal situation most women are silent out of fear that their lesbianism will be made public. Most women remain "in the closet" about their sexuality because they fear rejection and discrimination from family, friends, and colleagues.

These problems are particularly acute for young women. Recently, two young lesbians, ages 19 and 15, were caught trying to escape to Costa Rica. A newspaper report stated that the two were fleeing from home because their families were trying to break up their relationship. The family of S.M.M.—the older of the two—accepted her lesbianism, but the younger woman's family would not tolerate her lesbianism and, according to the report, had initiated court proceedings against S.M.M., who was being detained by the police. While no further information was stated regarding this case, it is not difficult to see how Article 204 could be used in such a situation.[1]

Allegations of lesbianism can be used as a threat against women involved in custody cases, as was illustrated by a recent dispute over the custody of a six-year-old boy. When the father accused the mother of being a lesbian, she denied the accusation and insisted that it was simply a ploy on the part of her ex-husband to gain custody of their son. Nowhere in the newspaper coverage was the possibility raised that lesbians could in fact be good mothers.[2]

In general, the low level of education in Nicaragua leads to ignorance and fear, particularly for lesbians who are trying to come to terms with their sexuality. This fear results in a great deal of self-doubt and isolation and can lead to depression and even suicide. To counter this isolation, the lesbian and gay movement is seeking to create greater visibility within Nicaraguan society and to provide as much information as possible through events, such as the annual pride parade.

NOTES

1 "Captura rompe idilio de lesbianas" ("Capture breaks lesbians' idyll"), *Barricada*, 16 June 1995.
2 "Acusan a madre soltera de lesbiana" ("Single mother accused of being lesbian"), *Barricada*, 12 May 1995.

ABOUT THE AUTHOR

María Bolt González is a feminist activist, a psychologist, an educator, and the sub-director of Fundación Xochiquetzal. She is one of the organizers of the annual Day for a Sexuality Free from Prejudices.

Norway

● ● ● ● ● ● ● ●

Gro Lindstad

Norway has a reputation for being a liberal country with a strong tradition of solidarity and of working towards equality for all members of society. The legal system affords lesbians and gay men many protections although same-sex couples are still not equal to heterosexual couples in all respects.

Lesbians also benefit from progressive legislation on women's issues and a notable presence of women in public life. In 1977 the Norwegian Parliament passed a law on gender equality covering all areas of society except for religious institutions. The current prime minister is a woman, as are close to 40% of the cabinet ministers and state secretaries.

LEGAL SITUATION AND HISTORY

Until 1973, male homosexual acts were illegal in Norway under Section 213 of the Penal Code. There have never been any legal restrictions on sex between women, probably because the Norwegian Penal Code dates from 1902, and at that time women's sexuality was in general not taken seriously.

In 1981, the Norwegian Parliament added two clauses to the Norwegian Penal Code prohibiting discrimination on the basis of sexual orientation. Section 135a makes it illegal to "threaten or deride, or to incite to hatred, persecution or contempt" against anyone on account of his or her "homosexual inclination, lifestyle, or orientation." Section 349a makes it illegal to refuse to give goods or services to anyone on these grounds. The maximum penalty is six months' imprisonment. These provisions made Norwegian lesbians and gay men the first in the world to be specifically afforded legal protection against discrimination.

Section 135a makes it illegal to "threaten or deride, or to incite to hatred, persecution or contempt" against anyone on account of his or her "homosexual inclination, lifestyle, or orientation."

On April 1, 1993, the Norwegian Parliament passed a partnership law giving lesbians and gay men the right to marry. The Norwegian partnership law is based on the laws that apply to heterosexual married couples. However, there are several distinct differences. Lesbians and gay men cannot get married in church, and lesbian and gay couples do not have the right to adopt children. In addition, members of same-sex partnerships are not accorded any rights regarding their partner's children. Thus, while lesbian and gay relationships are legally recognized, they are still not seen as morally equivalent to heterosexual marriages.

LESBIANS AND GAY MEN AT WORK

The Landsforeningen for Lesbisk og Homfil Frigjøring (LLH, Norwegian National Organization for Lesbian and Gay Liberation) has documented a large number of cases concerning discrimination in the work-place. We see cases where lesbians are harassed by colleagues and superiors. In some cases the harassment is so severe that lesbians are forced to quit their jobs.

For example, a lesbian working as a service person for local county health care authorities entered into partnership with her lover. They were the first couple to do so in a large city in Norway and the event received media attention. After this event her male colleagues started harassing her verbally to the point where she quit her job. Nobody effectively stepped in to stop the harassment.

In another instance, during reorganization of the county health services, a lesbian working in a high position in a county health administration was pressured from her job for being an open lesbian. The official reason given was that she was not competent to run the health administration after the reorganization.

LESBIAN PARENTING

Only married heterosexual couples are permitted to adopt under Norwegian law. There are no national guidelines for foster care, and the ability of lesbian couples to become foster parents varies from county to county depending on local guidelines. The prejudice that lesbians and gay men cannot be good and competent parents is widespread in Norwegian society. Lesbians who have become pregnant through donor insemination find that their lifetime companions have no legal rights to the children, although their combined income is counted when the local county authorities calculate how much they should pay for day-care.

EDUCATION

Although the Norwegian government and Norwegian society seem to have increasingly liberal attitudes towards lesbians, the educational system has generally failed to provide adequate sex education. On occasion, lesbians and gay men are invited to make presentations, but information on homosexuality is not systematically included in school curricula. Norwegian authorities are now in the process of revising national guidelines on education, and the proposal currently under consideration would limit sex education to basic information on reproduction, eliminating all discussion of sexuality more generally.

HIV/AIDS

The Norwegian Parliament recently passed a law giving the authorities the right to forcibly isolate a person with AIDS if he or she is considered a health hazard. The law also opens the possibility of forcibly testing people for HIV.

MENTAL HEALTH

LLH has received reports of psychologists who are not competent to counsel lesbians. The Norwegian Psychologists Association removed homosexuality as a disease and mental disturbance from its lists in 1978. However, LLH has also received reports of mental health professionals who try to convert lesbians to heterosexuality, and reports of ones who refuse to see clients because they are lesbians.

ASYLUM

While some lesbian and gay refugees have been granted asylum, Norwegian authorities are still hesitant to view persecution against sexual minorities as valid grounds for granting asylum. Some gains have been made on a case by case basis, but no clear policy has been established.

LESBIANS AND THE CHURCH

The Lutheran Church, which is the Norwegian state church, is run by the Department of Church Matters, Education, and Research. Eleven bishops, who form the top of the church hierarchy, make decisions concerning moral and ethical questions. For many years, one of these questions has been homosexuality, and since 1977 the church's official position has been that being homosexual is no problem, but same-sex sexual practices are. This attitude causes intense conflict and suffering for many lesbians and gay men who have wanted to belong to the church, and for some it has led to suicide. We know of several lesbians who are not allowed to practice as priests within the Lutheran Church because they are in long-term relationships with other women.

In April 1995, the bishops once again discussed the issue of homosexuality. This time three of the bishops expressed the view that lesbians and gay men should have a place in the church and that the church should allow lesbians and gay men to be priests even if they are in relationships.

LESBIAN LIFE IN NORWAY

In 1950, the first lesbian and gay organization formed under the name DNF-48. This organization operated secretly because of the criminalization of male homosexual acts at that time. The first visible spokesperson and secretary general of the organization, Kim Friele, was a lesbian, known today for her great work for the Norwegian lesbian/gay movement. Over the years lesbians have organized both in mixed lesbian and gay groups and in lesbian groups.

In 1988, a group of lesbians toured the country in a bus to inform Norwegians about lesbian life. The bus traveled all over Norway, making stops to hand out brochures, show videos about lesbian life, give lectures, and talk to people. Lesbians who live in larger cities enjoy a range of athletic, social, and cultural groups, but lesbians living in smaller cities and more rural areas have few bars or public spaces of any sort in which to meet one another.

ABOUT THE AUTHOR

Gro Lindstad, 35, is a lesbian living in Oslo, Norway. She has been an activist in the Norwegian lesbian and gay movement for the past 13 years. She works for the Norwegian State Authorities as a senior executive officer for child support reciprocity agreements with the U.S.

Philippines

●　●　●　●　●　●　●　●　●　●

Malu S. Marin

In the Philippines, lesbianism is considered a taboo subject, and any public manifestations of lesbianism are viewed as signs of a decadent society. The "forbidden" nature of lesbianism has created a general perception that lesbians do not exist in the Philippines, and that if there are Philippine lesbians, they are aberrant. This invisibility means that lesbians are excluded from mainstream cultural and political discourse.

In recent years more and more lesbians within the women's movement have dared to come out and become more visible. The groups that they have formed, such as Lesbond, Can't Live in the Closet (CLIC), LINK Davao, the Group, and the Women Supporting Women Committee, among others, are for the most part limited to urban centers. These groups have a decidedly political orientation and work to provide services for the lesbian community and to advocate for lesbian visibility and lesbian rights. Lesbian subcultures, which do not have a feminist or political orientation, predate these organized efforts and exist even in rural areas.

Unfortunately, the recent upsurge in awareness and advocacy for lesbian rights has not significantly impacted the mainstream human rights community. The first item in this report documents a concrete case of failure by the human rights community to redefine their framework to take into account discrimination on the basis of sexual orientation.

FIRST LEGAL COMPLAINT FILED BY
LESBIAN COUPLE IN THE PHILIPPINES

On September 6, 1994, Evangeline (Vangie) Castronuevo and Elizabeth (Beth) Lim each received notice that their employment at Balay Rehabilitation Center Inc. had been terminated. Balay, a human rights organization, provides services for political detainees and other victims of human rights abuses. Vangie has been working as a counselor for the Integrated Rehabilitation Program of Balay while Beth was the coordinator of the Expansion Program and a member of the Executive Committee.[1]

Beth and Vangie's saga began in April 1994 when their relationship was revealed to a friend and co-worker in Balay. Their relationship was eventually disclosed to everyone in the office and in the weeks that followed, the two women were subjected to varying degrees of isolation and harassment. The atmosphere in the office became so intolerable that Beth had to take a leave of absence from her job. An official inquiry was later conducted to solve the "organizational crisis" caused by the revelation of Beth's and Vangie's relationship.

Both women contend that their performance at work was not affected by their relationship and that their co-worker's reaction to their lesbianism, which was marked by intolerance and animosity, led to the "crisis." The predominant sentiment of the Balay personnel was that the marital status of Vangie was endangered and subsequently "ruined" because of her extra-marital relationship with Beth.[2] The Board of Directors stated that the two were terminated "because they committed acts grossly damaging to Balay, the staff and other people by engaging in [an] extra-marital affair and flaunting this affair before the staff which resulted in the subsequent breakup of Ruga's [Vangie's] marriage."[3] The double-standard at work in this decision is evident from the fact that the board made mention of Vangie's previously married status when it had long tolerated another female worker's relationship with a married man. The absence of protests against the heterosexual woman belie the claim that the extra-marital affair was the issue.

The Balay Board of Directors was split on the question of Beth and Vangie's dismissal: five were in favor of the termination and four refused to take part in it. In a letter to the five other members of the board, the four who opposed dismissal stated that "fundamental principles, such as respect for human dignity and individuality, lead us to take the position that the issue of the extra-marital relationship is not within the ambit of any action or interference which Balay may permissibly take. What we are doing is an invasion of private lives of two individuals, in total disrespect for their individualities and personal decisions which they have made at this time." The letter concluded by saying that the four board members refused to take part any further in the process.[4]

A week after their termination, Beth and Vangie filed a complaint for illegal dismissal with the National Labor Relations Commission. In the complaint, the two are seeking reinstatement to their former positions and payment of damages. This is the first lawsuit in the Philippines in which a complaint regarding discrimination against lesbians on the

Elizabeth Lim and Evangeline Castronuevo

basis of sexual orientation has been filed. As of this writing, the case is still pending. The issue of legal protection for lesbians is at this point nonexistent in Philippine jurisprudence, and the outcome of this case is likely to have a significant impact on opportunities for future lesbian rights advocacy.

The case has enabled lesbian and gay activists and supportive nonlesbian feminists to come together on several occasions to protest the actions of Balay and to challenge the human rights community to expand its definition of human rights to include lesbian and gay rights.[5] The human rights community, however, was silent throughout the time that the case was garnering media coverage, and not a single human rights organization in the country has offered a statement of support.

LEGISLATION

There are no concrete and specific laws that make lesbianism or homosexuality illegal in the Philippines. The only law that specifically mentions lesbianism or homosexuality is the Family Code. Promulgated in 1988 after several years of drafting, the Family Code is a revision of certain sections of the Civil Code (enacted in 1953) that deal with family relations. Article 45 states the conditions under which marriages may be annulled; one such condition is if "the consent of either party was obtained by fraud." Among the circumstances constituting fraud are "[c]oncealment of drug addiction, habitual alcoholism, homosexuality or lesbianism existing at the time of marriage" (Art. 46). Thus, if a husband "discovers" that he is married to a lesbian, and that his spouse's sexual orientation was concealed from him before the marriage, he may sue for annulment. In this case, the lesbian partner is the guilty party, and she may consequently lose her rights to joint property and may also jeopardize her right to retain custody of her children.

The other provision that mentions lesbianism and homosexuality in the Family Code relates to legal separation. In Article 55, lesbianism and homosexuality are listed as grounds for filing a petition for legal separation. This provision is similar to the previous one on annulment. In this case, the lesbianism of the female spouse is presumed to have begun during the marriage. A review of other grounds for legal separation sheds some light on the context in which lesbianism is viewed under Philippine law. These grounds include repeated physical violence or grossly abusive conduct directed against petitioner; physical violence or moral pressure to compel the petitioner to change religious or political affiliation; attempt of respondent to corrupt or induce petitioner to engage in prostitution; final judgment sentencing the respondent to imprisonment of more than six years; drug addiction or habitual alcoholism; sexual infidelity or perversion; and an attempt by the respondent against the life of the petitioner (Art. 55). It's clear from these brief mentions in the Family Code that under the law lesbianism is viewed as a crime or behavior responsible for the destruction of the (heterosexual) family.

Like the Family Code, the Philippine Constitution reflects the importance the state gives to the family. The constitutional provisions are as follows:

Sect. 12, Art. II: The State recognizes the sanctity of family life and shall protect and strengthen the family as a basic social institution.

Sect. 1, Art. XV.: The State recognizes the Filipino family as the foundation of the nation. Accordingly, it shall strengthen its solidarity and actively promote its total development.

Sect. 2, Art. XV.: Marriage, as an inviolable social institution, is the foundation of the family and shall be protected by the State.

To prevent any possible alternative interpretations of marriage, the Family Code clearly delineates marriage as a heterosexual institution. Article 1 of the Family Code which states: "Marriage is a special contract of permanent union between a man and a woman entered into accordance with law for the establishment of conjugal and family life." In the old Civil Code, marriage is defined as "not a mere contract but an inviolable social institution."[6] And although under the old Civil Code marriage was assumed to be heterosexual, the gender of the parties was not expressly articulated. In the current definition of a marriage, homosexual marriage is rendered impossible without being explicitly prohibited.

ATTITUDES TOWARD LESBIANS

With or without any legal instrument, there are other ways in which homophobia exists in all other socio-cultural and political apparatuses in Philippine society. While there has been no reported incidence of state violence against lesbians, homophobia remains pervasive in many institutions, such as the church, the education system, the mass media, and the family. There are occasions where lesbianism or homosexuality is denounced publicly, but in most instances, there is no need for verbal or written articulation of homophobia.

RELIGION

The Philippine Catholic Church is perhaps the most resolute and persistent of all the institutions that promote and perpetuate homophobia. Through centuries of religious colonization, the Catholic Church has achieved the status of being the only legitimate arbiter of morality, a position that remains in force up to the present day, and is evident in the church hierarchy's frequent involvement in state affairs.

The church has issued explicit pronouncements of its views on lesbianism and homosexuality. Its homophobia was concretely demonstrated during the height of the preparations for the International Conference on Population and Development (ICPD) in August-September 1994. Fearful that progressive and liberal-thinking official delegates to the conference would recognize, acknowledge, and support the growing calls to redefine the concept of family—such redefinition in the broadest interpretation would include homosexual unions—the church rallied its millions of followers to condemn these elements in the Philippine delegation. While the center of attack was the government's family planning program, which included the use of contraception as birth control, lesbians and gays were included in the vitriolic exchange of attacks and charges between the church and the state. In a "letter to parents," Jaime Cardinal Sin, the Archbishop of Manila, declared, "our children...are being brainwashed to accept as normal, attractive, and even glamorous certain abnormal and perverse relationships and behavior such as homosexuality, lesbianism, incest, sodomy, oral sex, contraception, sterilization, and abortion."[7]

Priests were instructed by the Cardinal to read the "letter to parents" during their homilies on August 7, 1994. This is just one example of the church's campaign to rid the Philippines of what it perceives as abnormal and perverse sexual relationships, practices, and behavior. Further, the incidence of born-again fundamentalist groups promising to "cure" lesbianism both within and outside the Catholic Church has increased in recent years.

The church is not an isolated power, and its reach and influence are well-entrenched in Philippine societal structures. The state, even if headed by a Protestant president, constantly reckons with the church position on crucial issues. The power of the church can be seen, for instance, in the case of advice columnists who counsel confused young lesbians to change their ways because being lesbian is against Catholic dogma. The same is true for teachers in secular or public schools who punish their lesbian students and send them to the confessional box to confess their "sin and immorality."

MEDIA

Lesbians still have a long way to go in their struggle for positive and honest media portrayal. Lesbians appear in the mainstream media only occasionally and in passing, playing stereotyped roles of men trapped in women's bodies. They are feared or shunned by women, and they possess power only by aping men. In some instances, popular female actresses who play lesbian roles are made to alter their feminine appearances in order to look masculine. Their characterization has become very predictable—in the end, a man sweeps them off their feet and they get transformed into their pristine and feminine heterosexual selves.[8]

The print media's coverage of lesbian- and gay-related events is also worth noting. While there has been a recent increase in the coverage of local and international lesbian and gay news, the scales of balanced reporting are still tipped in favor of heterosexist assumptions and notions. Tabloids report in screaming headlines about violence committed by lesbians or gays, in an attempt to portray them as violent, irrational, and dangerous persons, but there is no such coverage devoted to the violence that is done to lesbians and gays, except in very few instances where gays get killed or robbed by unidentified persons. Oftentimes, the sexual orientation of these crime victims are treated as incidental; there is no actual probe to determine if these crimes were committed against them because of their sexual orientation. The content of news concerning lesbians and gays is still confined to behavior that is perceived as abnormal or aberrant.

EDUCATION

In October 1994, the Department of Education, Culture, and Sports (DECS) announced its plans to encourage and give incentives to men who would be interested in entering the teaching profession. According to DECS Technical Service Director Ma. Lourdes V. Macatangay, there is a demand for male teachers in public elementary schools, where (as is the case in private schools) female teachers comprise the bulk of the teaching force. She argued that the predominantly female teaching force is the reason that "children become more susceptible to becoming gay." Thus, the presence of male teachers is intended to "help curb the homosexual tendency among young boys." Some officials even went so far as to suggest that homosexual tutors be banned altogether from teaching in schools below the college level.[9]

In order to achieve this plan, DECS proposed that prospective male teachers who had outstanding performance in high school be exempted from taking college entrance examinations or that they be offered scholarships. The department official likewise stated that they are studying the possibility of increasing salaries for teachers as an incentive to attract more male teachers. The plan has been criticized and attacked, not only by the secretary and some officials of the department but also by other concerned groups. That such an ill-conceived proposal is treated seriously, however, is an indication of how pervasive such attitudes are within the educational establishment.

Any assessment of homophobia within the educational system must take into account the Catholic schools which comprise an estimated 70% of the total number of private schools in the Philippines. In Catholic schools, homophobia is a fundamental element of the dominant culture. In some cases, it can be translated into concrete policies —for example, the requirement that students exhibit "good moral character." Lesbianism would be interpreted as a violation of this requirement.

These attitudes, manifested in the church, the media, the education system, and many other aspects of life, shape the everyday experience of lesbians in the Philippines. While legal challenges such as Beth and Vangie's demonstrate the progress that has been made in the struggle for lesbian rights, a great deal of work remains to be done to change societal attitudes.

NOTES

1 The information in this section was obtained through interviews with Evangeline Castronuevo and Elizabeth Lim by the author in October 1994.

2 At the time of her dismissal, Vangie was separated from her husband.

3 Nelson Flores, "Balay row more than 'gay' rights issue," *Philippine Daily Inquirer*, 22 September 1995.

4 Letter dated 1 September 1994. A copy is on file with CLIC.

5 Natasha Vizcarra, "2 dismissed lesbians seek aid of rights groups, unions," *Philippine Daily Inquirer*, 20 October 1994.

6 Article 52.

7 "Sin Appeals For Rally," *Manila Bulletin*, 4 August 1994, p.1 ; "Cardinal Hits Cairo Conference," *Manila Bulletin*, 27 July 1994, p.5

8 For instance, *Manong Gang* is a film about a tomboy who is a member of a syndicate that commits large scale robbery. She meets a fellow criminal (male) and they later join forces in eluding law enforcers. She falls in love with him and sheds her mannish and "masculine" ways towards the end of the film. Another example of popular representations of lesbians is *Bubbles*, a film about the criminal activities of a lesbian named Bubbles. It shows her preying on her victims and stripping them of cash, jewelry, and other personal belongings after lacing their drinks with drugs. The film also shows that Bubbles has murdered several people including a girlfriend of hers in a fit of jealous rage. The film ends with Bubbles' sensational capture and eventual imprisonment.

9 "DECS wants more male teachers in public schools," *Reprowatch (Newsletter of the Institute for Social Studies and Action, Philippines)*, 8-14 October 1994; "Ban on gay teachers discriminatory," *Today*, 20 October 1994.

ABOUT THE AUTHOR

Malu S. Marin is a co-founder of CLIC(Can't Live in the Closet). She is a freelance writer/researcher, desktop layout artist and a council member of the feminist collective, KALAYAAN. CLIC is a Philippine-based organization working for lesbian rights through media advocacy. CLIC also operates a library and resource center.

Poland

● ● ● ● ● ●

Joanna Garnier

Very little research has been conducted on lesbians in Poland. Studies of homosexuality have primarily focused on gay men, while research concerning women has not taken into consideration the issue of sexual orientation. This report is based upon information obtained from informal interviews with lesbians in Warsaw. It also makes use of the results of a report entitled *Lesbians and the Church*, written by Marzena Stana and published in Berlin in 1993.

THE LAW

Polish legislation on homosexuality is rather liberal. The legal age of consent for sexual contact is 15, and this law applies equally to heterosexual and homosexual couples. Same-sex sexual relations are not and have never been outlawed in Poland. While Polish law currently contains no prohibition of discrimination on the basis of sexual orientation, this may soon change. In April, 1995, the Constitutional Committee, which is in the process of drafting Poland's new constitution, proposed the following language for Paragraph 2, Article 22 :

> Nobody can be discriminated against because of their sex, race, national or ethnic background, health, physical or mental disability, social background, place of birth, sexual orientation, language spoken, religious faith or lack thereof, opinions, material status or for any other reason.

At this time, debate is continuing and there is significant opposition to the inclusion of sexual orientation in this paragraph. The opposition is particularly strong from the church, which has unanimously criticized the proposed clause. Bishop Tadeusz Pieronek has called it "an example leading toward extremes which cannot be accepted by any normal society."[1]

DISCRIMINATION

As Bishop Pieronek's words illustrate, the liberal tendency of Polish law is not necessarily reflected in social attitudes, and for lesbians, prejudices regarding homosexuality are compounded by the discrimination that they suffer as women. Legally, women are guaranteed the same rights as men. However, in practice women have more difficulty finding work, earn less, and receive fewer promotions.

Very few lesbians are open about their sexual orientation in the workplace for fear of being fired or harassed. This is particularly true of lesbians working as teachers in schools or in other professions that bring them into contact with children; the belief that lesbians and gay men should not be involved in raising children and young people is widespread in Poland.

The art of camouflage has been perfected by lesbians living in villages and small towns. Fearing discrimination and ostracism, such women rarely decide to "come out of the closet" about their lesbianism. If they are able to, many flee to large cities, such as Warsaw, Cracow, or Gdansk, where it is easier for them to conceal their sexuality and maintain anonymity. People in large towns and cities are more likely to accept differences of all types than are residents of villages or small towns.

MARRIAGE

The assumption of heterosexuality is so strong in Polish society that in certain ways it protects lesbians from scrutiny: women who live together, hold hands, or demonstrate affection for one another do not necessarily meet with any suspicion, and single women are not automatically assumed to be lesbians. While this can create some room for lesbian relationships to exist without persecution, the centrality of heterosexual marriage in Polish society also has negative consequences for lesbians. Marriage adds considerably to a woman's status, and women who are not married are often treated with contempt. According to Marzena Stana's study on lesbians and the church, many Polish lesbians are in fact married to men. Many young lesbians decide to get married

Many young lesbians decide to get married because of pressure from their families or out of the desire to be accepted and to lead a "normal life."

because of pressure from their families or out of the desire to be accepted and to lead a "normal life." Many get married before they are even conscious of their sexual orientation, and others believe that they will get over their lesbianism after they get married. The patriarchal model is so pervasive in Poland that many young lesbians accept the idea that their fundamental task in life is to get married and have children. They may discover their lesbianism years later and then find themselves unable to leave their husbands for financial or other reasons. Some lesbians enter into marriages with gay men in order to pacify their families.

ADOPTION AND DONOR INSEMINATION

Heterosexual married couples and single people are permitted to adopt children in Poland. Lesbians are not allowed to adopt children as a couple, and an individual lesbian would not be able to adopt if her sexual orientation were known. Donor insemination is available only to married couples. By and large the Polish public believes that lesbians and gay men should not raise children, even their own.

CHURCH

Poles are raised in a society which has been shaped by Christianity for centuries and in which the Catholic Church has a great deal of influence on the political life of the country. As is the case elsewhere, the Catholic Church in Poland condemns homosexuality as a sin. Lesbians who look for help and support from the church and the clergy often meet with rejection. Many lesbians report feeling discriminated against or even psychologically harassed by their confessors. Lesbians who discuss their sexual orientation are frequently told that lesbian sexual behavior is a sin and a deviation. They are told that they should change themselves, get married, have children, and devote themselves to their family. As a consequence of this type of attitude on the part of the church many lesbians give up their religious practices or leave the Catholic Church in search of more tolerant faiths. However, they cannot completely escape the church's teachings because the Catholic Church is the moral authority for the majority of Polish society, and its role in shaping people's attitudes is extensive.

THE LESBIAN MOVEMENT

In Poland, the lesbian movement is integrally tied to the gay male movement. Lambda, a national group, and the Warsaw-based Ruch Lesbljek Gajow (Lesbian and Gay Movement) both have male and female members. Men, however, are in the majority in both organizations. Lesbians are very reluctant to become active in any organizations, partly because like all Polish women they are socialized from a very early age into passive social roles. This contributes to the lack of visibility of lesbians in Poland.

Two lesbian publications have appeared but neither is currently active. Aside from these periodicals there have been only two publications addressed to lesbians: one, a photocopied leaflet on safe sex and the other, a photocopied selection of lesbian poetry. There are several gay male publications, but they include little material written by or for lesbians.

While the state of lesbian organizing leaves much to be desired, things do seem to be improving. In Warsaw, more lesbians are becoming active in Ruch Lesbljek Gajow. Activists are currently planning to establish a crisis telephone line for lesbians and are preparing another pamphlet on safe sex for lesbians. However, these efforts are hampered by a lack of resources; without an office or meeting place, and with few people willing to sponsor "deviants," lesbian organizing continues to grow at a very slow pace.

NOTES

1 Piotr Dukaczewski and Grzegorz Witkowski, "Homosexual Rights Provision — Love's Close-Call Clause," *Warsaw Voice*, 24 April 1995.

ABOUT THE AUTHOR

Joanna Garnier, 30, is a librarian, mother of little Justyna, and a member of Ruch Lesbljek Gajow, a new organization for gay people in Poland. The organization is especially interested in human rights and issues around "coming out."

Romania

●　●　●　●　●　●　●　●　●

Ingrid Baciu, Vera Cîmpeanu, and Mona Nicoara

Romania is one of the few European states that makes homosexuality a crime. Consensual same-sex relations between adults, even if they take place in private, are illegal. A 1994 decision of the Constitutional Court overruled some of these legal restrictions, but maintained a discriminatory age of consent for same-sex sexual relations as compared to heterosexual sex. The Parliament has been reviewing the law for the past two years, but, as of April 1995, no final decision has been made. Moreover, some of the legal formulations under consideration before the Parliament hardly represent a step forward from the current statute. The criminalization of same-sex relations has hampered the development of a lesbian community, much less the development of any lesbian advocacy groups.

Lesbians experience the same disadvantages as all women in Romanian society, and in addition, they are subject to the stigma that the general public attaches to homosexuality.

LEGAL RESTRICTIONS

Same-sex relations are criminalized in Romania under Article 200 of the Penal Code, which specifies that:

> Same-sex relations shall be punished by prison from one to five years.
>
> If the deed provided under Para. 1 is perpetrated upon a minor or upon an individual unable to protect him/herself or to express his/her will, or by means of force, the punishment shall be prison from two to seven years.
>
> If the deed provided in Para. 2 results in serious physical damage for the victim, the punishment shall be three to ten years in prison; if the deed results in the death or suicide of the victim, the punishment shall be prison from seven to fifteen years.
>
> Enticing or luring of a person into the perpetration of the deed provided under Para. 1 shall be punished by prison from one to five years.[1]

This criminalization violates the provisions of the 1991 Constitution, which, under Article 26, enshrines "the right to intimate, private, and family life" and the binding international human rights documents ratified by Romania.[2] Further, the criminal code provides for a higher age of consent (Romanian citizens reach legal adulthood at 18) for same-sex relations than for heterosexual sex, for which the age of consent is 14.[3]

Article 200 of the Penal Code is known to have been enforced in a number of cases. Indeed, as of November 1994, the listings of detainees convicted under Article 200 provided by the Romanian Ministry of Justice showed 56 prisoners, all male, serving sentences under the various paragraphs of Article 200.

This provision of the Penal Code dates back to 1968, when the version currently in force was adopted. Following the 1989 Revolution, which led to the demise of the communist regime, there have been several attempts to review the whole Romanian penal system. However, only during the past two years has the Parliament taken up the issue in a more systematic way.

Article 200 of the Penal Code has a complicated procedural history. The first attempt to revise the current version of Article 200 dates back to early 1993 when, on the initiative of a Romanian human rights group, the Romanian Helsinki Committee, a deputy forwarded a proposal to amend Article 200 so as to eliminate Paragraph 1 altogether. The proposal was shelved at the level of the Chamber of Deputies, but the debate was revived upon Romania's accession to the Council of Europe. One of the recommendations made by the Parliamentary Assembly at that time was that "Romania will shortly change its legislation in such a way that...Article 200 of the Penal Code will no longer consider as a criminal offense homosexual acts in private between consenting adults."[4]

Thus, in autumn 1993, the Romanian government forwarded the Senate a package reform of the Penal Code and Penal Procedure Code. While increasing the penalties provided under Paragraphs 2-3 of the current formulation of the Penal Code, the bill proposed to amend the wording of the first paragraph, so as to criminalize same sex relations "resulting in a public scandal." This formulation coincides with the one included in the 1938 Penal Code, but would by no means bring a real liberalization of same-sex relations: the vagueness of the notion of "public scandal" would allow for abusive interpretation by law enforcement agencies and national courts. In early 1994, the plenum of the Senate decided upon another major point of concern for human rights activists in Romania, adopting the following wording for the last paragraph of Article 200:

> "Enticing or seducing a person with a view to perpetrate the deeds provided in the above paragraphs, as well as propaganda, association, or any acts of proselytizing carried out to the same effect shall be punished by 1 to 5 years in prison."

This provision seriously jeopardized the rights to freedom of expression and association, enshrined both by the Romanian Constitution and by the international documents to which Romania is a party. The bill was submitted to the Chamber of Deputies, which has often shown itself to be more responsive to the human rights organizations advocating the decriminalization of same-sex relations. However, in October 1994, the plenum of the chamber decided to maintain the formulation contained in the Penal Code currently in force, notwithstanding the recommendations of the Council of Europe, and disregarding an earlier decision of the Constitutional Court (see below). Following a letter-writing campaign initiated by Romanian and international human rights groups, the chamber decided to review the vote a week later, maintaining the formulation of the last paragraph of Article 200 and adopting a less vague and somewhat more liberal version for the first paragraph: "Same-sex relations, if perpetrated in public or under conditions of a nature to disturb public order, shall be punished by prison from one to 5 years." The debate is currently continuing over the exact status and wording of the law.

Recently, the constitutionality of the law was challenged by six male defendants prosecuted under the first two paragraphs of Article 200. While the Constitutional Court ruled that the law prohibiting same-sex relations among adults is unconstitutional, the wording of the decision was such that the Court would accept any of the versions of the law currently being circulated. The provisions relating to minors and sexual assault between same-sex parties were upheld by the court.[5]

NEGATIVE PUBLIC ATTITUDES TOWARDS LESBIANS

Prevailing attitudes in Romanian society toward lesbians and gay men are, in general, negative. However, the public and parliamentary debate around Article 200 in Romania seems to have focused almost entirely upon gay men, leaving out lesbians altogether. For instance, the above-mentioned parliamentary debate has concentrated almost exclusively on "homosexuals,"[6] even though the legislation in question would affect both lesbians and gay men.

This omission is reflective of the relative invisibility of lesbians in Romanian society; while an individual lesbian is likely to encounter condemnation and discrimination, homosexuality in the abstract is most often discussed in male terms. This is in part a reflection of the relative positions of women versus men in Romanian society. In a country where patriarchal values are at the core of the social structure and men are seen as the sole decision-makers, homosexuality among men is more of an issue precisely because it threatens the gendered organization of priorities. Women are much less represented than men in decision-making structures, domestic violence is widely accepted as a fact of life, and women's private lives are supposed to be entirely dedicated to family issues. Indeed, apart from a few educational pieces included among the sex education features of Romanian publications, lesbianism has been visible only in pornographic magazines, displayed for the pleasure of a male viewer.

Prior to the 1989 Revolution, sex education was nonexistent in Romania. The silence surrounding homosexuality within Romanian society made it difficult for girls to consider any alternatives to hetero-sexuality. I.B., a lesbian activist and journalism student, says: "At the time, I did not even know that words such as 'lesbianism' or 'homosexu-ality' existed. In a closed society like pre-1989 Romania, the issue was more than a taboo: it simply did not exist. But I had been attracted to women from a very early age and was wondering as to what was happen-ing to me. I was lucky enough to get a hold on the black market of a magazine featuring two women making love. I realized then that this was what I wanted, but I knew it was hard to get it in a society where you have to pay with your freedom for being attracted to someone of the same sex as you."[7]

The few opinion polls focusing on sexual orientation and the response of the population to homosexuality show equal degrees of intolerance towards lesbians and gay men. A March 1995 poll shows that as many as 53% of the interviewed subjects believe that lesbians should not be accepted into society, whereas only 30% are willing to accept them with no reservations. An additional 10% would accept them with some reservations, while 7% expressed no opinion. Youth and more educated people seem to be most tolerant of lesbians, gener-ally.[8]

Religious beliefs play an important role in determining the attitude of the majority towards gay and lesbian issues (according to the 1992 census, 99.3% of the population declared themselves religious) and are increasingly used to justify conservative political decisions on the issue. Many of the parliamentary factions have used the fact that the majority of their constituents are religious as a rationale to oppose the decrimi-nalization of same-sex relations. Likewise, many religious denomina-tions, and particularly the Romanian Christian Orthodox Church, have been very vocal in opposing the liberalization of same-sex relations. A national Christian Orthodox students' organization, supported by the church and by other student groups, even started a campaign in the summer of 1994 to collect signatures in order to push for a popular legislative initiative to criminalize same-sex relations, in case the Parliament would have decided otherwise.

However, the media are finding stories about homosexuality increasingly marketable. Since 1993, a number of television and radio shows dealing with homosexuality have been produced. The written press is also picking up on the subject, publishing more and more sensational stories. Such features show little serious understanding of the issue. Often, by presenting lesbians as sensational "others," they perpetuate the negative stereotypes that the public seems to have already formed. The shock value of the subject seems to outweigh journalistic ethics: lesbian activist I.B. was "outed" as a lesbian during a show on Romanian public television in November 1993, even though she had agreed to participate only under the conditions that her face would not be shown and her name would not be disclosed. The producer of the show used sensational tactics and disregarded his agreement to maintain I.B.'s anonymity. As a result, her relations to family and friends have deteriorated, and she has been recognized and harassed on the street numerous times.

M.P., a lesbian, a mother of two, a victim of domestic violence, and a former sex worker, was arrested under the pre-1989 regime for revealing her sexual orientation and refusing to accept propositions made to her by a local political leader. She was taken into police custody to be charged under Article 200, but through her family's connections managed to get the charge reduced to "illegal abortion." She was released three months later, never having been brought before the court. She took a job as an accountant after 1989, only to find herself fired for being outspoken about her sexuality and refusing to yield to the sexual advances of a male colleague. She has repeatedly been offered money to have sex with her girlfriend in front of men.[9]

Under such circumstances, revealing one's sexual orientation to friends, family, and co-workers can be extremely difficult. Of the nine lesbians interviewed by the authors only one, C.D. (a high school student), seems to have benefited from a more tolerant family environment. Her family accepts her lesbianism and has not tried to stop her from living with her girlfriend.[10]

ADVOCACY AND THE DEVELOPING
LESBIAN COMMUNITY

The battle for the decriminalization of same-sex relations has so far been led by independent human rights groups, such as the Romanian Helsinki Committee (through its legislative advocacy and minorities projects) or the Independent Romanian Society for Human Rights. The Romanian Helsinki Committee has been lobbying the Parliament on the issue for the past two years and has initiated a series of letter-writing campaigns for the Parliament and the Constitutional Court. International organizations, such as Amnesty International, Human Rights Watch/Helsinki, the International Human Rights Law Group, the International Gay and Lesbian Human Rights Commission, and the International Lesbian and Gay Association, have been actively

None of the approximately 40 women's groups in Romania has shown any interest in lesbian issues.

involved in such campaigns.

In 1993, the Independent Romanian Society for Human Rights developed a program for sexual minorities, the only one of its kind among public interest groups. However, despite efforts to promote lesbian issues, the project was not successful in bringing together and organizing lesbians. "My experience has been that lesbians are not visible or active, possibly due to fear. Gay men are more united and have proven to be able to stand up for their rights better than lesbians so far. During my stay in the Romanian Independent Society for Human Rights I have managed to bring together only a few women: some were feminists, others simply got involved because they had a lot of spare time on their hands. None of them were lesbians, however, and, despite the fact that we publicized our activity throughout the country, no lesbians contacted our project," says I.B.[11]

No other organizations are known to have addressed lesbian issues. None of the approximately 40 women's groups in Romania has shown any interest in this area. AIDS prevention and education groups have focused primarily on heterosexuals; some have worked covertly with gay men, but none have sought to reach lesbians.

Starting in 1992, a few underground gay and lesbian groups, such as Total Relations and Group 200, functioned, each for a rather brief period of time. An underground lesbian group was reported to exist in Ploiesti, a city 60 kilometers north of Bucharest. The main reason that such groups are forced to remain underground is that the existence of Article 200 makes official registration of any gay and lesbian group virtually impossible. For instance, the leader of Group 200 was requested to present approvals from several ministries before registering the group in court. Several of the ministries refused to do so, based on the provisions of Article 200 of the Penal Code. Without an official registration, these groups cannot open bank accounts, hold assets, or rent an office. Article 200 thus results in serious infringements on free speech and association. Despite these obstacles, as of this writing several gay and lesbian groups, such as the Bucharest Acceptance Group and the Commission for the Rights of Sexual Minorities, are trying to get organized and registered in Bucharest.

The lesbian cultural scene has been no more lively than the organizational history presented above. The only gay and lesbian publication known is *Gay '45*, edited by the director of the sexual minorities project of the Romanian Independent Society for Human Rights. However, apparently due to lack of financial resources and difficulties relating to distribution (few newsstands agreed to carry the magazine), only two issues have been published so far, both in 1993. A gay and lesbian festival with international participation was prevented from taking place by the Romanian authorities in the summer of 1994; police troops surrounded the building and prevented organizers, performers, and the public from entering. No safe meeting places for lesbians are known. A few regular bars are known to be more popular among lesbians than others, but the vast majority of customers in such places are heterosexual. The absence of a space for debate and consciousness raising among lesbians is one of the major impediments to developing a strong lesbian community.

NOTES

The authors acknowledge the support of the Romanian Helsinki Committee in drafting this report.

1 All quotations from Romanian statutes and court decisions follow unofficial translations, with the exception of the Romanian Constitution.

2 According to Art. 11 and 20 of the 1991 Constitution, international human rights documents ratified by Romania are integral part of the domestic law and prevail over conflicting national legislation. These include the Universal Declaration of Human Rights, the International Covenant on Civil and Political Rights, and the European Convention for the Protection of Fundamental Rights and Freedoms.

3 See Art. 197 and 198 of the Romanian Penal Code. The age of consent for women to engage in heterosexual sex is 14 ; Romanian law does not specify an age of consent for men to engage in heterosexual sex.

4 "On the Application by Romania for Membership of the Council of Europe," Op. No. 176, Eur. Parl. Ass., 44th Sess. para. 7, 1993.

5 The Constitutional Court decision, no. 81/July 15, 1994, reads: "1. [The Constitutional Court of Romania] partially admits the exception of unconstitutionality relating to Art. 200 para. 1 of the Penal Code, invoked by B.O.N., B.O., B.L., S.I.C., H.F.P., and N.G.C. by means of files no. 5298/1993, 5711/1993, and 5943/1993 with the Sibiu Court, and notes that the provisions of this paragraph are unconstitutional to the extent to which they apply to same-sex relations between freely consenting adults, not perpetrated in public or not producing a public scandal.

6 "[The Constitutional Court of Romania] rules against the claim of unconstitutionality related to Art. 200 para. 2 of the Penal Code, raised by B.O.N. by means of file no. 5298/1993 and by B.L. in file no. 5711/1993, both pending before the Sibiu Court."

7 In Romanian, as in many languages, "homosexual" has come to mean almost exclusively "gay man," losing its generic meaning.

8 Interview with I.B. by Mona Nicoara, 17 March 1995

9 The results were kindly provided to the authors by the Center for Urban and Regional Sociology in Bucharest. This poll is representative only of Romania's capital, Bucharest, which has in past polls appeared to have the highest degree of tolerance towards any minorities. For instance, a June 1993

nationwide poll conducted by the Institute for the Research of Life Quality showed that 85% of the interviewed subjects were not willing to accept homosexuals in society. (Quoted by Catalin-Augustin Stoica in "Homosexuals: Premises on their Acceptance in Today's Romania," presented at the Conference on National Reconciliation, Bucharest, May 1994.)

10 Interview with M.P. by Mona Nicoara, 19 March 1995.

11 Interview with C.D. by Mona Nicoara, 10 April 1995.

12 Interview with I.B. by Mona Nicoara, 17 March 1995.

ABOUT THE AUTHORS

Ingrid Baciu is a journalist and Romanian lesbian activist.

Vera Cîmpeanu is a women's rights and human rights activist, associated with the Romanian Helsinki Committee for Human Rights, where she coordinates a project on ethnic and sexual minorities.

Mona Nicoara is a board member of Gender - Center for Women's Studies, Bucharest, and a parliamentary liaison for the Romanian Helsinki Committee for Human Rights.

Russia

● ● ● ● ● ●

Masha Gessen

In the last five years, with the general liberalization of Russian society and the emergence of a gay and lesbian movement, the situation for lesbians has improved a great deal. The prevailing attitude toward lesbians appears to have become more tolerant: we have no studies that measure the public's opinion of lesbians separately from gay men, but the most recent opinion surveys show that, though most people continue to believe that homosexuals in general are sick, the number of people who believe homosexuals should be left alone is growing steadily.[1] A number of lesbian and gay groups have formed in the last five years, making it easier for women to meet others like them—though isolation continues to be perhaps the most pressing problem for most lesbians. In general, official persecution of lesbians has declined drastically. Still, it continues to exist.

Since the early 1930s, when the Soviet government began its six-decade-long anti-homosexual witch-hunt, the psychiatric institutions have posed the greatest threat to lesbians. Whereas gay men faced the risk of arrest, lesbians had to fear being institutionalized. And while the criminal law banning gay male sex was repealed in 1993,[2] the professional provisions that compel psychiatrists to "treat" lesbians have remained unchanged.

Two things have set the institution of Russian psychiatry against lesbians. One was a theory advanced by the founder of Soviet psychiatry, Andrey V. Snezhnevsky, who in the 1930s maintained that schizophrenia can manifest itself years or even decades before the onset of clinical symptoms through such signs as sleep disturbances, unconventional thought patterns (this idea proved lethal to political dissidents), homosexual behavior, and so on. This theory led to a diagnosis known as "slow-going schizophrenia" (*vialotekushaya shizofreniya*; this phrase is often erroneously translated by Russian doctors as "borderline personality," when in fact there is no direct equivalent among conventional English-language diagnoses). The second factor was the inclusion of "homosexual orientation" in the section on personality disturbances in the diagnostic manual issued by the Ministry of Health.[3]

Until recently, it was exceedingly easy in Russia to commit someone

---

Olga, committed to a psychiatric institution for being a lesbian, was subjected to electroshock treatments and given drugs that severely altered her consciousness and caused hallucinations.

---

to a psychiatric institution. Olga, 24, reports that when she was 17, a teacher at the technical school where she was a student found out she was having a relationship with another female student. The teacher contacted a psychiatric institution, and both young women were committed. Olga's friend was released through the intervention of her parents, but Olga, who had only a mother who lived far away, remained in the hospital for three months. She says she was subjected to electroshock treatments and given drugs that severely altered her consciousness and caused hallucinations. After she was released from the hospital, she was compelled to register with a local psychiatric clinic, where she was required to check in regularly, and her passport was stamped to indicate she had a psychiatric illness. All this was standard procedure for people being released from psychiatric hospitals. Her status as a mental patient meant she could not go back to her studies since she was banned from any vocation that would put her in contact with people.[4]

A law passed in 1992 now makes it more difficult to commit a person to a mental institution against her will. However, according to an assessment done by the New York-based Lawyers Committee for Human Rights, the law is difficult to enforce. In any case, it does not protect the most vulnerable group of lesbians: young women who have not reached legal majority and continue to be legally in the guardianship of their elders. Lena, 19, was committed to a psychiatric institution at the age of 17 by her mother. Her mother took this step because Lena wanted a sex-change operation. Such operations are legal in Russia and are carried out (under psychiatric supervision) far more frequently than in many countries. Lena had applied for the operation at the age of 15, when she was too young to have it legally. But when her mother found out about the application two years later, she had Lena committed. Over the months of "treatment," the doctors attempted to "correct" her gender and sexual identification with the help of various drugs.

The diagnostic manual used by Russian psychiatrists has been due to be revised for years now. The edition currently used dates back to 1982; professionals familiar with the revision process say a new edition will be years in coming. The fact that "homosexual orientation" continues to be listed as a personality disorder has a dual negative effect: on the one hand, it means that those who enter psychiatric institutions involuntarily are given "treatment," and, on the other hand, it means that lesbians who may need or seek counseling are denied appropriate care. "Vera," 19, was involuntarily committed to a mental institution following a suicide attempt after being rejected by the young woman with whom she had fallen in love. In the hospital, the doctors began, as she says, "treating everything at once"—that is, her suicidal tendencies and her sexual orientation. Now out of the hospital, she continues to take medication in the hopes of "curing" her condition.

According to Aleksandr M. Poleyev, a professor at a Moscow postgraduate school for psychiatrists, where doctors from around the country come for periodic mandatory courses, while Moscow psychiatrists of great authority have come to believe that homosexuality is not a mental illness, local doctors—the ones who actually treat people—hold the opposite view. The existing diagnostic manual gives them a way to put their convictions to work.[5]

THE LEGAL STATUS OF LESBIANS

Lesbian sex, unlike gay male sex, has never been criminalized in Russia. The law against consensual gay male sex was repealed in 1993. However, the Criminal Code continues to make a distinction between heterosexual rape and homosexual rape. For nearly a decade now various groups have been working on a new code. Early this year, a draft of a new code made it through Parliament. When first submitted, the draft contained an article that punished nonconsensual "satisfaction of sexual desire through homosexual, lesbian or other perverted means." This article prescribed a milder sentence than the law against missionary-position heterosexual rape. As one lawyer who worked on the draft explained, the logic behind that was that non-missionary sexual acts could not result in pregnancy.

In Parliament, the draft code changed for the better. The words *lesbian* and *homosexual* were removed, leaving just "perverted means," and the penalties for all rapes were made equal. In March, however, President Boris N. Yeltsin rejected the draft and sent it back to Parliament for further work. Lesbian and gay activists fear that the word lesbian may make it back into the document. Even if it does not, the phrasing "perverted means" is cause for concern: there is no definition of "perversion" in Russian law, but it is probably fair to assume that lesbian sex would be deemed to fit the term. The existence of separate laws concerning heterosexual and "perverted" rape paves the way for unequal enforcement of the laws. Many gay men who have served time in prison say they ended up there on trumped-up rape charges in part because of the homophobia of the police, who could not conceive of two men actually wanting to have sex with each other, and therefore assumed it to be rape. Lesbians fear that under the proposed new law the same charges may be used against them.

THE SOCIAL STATUS OF LESBIANS

Until five years ago, lesbian networks in Russia—the only ways for lesbians to make contact with one another—were informal and largely closed (newcomers could not be trusted, and the fear of persecution was too great to take risks). Now there are more formal lesbian organizations in Moscow, St. Petersburg, and the Siberian cities of Omsk and Novosibirsk. (None of these groups, however, are formally recognized by the governments.) All four cities have services to introduce lesbians to other lesbians (in Omsk and Novosibirsk, though, they are quite informal at this point); in addition, in Moscow there is an organization called Moscow Organization of Lesbians in Literature and the Arts (MOLLI), which produces concerts, and in St. Petersburg a lesbian consciousness-raising group meets at the St. Petersburg Center for Gender Issues, a feminist organization. Occasional semi-public parties for lesbians are held in Moscow and St. Petersburg.

The situation is significantly better than it was a few years ago, but it compares very unfavorably to that of gay men. In Moscow, there are two full-time gay clubs and numerous weekend gay discos, but these do not give lesbians the opportunity to meet one another. In all four cities where there are lesbian networks, organizers report that the people who come to them suffer from intense loneliness, often having never met other lesbians.

Fear of repression continues to make lesbian organizing—even of the purely social variety—extremely difficult. In Omsk, for example, an attempt to create a lesbian group at the local AIDS center failed not because there were not enough women who wanted to take part but because they feared they would be seen at the center, even if only by gay men, who used the same time slot.[6] Isolation continues to be the central problem for Russian lesbians, and the gains of the last few years have made barely a dent in it.

NOTES

1 Nationwide survey conducted by the All-Russian Center for Reseach on Public Opinion, as contrasted with a survey conducted by the same center (then called the All-Union Center) in 1989.

2 Masha Gessen, *The Rights of Lesbians and Gay Men in the Russian Federation*. San Francisco: International Gay and Lesbian Human Rights Commission, 1994, pp. 24-33.

3 *Mezhdunarodnaya statisticheskaya klassifikatsiya bolezney, travm i prichin smerti,* 9th edition adapted for use in the USSR, Moscow, 1982, Section V.

4 The scenario was repeated in more than a dozen interviews done by the author in 1991-93. All respondents spoke on condition of anonymity. The ages of women most often described ranged in age from 15 to 19.

5 Interview by the author with Dr. Aleksandr M. Poleyev, a psychiatrist, an assistant professor at Moscow State University, and a senior researcher at the Ministry of Health's Moscow scientific Research Institute of Psychiatry, 9 August 1993.

6 Interview with Yelena Chernykh, director of the Center's press center, March 1995.

ABOUT THE AUTHOR

Masha Gessen is a Moscow journalist and lesbian activist. She is the author of The Rights of Lesbians and Gay Men in the Russian Federation, *an International Gay and Lesbian Human Rights Commission report published in 1994.*

Serbia

• • • • •

Jelica Todosijevic

eing a lesbian in Serbia means that you don't exist at all. You
don't exist legally; you don't exist illegally. You are an offensive
word, a bad character from a cheap novel or a character from a
pornographic film. But being a woman who loves other women, or any
woman without a man to stand behind, means that you live in fear.

Women in Serbia are validated by their husbands. If a lesbian
chooses the way of living she desires, it means that she's condemning
herself to the endless battle for her integrity. No one imagines that a
woman living without a man could be part of a couple. Lesbians aren't
even lesbians here—they are single women, and as single women they
encounter many forms of discrimination. A single woman will be the
second choice for a job offer if there is a married woman who applies for
the same position. Married women are seen as those who have learned
to obey and respect authority. It's thought, why take a chance on a single woman? A single woman will have a difficult time finding a decent
apartment for herself; landlords will be suspicious of her morality. A single woman will get fired from her job if there is a need for reducing the
staff; she eats less. A single woman will be put on graveyard shift all of

the time; she doesn't have any family obligations. A single woman should be at home before dark; there is nobody to protect her from being harassed or raped on the street; if she encounters any kind of violence, she asked for it by being on the street alone. A single woman is never thought to be single because she decided to be that way. She is always seen as abandoned, unable to find a man, immoral, crazy, or unable to have children. Two women living together may not be seen as lesbians, but they will nevertheless be the object of their neighbors' suspicions. People prefer "normal" families with children and a male head of the family. Who could imagine women having a family together?

THE STATUS OF THE LAW

The Yugoslav Constitution does not mention the existence of lesbians in any way, positive or negative. On July 14, 1994, the Serbian government adopted a new criminal law lifting the ban on male homosexuality. However, the age of consent for male homosexuals remains higher (age 18) than that for heterosexuals (age 14). Lesbianism was not included in the original legislation, and lesbians are not covered by the current age of consent law.[1]

The reform came as a surprise to the Serbian gay and lesbian community. Many assume that the change came from someone high up in government. In the current political climate, there is little opportunity for ordinary citizens to influence legislation in Serbia. This is particularly the case for lesbian and gay activists, for whom lobbying means calling attention to themselves publicly as members of an "undesirable" group. Given the war and the current state of lawlessness in Serbia, this could provoke a dangerous reaction from the government or its agents. In general, those who demand their rights are seen as threat to nationalist ideals, and diversity among women is particularly seen as an affront to the nation. There is presently a strong campaign against abortion backed by an explicitly nationalist and pro-natalist ideology, and lesbians, who do not fit into the image of "mothers of the nation," are viewed as useless elements of society.

ATTITUDES TOWARDS LESBIANS

In October 1994, Arkadija's Lesbian Working Group conducted a street survey in Belgrade on attitudes toward lesbians. Fifty people were

asked the following questions:
1. Do you know what a lesbian is?
2. Do you know any lesbians?
3. Would you allow your daughter/wife to have a lesbian friend?
4. Would you mind if you discovered that one of your colleagues is a lesbian?
5. Would you still go to the same store if you knew that the shopkeeper was a lesbian?
6. Would you allow your child to have a lesbian teacher?
7. Do you think that lesbianism is 1) hereditary, 2) acquired, 3) illness, 0) none of the above?
8. What would you do with such a person?

Responses

Younger Women (avg. age, 23)	Older Women (avg. age, 45)	Younger Men (avg. age, 22)	Older Men (avg. age, 54)
1. Yes - 100%	Yes - 100%	Yes - 100%	Yes - 100%
2. Yes - 22% No - 72%	Yes - 20% No - 80%	Yes - 28% No - 72%	Yes - 25% No - 75%
3. Yes - 44% No - 56%	100% - No	Yes (wife) - 57% No - 43%	Yes (wife) - 75% No - 25%
4. Yes - 57% No - 43%	Yes - 70% No - 30%	No - 100%	Yes - 25% No - 75%
5. Yes - 100%	Yes - 80% No - 20%	Yes - 100%	Yes - 75% No - 25%
6. Yes - 44% No - 56%	Yes - 20% No - 80%	Yes - 72% No - 28%	Yes - 75% No - 25%
7. (2) 44% (3) 56%	(2) 20% (3) 80%	(1) 14% (2) 14% (3) 49% (0) 23%	(2) 100%
8. 35% Nothing 31% Medical Treatment 11% Isolation 23% Friends	20% Nothing 60% Medical Treatment 10% Isolation 10% Aggressive Treatment	61% Nothing 39% Sex	25% Nothing 75% Sex

According to the survey results, women are more homophobic than men, but it is obvious that most men have a voyeuristic attitude. They would allow their wives to have a lesbian friend, but not their daughters, and most of older men who were questioned would "treat" lesbians sexually in order to "cure" them. It is obvious that a large majority of the population believes that lesbianism is an illness and that it should be medically treated. Some of the women respondents suggested isolating lesbians in ghettos; some even suggested sewing up the genitals of lesbians. While less homophobic than the older generation, the younger respondents still exhibited many prejudices against lesbians, saying that lesbians are sick and need to be cured.

CHILD CUSTODY

As previously mentioned, there are no laws that explicitly criminalize lesbianism. However, in the homophobic atmosphere in which we are living, it is impossible to even hope that anybody would try to understand a lesbian mother who claims her right to obtain custody of her child. Lesbians are considered to be immoral, irresponsible, mentally disturbed, and dangerous. Women are forced to hide their lesbianism in order to retain custody of their children; accusations of lesbianism (whether true or not) can be used as a reason to take a child away. Many lesbians in Serbia have children, but they live as quietly as possible, often sacrificing themselves for their children.

> "We had to sue him for libel because if he proved that J. and I had a lesbian relationship, the Court would not permit J. to see her child at all" a forty-year-old lesbian, B., commented on her girlfriend's process of divorcing. "Her husband wanted to keep J. away from their daughter, but fortunately we had a good lawyer. M. [the daughter] is living with her father now in the other town, but she is coming to visit us for holidays. I love her as if she is my own child, and I miss her a lot every time she goes back to her father."[2]

An issue which compounds this problem is that divorced women often live with their parents. In constant fear of being discovered, lesbian mothers are in a "double closet"—hiding their sexuality from the state but also from their parents, children, colleagues, and friends.

EMPLOYMENT DISCRIMINATION

"If there was a homosexual in this office, I would fire this person immediately," stated the director of a large legal research firm in Belgrade. "How do you know that there is not such a person in here?" one of the employees remarked. "I have heard something about that, but I don't know it for sure. If I was positive, I would expel them from the job," the director continued. "But there is no legal basis for something like that; what would be your excuse for firing that person?" frightened Z. asked her superior. "I would just make sure that I found something and make that person withdraw their documents on their own and leave the firm," he declared.[3]

Z. has been living in fear of being exposed to her supervisor for three years. She is afraid that any of her colleagues might see her walking with

---

Even a single allegation of lesbianism can have disastrous effects.

---

her girlfriend and suspect something. She knows that she could lose her position and her future if somebody finds out that she is a lesbian.

Discrimination against lesbians is particularly strong in professions that involve work with children. At an April 1994 meeting of one of the humanitarian foundations in Belgrade, a group of Belgrade University psychology professors suggested that L.M., a lesbian psychologist at the Center for Women and Children Victims of Violence, should be barred from working with young victims of rape and domestic violence because of her sexuality. These professors eventually managed to have Arkadija, a lesbian and gay organization, prohibited from holding meetings at the Women's Studies Center because the group was "incompatible" with the refugee project on which they were working. "It is ironic," they said, "that we must share a space with perverts when people who really need help come here." (The true irony of this statement is that some of Arkadija's members are themselves refugees.)[4]

Even a single allegation of lesbianism can have disastrous effects:

> G. was a successful musician in a local cafe. She always attracted a big crowd and her boss was always happy with her. Then one day, in the middle of her act, a drunk man stood up and shouted "lesbian" at her. He continued to verbally abuse her and threatened physical violence. The next day, the owner of the cafe told G. that she was fired.[5]

These are just three examples of the kind of harassment lesbians have on the job. No laws protect lesbians from being fired or discriminated against on the basis of their sexual orientation. With few exceptions, lesbians must hide all aspects of their lives that might reveal their sexual orientation at their place of employment.

STREET HARASSMENT

In Serbia, lesbians are utterly invisible. Boys and men use the word "lesbian," but they use it as one insult among many to harass women as women and not necessarily as lesbians. Street harassment and other forms of violence against women, both on the streets and at home, have increased since the start of the war. Some of the women who experience this violence are lesbians but again, they are invisible.

SOCIAL ISOLATION

The examples of social isolation are too numerous to list. Being a single woman in Serbia means being marked because you don't fit into the pattern of "the mother of the nation." Under very hard conditions, marked by a complete breakdown in the legal system, virulent nationalism and pro-fascistic propaganda, those whose "devotion to the fatherland" is questioned have few chances of advancing in any realm of life.

EDUCATION

The stigma attached to homosexuality can make it difficult for young lesbians to obtain an education. Those whose sexuality becomes known often face discrimination in school.

> A 17 year old high school student , S., fell in love with one of her female professors. She sent the professor a letter of admiration and some flowers. When the professor found out who sent the love note, she made a remark about it at a board meeting. Soon every-body in the school knew about S., and S. was ultimately forced to leave the school. She was unable to attend classes without being constantly insulted by her schoolmates and mistreated by her pro-fessors.[6]

DISCRIMINATION WITHIN THE FAMILY

Due to the poor economic situation in the country, single people are often forced to share the same space with their parents. This is especially true for women because they cannot afford to move out and become independent of their families. Very few lesbians live alone or in couples. Their incomes are usually not high enough to cover the basic costs of living, and they are thus dependent on the good will of their parents. In such situations, families often feel that they have the right to regulate the private life of their members. It is not uncommon for a lesbian to be blackmailed with the threat that her sexual orientation will be revealed to her family. In cases where their secret is somehow revealed, many les-bians immediately lose the financial and emotional support of their fam-ily.

Lesbians are seen as a disgrace and an affront to the family's honor. One of the lawyers of the Belgrade Women's Law Group recently received a phone call from a woman seeking advice. Her "problem" was that she had a neighbor with a lesbian granddaughter. According to her complaint, the young woman was mistreating her grandmother by bring-ing her lesbian partner home. Except for that, the "concerned" neighbor had no other facts to prove that the "unfortunate grandmother" had been mistreated in any other way.[7]

HEALTH CARE

When J.T. reached her late forties, she visited a gynecologist for menstrual problems she was experiencing. She had seen a gynecologist only once before, when she was 20. At the second examination, she was subject to harassment and humiliation by the doctor when he discovered that her hymen was intact. "Why didn't you pay somebody to sleep with you?" he screamed at her after performing the exam.[8]

Many lesbians do not visit gynecologists because medical practitioners assume that all women are sexually active with men, and lesbians are often forced to lie or risk the consequences of revealing their lesbianism. Many lesbians not only forego preventative care; they also delay treatment for medical conditions until they become acute.

Medical professionals are not educated to be sensitive to the needs and concerns of lesbian patients. On the contrary, homosexuality is discussed in the medical textbooks as a disease.[9] Although lesbian and gay activists have begun talking to women's groups about calling for the demedicalization of homosexuality, no other groups have yet taken on the campaign.

ORGANIZING FOR CHANGE

Arkadija, the only lesbian and gay organization in Serbia, has existed since 1990. The decriminalization of male homosexuality in 1994 has enabled Arkadija to become for the first time somewhat open in its work. Arkadija's Lesbian Working Group is holding workshops once a week with the primary goal of the increasing self-awareness, self-respect, and self-confidence of the women who attend. There are more and more women interested in gathering and sharing opinions and experiences. For some women, these meetings are the first time that they have been able to express their lesbianism openly to anyone. Last fall, the Working Group held a safe-sex workshop for lesbians; never before had lesbians gathered to discuss HIV among lesbians. Still, there is very little information on HIV and AIDS, and little on lesbian health care in general.

Arkadija has also begun to explore the possibilities of publicizing the group through the media. In the summer of 1994, an "out" lesbian appeared on television for the first time in Serbian history. This show received several positive responses from the public and it was carried by the regular Belgrade Art Channel. Arkadija has also encountered some success in the print media. The daily *Borba* ran several positive articles about lesbians in late 1994 and early 1995, three of which were written by Arkadija members. However, *Borba* was one of the last remaining independent papers and has recently been banned by the government.

In addition to building links with lesbian and gay organizations in other countries, Arkadija is also reaching out to women at home through a bimonthly bulletin. Arkadija views the struggle for the human rights of lesbians and gay men as one part of a much larger struggle to increase tolerance within Serbian society for minorities of all sorts.

NOTES

1 Article 10 of the Criminal Law of the Republic of Serbia, 14 July 1994, Section on Indecent Acts Against Nature, reads: "For indecent acts against nature with the under-aged male person over the age of 14, the actor will be punished by the imprisonment of up to one year." The former version criminalized "indecent acts against nature" between two males regardless of age.

2 Interview with B. by the author, 1995.

3 Interview with Z. by the author, 1995.

4 Interview with L.M. by the author, 1994.

5 Interview with G. by the author, 1995.

6 Information on file with Arkadija.

7 Interview with employee of Belgrade Women's Law Group by the author, 1995.

8 Interview with J.T. by the author, 1995.

9 See for instance Drs. Radoslav Lopasic, Stjepan Betlheim, and Sergije Dogan, *Psychiatry*, Belgrade, 1965 and Dr. Strboljub Stojanovic, *Psychiatry with Medical Psychology*, Belgrade: 1975.

ABOUT THE AUTHOR

Jelica Todosijevic is a member of the Lesbian Working Group of Arkadija.

South Africa

● ● ● ● ● ● ● ● ● ● ●

Karin Koen and Patricia Terry

The legal position of lesbians in South Africa is unique in the world today. Currently, South Africa is the only country to have a constitution that explicitly affords lesbians protection against discrimination.

The Constitution of the Republic of South Africa,[1] which is interim in nature, includes a justiciable Charter of Fundamental Rights, which expressly prohibits direct or indirect discrimination on the basis of sexual orientation. The pertinent provision in the Charter of Fundamental Rights, Section 8, guarantees equality before the law and equal protection of the law. It also protects persons against discrimination on "one or more of the following grounds: race, gender, ethnic or social origin, color, sexual orientation, age, disability, religion, conscience, belief, culture or language."[2] Despite this provision, lesbians are still largely invisible in South African society and face discrimination and oppression in their everyday lives.

LESBIANS AND THE LAW

There are two serious weaknesses in the legal protection currently enjoyed by South African lesbians. The first is that the constitution is of recent vintage and laws and practices that discriminate against lesbians remain valid until challenged and defeated in court, or until the government abolishes the provisions at issue. No such litigation has occurred to date; however, the South African Department of Justice is currently examining some of the relevant legislation.

The second weakness in this legal protection is that the country is currently rewriting the constitution, which had been designed to be an interim one until a democratically representative body could be elected to write a final text. The process of drafting the permanent constitution has just begun. Among other things, it involves the taking of submissions on all aspects of the constitution from all those who are interested. This includes political parties, institutions, organizations, and individuals. The Constitutional Assembly is making a special effort to involve even those people who by virtue of their poor education or other factors are generally excluded from such debates.

The lesbian community in South Africa is specifically seeking to influence the constitution-making process so that it can retain the explicit protection against discrimination on the basis of sexual orientation in the equality clause of the constitution. In this effort South African lesbians are represented by a new national body, The National Coalition for Gay and Lesbian Equality (NCGLE), as well as regional coalitions in four of the nine provinces in the country. The NCGLE was mandated by its 52 constituent organizations to appoint a lobbyist whose specific task it is to lobby influential individuals and organizations both inside and outside of Parliament. The regional coalitions are also expected to lobby in their respective regions. It is the aim of the NCGLE to have a coordinated national strategy to ensure the retention of the sexual orientation clause.

The second aim of the NCGLE is to have old discriminatory legislation removed from the statute books. There are few laws predating the constitution that influence the lives of lesbians directly. Although male same-sex conduct was regarded as a criminal offense[3], the same sanctions did not apply to lesbians. The reason for this probably lies in South Africa's British colonial past and the Victorian notion that women simply did not "do such things." Despite this historic omission, there are some laws that discriminate against lesbians specifically. In 1988, it became a criminal offense for a woman to engage in sexual acts with a girl under the age of 19[4] while the heterosexual age of consent is 16. This particular piece of legislation contradicts the provisions of the new constitution and is one of the issues currently being examined by members of the Department of Justice.

Lesbians face additional discrimination in the context of donor insemination. Under the terms of the Human Tissue Act of 1983, only women who are married may benefit from this procedure.[5] Currently, there is lobbying by the Lesbian Health Group to change the Act to remove this restriction so that it no longer discriminates against all single women and against lesbians—regardless of whether or not they are in long-term partnerships. Additionally, attention was drawn to the matter in a conference on Reproductive Health in June 1994.

Finally, we must point out that although the protection offered to lesbians in terms of the new constitution is all-encompassing, it is not perfect. Unfortunately, the Charter of Fundamental Rights is only binding on organs of the state. This is a serious gap in the law. It means that institutions, organizations, and businesses that are not organs of the state may discriminate against lesbians and there is no explicit legal protection against such "private" discrimination. The same applies to individuals acting in their private capacity. Various organizations are making submissions to the Constitutional Assembly to extend the application of fundamental rights enshrined in the constitution to all institutions, organizations, businesses, and individuals.

PARENTING

Natural and Adoptive

Whatever the method of conception, by South African law, a child born to a single woman is illegitimate. Fortunately, with only a few narrow exceptions (which affect paternity and not maternity rights), the legal position of legitimate and illegitimate children is now the same.

The Child Adoption Act[6] governs adoption. This Act contains no explicit prohibition against lesbian adoption. In fact, it could be argued that Section 17 of the Act, which refers to an "unmarried person" as one of the categories of persons who can adopt a child, includes lesbians. Unfortunately, although the law does not forbid lesbians to adopt, lesbians often do not attempt it because of the perceived discriminatory attitudes and practices of state departments responsible for adoption. Many lesbians have pretended to be heterosexual to adopt and have suffered considerable emotional stress as a result.

One lesbian—a white Cape Town resident who adopted a Black child—has described the precarious emotional and legal position in which the adoption placed her, her partner of 13 years, and their daughter, Jessy:

> For the three years in which we have raised and loved Jessy, we have lived in fear of having the adoption reversed should our sexual orientation be discovered. This is an inhuman state of affairs. We are hoping that the final constitution will protect us and our child.
>
> Because I had to adopt as a single parent, Kerry has no legal protection. Legally and emotionally she is in a wilderness. She has loved, supported and cared for our child from birth, yet has no legal hold over her whatsoever. The laws should be amended to take cognizance of the existence of alternative families such as ours.
>
> Socially all three of us are in a wilderness—society has managed to ignore and ostracize lesbians and gays, and where does this leave a minority-within-a-minority, such as a lesbian family? I would like to see social education programmes which recognise and help to legitimize all forms of alternative families.[7]

Beyond the ambit of the law and the courts, parenting by lesbians is a controversial issue in South Africa. It causes considerable disquiet among many heterosexuals, and lesbian mothers often have to contend with family members who threaten to have their children taken away unless they change their "lifestyle."[8] Such family members tend to subscribe to all the myths concerning the unfitness of lesbians and gay men as parents. These views are beyond legislation of any kind.

Custody

Historically in South Africa, it has been almost impossible for openly lesbian mothers to retain custody of their children after divorce. Most end up with only access rights to their children. This obviously causes great hardship. The position of lesbian mothers who divorce is aggravated by the distinction in South African law between guardianship (legal control) and custody (actual caregiving). Even where women are granted custody of their children on divorce, the notoriously conservative courts usually grant guardianship to their fathers.

HEALTH CARE

Psychological Health

Some lesbians experience little or no difficulty in coming to terms with their sexuality. Unfortunately, this is not always the case, and many others experience internal doubt, anxiety, and trauma. The psychological aspect of the position of lesbians in South Africa is a cause for concern. It is precisely in this respect that many lesbians are vulnerable. Because lesbians are an oppressed minority, some tend to be very susceptible to loneliness and isolation, confusion, and shame. This is particularly so in the case of "closeted" lesbians who have to be constantly vigilant in case their friends, family, or co-workers discover their secret.

Many lesbians are financially unable to seek psychological counseling. Working-class lesbians in general and many Black lesbians are also not likely to seek counseling as it is not regarded as culturally appropriate to discuss problems with psychologists, psychiatrists, or counselors. Added to this there is fear of being exposed as a lesbian and consequently seen as abnormal. From discussions with lesbians it emerged that some have very low self-esteem and generally feel isolated in the communities in which they live. This results in lesbians socializing among themselves and often involves consuming large quantities of alcohol.[9] There are no safe spaces for working-class lesbians to go. At a recent retreat for Black working-class lesbians organized by the Association for Bisexuals, Gays and Lesbians (ABIGALE), Black lesbians in their forties commented that it was the first time in their lives that they had spent time not only socializing with other lesbians but talking about what it means to be a lesbian and a woman.[10] And for those who do seek help the problem is not necessarily over. Until fairly recently, several psychology faculties at universities regarded homosexuality as an abnormality. It can therefore be difficult for lesbians to find good mental health care even when they know it is an option.

However, the picture is not all negative. As Julia Nicol of The Organization for Lesbian and Gay Action (OLGA) points out, "The courage and self-awareness required to come out may make the lesbian individual a more confident and more aware person." She adds that "...influenced by their own experiences of oppression [lesbians] are in the vanguard of movements for progressive societal change in numbers far outweighing their proportion in the population. " There are many lesbians in South Africa who fit these descriptions.

Physical Health

In terms of their physical health needs, lesbians often find themselves in a difficult situation. Health workers usually use heterosexuality as their point of departure in their thinking and in their face-to-face interaction with clients. Many lesbians remain "closeted" when they consult health workers. This can be detrimental to their health, especially if they do not reveal pertinent facts. Those who do "come out" may have to face negative attitudes from health workers. In addition, many lesbians do not have the same medical aid benefits as married heterosexuals because their partnerships are not recognized.

There are, however, signs of change. At a National Health Policy Conference in December 1994, a proposal concerning lesbian health issues was drafted by a group of about 70 women, most of whom were not lesbian. The proposal covers the above problems and others that are not uniquely South African, such as the reported high incidence of cervical cancer among lesbians. It also makes strong recommendations regarding the training of health workers, especially regarding the adoption of positive attitudes toward homosexuality. This policy document has been submitted to the Department of Health, which is currently drafting a new health policy for the nation.

LESBIANS IN SOCIETY

In addition to the homophobia that lesbians face in many parts of the world, several aspects of South African life have particular impact on the lives of South African lesbians. These are:

- The commonly held belief that lesbians are *stabane*—i.e., have both male and female sexual organs.
- The belief held by some people that homosexuality is un-African, that it is a European phenomenon or an import of European society.
- Lack of mobility, which keeps lesbians in rural areas or small towns, and working-class lesbians in urban centers from accessing the support systems that do exist.
- Pressure to marry, especially in more traditional communities such as the Muslim community.
- Peer pressure, particularly on young lesbians, to prove their "normality" by having sex with men.
- Physical harassment. Lesbians in the townships are scared to come out because there are gangs that go out in groups and rape women. One gang in particular, the Jackrollers, targets lesbians. In the words of one young lesbian, "…and when they catch one [a lesbian] they say 'We'll put you right.'"[11]
- Invisibility. The lesbian literature that is available is predominately western, white, concerned with middle-class issues, and urban. There is no indigenous lesbian literature available.
- Internal divisions. The lesbian community is characterized by the same divisions of race and class that characterize South African society as a whole.[12]

In addition, Tanya Chan-Sam of the Lesbian Forum recently highlighted the following societal pressures that affect Black lesbians specifically:

- Bars, clubs, and organizations are usually found in white areas and are frequented predominantly by white lesbians.
- Many Black gay men resist sharing skills with lesbians.

- Many Black lesbians are forced through economic necessity to live with their parents. As a result they have little privacy to explore their sexual identity.
- There are few strong Black female role models in the history books, let alone lesbian ones.[13]

These beliefs and restraints can have a profound and destructive impact on the lives of lesbians. A particularly acute testament to this reality is provided by one woman who describes her life after "coming out" to her family and community:

> Lots of attempts have been made to rape and assault me because of my sexual orientation. Insults have become the norm of the day. Even when I was going to praise my God for giving me life, churchgoers made insulting remarks. My family could not deal with the remarks they had to put up with because of the "dirty child" they keep.
>
> Being silent about this, especially to the public protectors, has made it even worse. Many culprits have gotten away with crimes, and many women have suffered and died as a result of them. I do not want to be added to those numbers.
>
> I would not like to see a situation where tomorrow, when I go looking for a job with the appropriate qualifications, I am denied the job because I am a "dyke." I want to go out and enjoy my youth without fearing being raped, assaulted and insulted. I want to be proud of who I am and for my family to be proud to talk about me without fearing that the issue of my lesbianism will come up.[14]

LESBIAN ACTIVISM

Lesbian activism in South Africa dates back to the early 1970s. Influenced by feminist activism and the gay liberation movement that emerged in Europe and North America in that period, white lesbians became involved in setting up feminist organizations. "For many women these were the first places they felt free to articulate feelings of attraction to other women and to consider what the political implications of this might be."[15]

South Africa's first lesbian organization, Lesbians in Love and Compromising Situations (LILACS), was formed in Cape Town in 1983. LILACS was disbanded in 1985 but in its wake followed a number of new organizations. Lesbians and Gays Against Oppression (LAGO) was founded in 1987, and later became the Organisation for Lesbian and

---

The early 1990s saw a dramatic increase in Black lesbian and gay activism.

Gay Activists (OLGA). OLGA was an affiliate of the anti-apartheid United Democratic Front (UDF) until 1991 when the UDF disbanded. OLGA changed its name to the Organisation for Lesbian and Gay Action in 1991, and retained its acronym. It is now defunct.

Black men and women had been involved with LAGO from the organization's founding. The early 1990s saw a dramatic increase in Black lesbian and gay activism, which led to the formation of groups such as the Gay and Lesbian Organisation of the Witwatersrand (GLOW) and the Association of Bisexuals, Gays and Lesbians (ABI-GALE).

South African lesbians are active within a broad range of organizations. There are political groups, social groups, organizations for sport and leisure activities, counseling services, AIDS-related organizations, Christian groups, Jewish groups, Alcoholics Anonymous groups, media groups, and professional groups. While these groups contain both men and women, there are also several organizations specifically for women: the Lesbian Forum in Johannesburg, Sunday's Women in Durban, and two groups in Cape Town—ABIGALE's Lesbian and Bisexual Women's Caucus and the Lesbian Action Project (LAP). An important point to make in relation to lesbian activism is that while lesbian issues have often remained invisible, many lesbians have been at the forefront of women's struggles in this country.

THE "L" WORD

In South African law it is a civil offense to defame someone. Being called a lesbian has been interpreted by the South African courts to be defamatory—unless, of course, the woman in question is in fact a lesbian. The term is considered to be an insult which diminishes a woman's good name and reputation in the eyes of what the courts refer to as "right thinking people." In 1981, a woman fought and won just such a case.[16]

It is debatable whether this judgment would still form a precedent in South African law, given the fact that it is inconsistent with the new protection afforded to lesbians in the constitution. Nevertheless, the existence of such judgments can be taken as an indicator of the attitudes that still prevail in South African society, and the work that will need to be done by lesbians whether they enjoy constitutional protection or not.

The fight is now on to retain the constitutional prohibition on discrimination based on sexual orientation. Already one political party, the African Christian Democratic Party, has stated that it regards homosexuality as contrary to "the will of God and African culture" and has made the abolition of lesbian and gay rights the main theme of its constitutional submissions. If the sexual orientation clause can be retained in the face of such opposition, South Africa may indeed be able to show other nations the way forward regarding lesbian and gay rights.

NOTES

1 Act No. 200 of 1993.

2 Section 8 (2).

3 Sexual Offences Act (No. 23 of 1957).

4 Section 14(3)(2) of the 1988 amendment to the Sexual Offences Act (No. 23 of 1957). The age of consent for gay men is also 19.

5 Act No. 65 of 1083.

6 Act No. 74 of 1983.

7 Personal testimonial by Josephine Stable (the author has used pseudonyms to protect her family), solicited by Karin Koen, spring 1995.

8 Interview with Sandra Adams by Karin Koen on 19 January 1995, in Cape Town.

9 Discussions by Karin Koen with lesbians on the Cape Flats on 4 and 11 February 1995.

10 From the ABIGALE Lesbian and Bisexual Women's Camp, 20 to 22 January 1995. We would like to thank the ABIGALE Caucus for permission to use their personal information for this report.

11 Bongie in Tanya Chan Sam, "Five Women: Black Lesbian Life on the Reef" in M. Gevisser and E. Cameron, eds., *Defiant Desire: Gay and Lesbian Lives in South Africa* Johannesburg: Raven Press, 1994, p. 147.

12 Bronwynne Perreira. "Lesbians in the Eastern Cape—A Report" (1995), p.1.

13 It is important to point out that there are in fact no female role models of any description in any South African history textbook.

14 Interview with Sylvia Vilakazi by Karin Koen on 26 May 1995, in Cape Town.

15 M. Armour and S. Lapinsky, "Lesbians in Love and Compromising Situations" in Gevisser and Cameron , eds., op. cit., p. 247.

16 Edwin Cameron, "'Unapprehended felons': Gays and lesbians and the law in South Africa," in Gevisser and Cameron, eds., op.cit., p. 89.

ABOUT THE AUTHORS

Karin Koen is a member of ABIGALE and is currently working with the National Coalition for Gay and Lesbian Equality.

Patricia Terry is a lawyer and a human rights educator and activist. She is a founding member of the Lesbian Action Project in Cape Town.

Spain

• • • • •

Mili Hernández

In the late 1960s and early 1970s, when the lesbian and gay liberation movement was gaining ground in North America and Northern Europe, life remained very difficult for lesbians in Spain. In 1970, Franco's government enacted the Law of Social Danger and Rehabilitation, under which same-sex sexual conduct was punishable by imprisonment. This law was repealed when the current Constitution came into effect in 1978.

Although lesbian and gay organizations were not allowed to exist openly under the Franco regime, El Movimiento Español de Liberación Homosexual (MELH, Spanish Movement for Homosexual Liberation) began operating illegally in 1971. When the political climate changed, MELH began making its existence more widely known, and several new gay and lesbian groups were formed beginning in 1976. In all of these groups, however, lesbians were far outnumbered by gay men.

The first lesbian organization, El Colectivo de Lesbianas (Collective of Lesbians), was formed in September 1977, within the Frente de Liberación Gay de Cataluña (Gay Liberation Front of Catalonia). It split off a year later, forming its own group called Grupo de Lucha para la Liberación de las Lesbianas (GLAL, Group for the Liberation of Lesbians). The majority of the lesbian organizations in the 1970s and 80s, including GLAL, grew out of and alongside the feminist movement. During this time, the focus of lesbian groups was primarily on political advocacy rather than on providing services to meet the needs of lesbians. More recently, however, lesbian groups have begun to move into different areas. Grants from state and private organizations have allowed these groups to improve their infrastructure and to develop services targeted toward lesbians, such as psychological counseling, legal counseling, and telephone information lines. There are approximately twelve exclusively lesbian groups currently in existence in Spain. In addition, there are approximately 25 lesbian and gay groups in which lesbians, while still in the minority, are increasingly vocal.

LESBIAN PARTNERSHIPS

Currently, as shown by a survey of the Centro de Investigaciones Sociológicas (CIS) carried out in April 1994, 53% of Spaniards feel that

The proposed legislation would give lesbian and gay couples the same rights as unmarried heterosexual couples in the areas of inheritance, pension, and property rights.

lesbian and gay partnerships should be legally recognized in the same way that heterosexual domestic partnerships are.[1] This has become a central focus of several lesbian and gay organizations. In November 1994, the Parliament voted in favor of such recognition and ordered the Ministry of Interior Affairs and the Ministry of Justice to draft the necessary legislation. The proposed legislation would give lesbian and gay couples the same rights as unmarried heterosexual couples in the areas of inheritance, pension, and property rights. In anticipation of its passage, many city and town halls have begun to set up procedures through which lesbians and gay men can register their partnerships.

PARENTHOOD

This proposed legislation marks a milestone in the history of the lesbian and gay movement. One major area that it does not address, however, is adoption. As an individual, a lesbian can adopt a child.[2] However, two women are not allowed to adopt as a couple, and a lesbian who is open about her sexual orientation would face great difficulty. There is still significant opposition in Spanish society to adoption by lesbians or gay men. According to the CIS survey, 55% of those polled are opposed to such adoptions, and only 33% are in favor. The Spanish Society of Pediatrics has stated that it is necessary for children to be placed in "a family environment in which the roles of the mother and the father are clearly established, each with a particular part to play in the care and training of the child,"[3] and the Catholic Church has issued statements explicitly opposing lesbian and gay adoption rights.

Lesbians who wish to bear children are able to obtain donor insemination without much difficulty. The Law of Assisted Reproduction does not specify any requirements regarding marital status. Legally, however, the biological mother is the child's only parent, and her partner has no legal rights regarding the child.

REPRESSION OF LESBIANISM IN THE FAMILY AND IN THE EDUCATIONAL SYSTEM

Many lesbians who reveal their sexual orientation to their family face rejection and condemnation. Due to tradition and difficult economic conditions most unmarried women live with their parents until their early thirties, making such rejection particularly difficult to bear. This dependence on the family is one of the primary reasons that many lesbians remain "in the closet," hiding all of the aspects of their lives that may reveal their lesbianism.

Young lesbians who do not receive the support of their families have few alternative sources of information. There is a tremendous lack of accurate information regarding homosexuality in the Spanish educational system. Currently, homosexuality is not discussed in most school curricula, although there are some isolated cases where schools request the help of lesbian and gay groups in giving presentations. Several organizations are currently calling for the progressive standardization of teaching about homosexuality in schools.

LESBIAN INSTITUTIONS

Recently, the first two bookstores specializing in gay and lesbian literature have opened, and they have helped to create visibility and community. At the same time, several new lesbian publications have recently appeared. However, beyond the existing social and political groups, lesbians have few public spaces in which to socialize. As opposed to gay men who have saunas, parks, and a varied selection of bars and discos, lesbians have only a few bars, which means that most lesbian socializing takes place in private homes. This contributes to the low visibility of lesbians in Spanish society and the consequent isolation of many individual lesbians. Thus, despite the promising new legislative developments, many lesbians remain "in the closet" and have internalized the negative images of lesbianism that they have learned from their families and their schooling. Progressive laws will be of little value if lesbians are not able to come to terms with their sexuality and feel able to take advantage of the protections that such laws establish.

NOTES

1 "Los gais no hemos de adoptar," *Entiendes...?* Jan-Feb. 1995, p. 13.
2 Civil Code, Chapter V, second section, Art. 175-180. Unmarried people are permitted to adopt.
3 "Los gais no hemos de adoptar," *Entiendes...?* Jan-Feb. 1995, p. 13.

ABOUT THE AUTHOR

Mili Hernández is a militant lesbian activist and owner of the first gay and lesbian bookstore in Spain.

Thailand

● ● ● ● ● ● ● ● ●

Kanokwan Tarawan

T hai law does not state anything regarding lesbians. In fact, there is no specific term in Thai for lesbianism. The closest equivalent is *len-peuhn* or "playing with friends." The verb *len* does not indicate playing as an innocent preoccupation but rather connotes disrespect and improper behavior. More appropriate to many lesbians are the labels *tom* and *dee*. These are shortened versions of "tom-boy" and "lady." *Toms* are the more "masculine" of the couple, while *dees* are the more "feminine." Anjaree, the first lesbian organization in Thailand, has created a new term in Thai for lesbianism and uses it officially to identify the group: *ying-rug-ying* or "women who love women."

ATTITUDES WITHIN THE FAMILY

Thai culture allows women to interact closely with one another. This often makes it hard to determine whether women couples are in fact lovers or just friends. Two women can live together for an extended amount of time, hold hands, hug in public, sleep in the same bed, and even raise a child together without much opposition, because such relationships are generally not seen as sexual. Unfortunately, such relation-ships are denied the social recognition that heterosexual marriages are accorded, and parents accept such relationships only so long as the sex-ual nature of the relationship remains hidden.

"Nobody accepts it when women would like to marry women. Now that she's dead, they say she deserved it."

For example, *tom* and *dee* relationships are often opposed by parents because the sexual nature of the relationship is clear. In such cases, par-ents often use forced marriages to "cure" the daughters' "abnormality." As a result, many lesbians suffer extreme confusion and self doubt. Many young women flee their homes due to the pressure to marry or to stop seeing their woman lover; some commit suicide.

One such case was reported at a recent seminar in Bangkok. A woman from Bokwan village, Muang district, Nongkhai province, gave the following report:

> The story started when a woman in Nadee Village in Nongkhai Province came to work at Udonthani Province. She was 16. At the workplace she met one woman from Udonthani. They fell in love and reached the level that they bought rings for each other and wanted to get married. But the parents of this young girl of 16 wanted her to get married to a man. She didn't know what to do. When we heard the news about this again she had already hung herself. The ring was still on her finger.

Asked if the parents felt sad about their daughter's suicide, the woman replied:

> Not at all. Nobody accepts it when women would like to marry women. Now that she's dead, they say she deserved it.... The vil-lagers talked amongst themselves that she should die, this kind of person.[1]

DISCRIMINATION IN THE WORKPLACE

Gender and sexuality are identities that are expressed in language, attitude, and behavior. *Toms*, who manifest "masculine" qualities such as short hair and pants and speak with the masculine form of language,[2] are often more visible than *dees*. *Toms* do not fit into the typical Thai image of a feminine woman and often face malicious gossip, harassment, and discrimination. Most decision-makers in workplaces in Thailand are men who hold strong views about "proper" (i.e., feminine) appearance, and many jobs require women to wear skirts. *Toms* often have to hide their identity in order to get a job, and the discrimination does not stop at the job interview. Many lesbians must hide their identity throughout their careers. They cannot speak or act in any way which would show that they are lesbians.

MASS MEDIA

If it is mentioned at all within Thai society, lesbianism is considered to be an abnormality or a passing phase. Reflecting the attitudes that prevail in Thai society, the media generally perpetuates the view that lesbians need to be "cured." News reporters of all sorts make fun of lesbian relationships and write about lesbianism as the result of a broken home or a woman's bad experiences or failure in having relationships with men. Few, if any, lesbians have confronted the mass media about these portrayals because such images are extremely entrenched in Thai society and are often internalized by lesbians themselves.

Thai academics and mental health professionals view lesbianism as a deviation from normal behavior. Most believe that homosexuality needs to be treated with therapy.[3]

LESBIAN ORGANIZING

Anjaree is the first lesbian organization in Thailand. It was founded by a small group of Thai lesbians in 1986. The first aim of the organization was for its members to have a safe space in which to meet and hold social events. The organization grew out of the women's movement, and

Anjaree at first served mainly lesbian feminists and their friends. However, the majority of Thai lesbians are not active within the feminist movement, and over the past few years Anjaree's membership (which currently numbers over 300) has grown to include a much broader spectrum of women.

Lesbian activist Anjana Suvarnananda, addressing an international lesbian and gay rally in New York City, 1994

In 1990, Anjaree hosted the first Asian Lesbian Network (ALN) meeting in Bangkok. This meeting had a strong impact on Anjaree, as did a 1991 workshop on violence against lesbians at an international conference held in Bangkok.[4] More lesbians paid attention to the organization, and the inspiration and strength acquired from these meeting encouraged Anjaree to become public about its existence. Anjaree did not trust the mainstream press and did not know how the public would respond to the organization. Many members feared being rejected by family and friends if their membership in the organization became known. Since no women had ever come out publicly as lesbians in Thailand, Anjaree members had no examples to follow.

As a result of the workshop, a small Bangkok paper interviewed a member of Anjaree. The paper was read only by a small number of people and Anjaree received hardly any response. In early 1993, Anjaree agreed that its name and address could be printed in a column in *Strange*, a sensational weekly magazine. The column in which Anjaree had its information printed was a question-and-answer column primarily aimed at gay men. The organization received a significant response from this particular coverage. Apparently, many of Anjaree's current members found out about the organization through this column.

Anjaree has increasingly drawn the public's attention in the past year. Articles on lesbianism with interviews of Anjaree members have appeared several times in both the Thai- and English-language press, and the tone of such articles is becoming more positive.[5] Anjaree has appeared in magazines, local papers, and on a national TV program. Anjaree holds regular meetings and social events, publishes a bimonthly newsletter, and receives letters from women all over Thailand.

Within the Thai women's movement, lesbianism is not widely accepted as part of feminism. In 1994, however, Anjaree representatives began to attend local, regional, national, and international meetings on issues concerning women. On International Women's Day on March 8, 1995, Anjaree appeared with other grassroots women's organizations in a march for women's rights in Bangkok and was among the organizations to present a letter to the Deputy Prime Minister. In the letter, the groups demanded changes in Thai laws and public policy to improve conditions for women.

NOTES

1 Supaporn Attamongkol, "Violence Against Women in Thai Society: The Quiet War Without Borders," in Krittaya Adohawanijkul, ed., *Khiang Rang Sang Phandin* (The History of Ordinary Women Struggling), Bangkok: Foundation for Women, 1995. This information was first reported in a seminar on "Thai Women in the Next Decade: Grassroots Women to the World Conference on Women in Beijing," Emergency Home for Women and Children, Bangkok, 29 November 1994.

2 In Thai, many forms of speech vary depending on the gender of the speaker and of the person being addressed.

3 For a discussion of homophobia within the psychiatric profession, see "Parents' protectionism 'tied to surge in lesbianism,'" *Nation*, 17 July 1994, p.A1.

4 The workshop took place at a 1991 conference on Violence Against Women organized by War Resisters International and five Thai women's groups.

5 For example, Varaporn Chamsanit, "Women who love women," *Nation*, 25 September 1994, Focus Section pp. C1-C2; Tessanee Vejponogsa, "Thai NGO to press for lesbians' rights," *Bangkok Post*, 29 July 1994; Panwa, "'Phuying' kap thang say ti saam" ("Women and the third way"), *City Life Magazine*, 5 July 1994, pp. 78-80.

ABOUT THE AUTHOR

Kanokwan Tarawan lives in Chiang Mai and is an active member of the Chiang Mai branch of Anjaree, the first and only lesbian organization in Thailand.

Turkey

● ● ● ● ● ● ●

Deniz Kiliç and Gaye Uncu

GENERAL OUTLOOK

Turkey has a secular system of government and operates nominally as a democracy. It is currently seeking membership in the European Community (EC) and has already become part of EC customs unity agreements. Many new laws have recently been introduced in Turkey, including a new national health service and laws that will increase penalties for rape and domestic violence.

Despite these promising changes, many marginalized groups, including ethnic, religious, and sexual minorities, continue to be denied their rights. Human rights violations in Turkey have been increasing as religious fundamentalism has gained strength over the past several years.

SOCIAL AND CULTURAL PRESSURE ON LESBIANS

The population of Turkey is 99% Muslim. Although the country has a long-standing tradition of secularism, religious fundamentalists are currently gaining political power and influence in the country. As is the case with any form of religious fundamentalism, Muslim fundamentalism threatens to make life very dangerous for all marginalized communities.

Homosexuality is prohibited within Islamic law. The Koran talks about the tribe of Lut, in which men had sex with men; as punishment for this transgression, Allah sent stones raining down on them from the sky. In many mosques in Turkey, religious authorities preach against homosexuality and talk about AIDS as another rain of stones on homosexuals. Through teachings such as these, Turkish children are brought up to believe that lesbians and gay men are sinners. Homosexuality is seen as a threat to the family and by extention to society as a whole.

LEGAL SITUATION

The Turkish Penal Code has been subject to a series of revisions, beginning in the early 19th century, that have been based largely on French law. Although homosexuality is not mentioned in Turkish law, however, there are several broad ranging provisions that have been selectively enforced against sexual minorities. These laws, which prohibit indecency and offenses against public morality,[1] are most often

---

In July 1993, the Istanbul city government intervened to stop Turkey's first lesbian and gay pride celebration.

---

used against transvestites, transsexuals, and gay men, particularly those who are sex workers. Because the terms of the laws are fairly broad and do not specifically single out lesbians or gay men, they are extremely difficult to challenge, even when they are enforced in a discriminatory manner.

In July 1993, the Istanbul city government intervened to stop a group of lesbians and gay men from organizing a lesbian and gay pride celebration. In the week prior to the event, the organizers also received calls from fundamentalist groups threatening to bomb the cinema where the activities were scheduled to take place. This harassment was provoked in part by inflammatory reports in the newspaper *Bügün*, which for an entire week devoted its back page to the event. Articles announced that "perverts" would be meeting in Istanbul and that "perverts" from abroad were coming to force Turkish youth into decadence. On the day the celebration was scheduled to begin, the Governor of Istanbul faxed hotels in the city instructing them not to accept foreign participants in the celebration. The next day, Turkish authorities arrested and expelled 28 foreign delegates who were there to take part in the celebration. In addition, three Turkish men were arrested for their efforts to organize the event. Letters protesting the government's action arrived from many different countries around the world, and the incident was included in the Human Rights Foundation's 1993 report on human rights abuses in Turkey.

There have been no reports of Turkish lesbians being arrested or otherwise subjected to state persecution on the basis of their sexual orientation. This is in part due to the invisibility of lesbians in Turkish public life. Lesbians are not a visible presence on the streets or in bars, and the events in 1993 have cast doubt on the ability of any lesbian or gay group to form a legal organization, since this would require registering with the government. Turkey's first lesbian group, Venüs'ün Kizkardesleri (Sisters of Venus), was established in July 1994 (see below), but the group does not exist legally and cannot hold a bank account or otherwise establish itself publicly.

ISOLATION OF LESBIANS

The pervasive prejudice within Turkish society puts lesbians under a great deal of pressure. It is very difficult for a lesbian, especially a young lesbian, to "come out" to herself or to her family or friends. Each lesbian has to find her own way, without the help of a visible lesbian community or any sort of support organizations. Forced marriages are very common, especially in rural areas, and girls are brought up to believe that there are no alternatives to heterosexual marriage. In big cities, the incidence of forced marriage is not as high, but younger lesbians are frequently sent to psychologists to be "cured."

LESBIAN ORGANIZING

Lesbians who have managed to live independently have a difficult time reaching other lesbians. The Sisters of Venus, the first lesbian group in Turkey, began meeting in July 1994. This group began with three lesbians; it has grown to over 20 women, and the membership continues to increase as more women learn of the group's existence. While the group is not yet strong enough to be a political pressure, it is nonetheless able to offer support to lesbians. The group holds regular meetings where members can share experiences and difficulties with one another. It has begun to print brochures and to assemble a small library of articles and books. The brochures focus on subjects, such as "coming out," homophobia, how to feel proud of one's sexual identity, and the like. At great risk Sisters of Venus lists its post office box number on these brochures and receives both positive and negative feedback. Sisters of Venus members also contribute to Turkey's only lesbian and gay publication, *KAOS GL*, which is an underground publication that cannot be distributed openly. The organization has also responded to the mainstream media's generally negative portrayal of lesbians by sending protest letters.

Sisters of Venus is beginning to work with other organizations in Turkey, including the AIDS Prevention Society; feminist groups such as Eksik Etek, Mor Cati, Pazartesi, and the Women's Human Rights Project; Lambda, a gay men's group in Istanbul; and KAOL GL, a lesbian and gay group in Ankara. The group has also begun to network with organizations in other countries, such as the Indian group Sakhi, the organizers of the Berlin Lesbian Week, and Frauenzeitung in Munich.

While Sisters of Venus has received support from many feminists, there is clearly a need for lesbians to organize independently of the feminist movement. Some lesbians work in feminist groups, but they can only be outspoken on heterosexual women's issues because even within such organizations anti-lesbian prejudice is pervasive.

CONCLUSION

The lesbian and gay movement is just beginning in Turkey and is limited to urban centers. The threat from the fundamentalist movement and, conversely, the possibility of Turkey's becoming a member of the European Community have created strong incentives to organize and to push for an increased emphasis on human rights.

NOTES

1 Articles 419, 547, and 576 of the Penal Code.

ABOUT THE AUTHORS

Deniz Kiliç and Gaye Uncu are members of Sisters of Venus, the first and only lesbian group in Turkey.

United States

● ● ● ● ● ● ● ● ● ● ● ●

Shannon Minter

I n the past three decades, lesbians in the United States have gained recognition for their rights in a number of areas. Nevertheless, the human rights of lesbians continue to be violated on a daily basis.

HATE VIOLENCE AGAINST LESBIANS

Hate violence against lesbians is pervasive throughout the United States. In recent years, numerous studies have documented a dramatic increase in the number of reported incidents of anti-lesbian and anti-gay violence. In the five major U.S. cities with agencies that monitor hate crimes against lesbians and gay men, reports of anti-gay and anti-lesbian incidents increased by 172% between 1988 and 1992.[1] In Colorado, reports of anti-lesbian and anti-gay violence tripled in November and December of 1992 after voters approved a state ballot initiative prohibiting enactment of laws to protect lesbians and gay men from discrimination.[2] According to the U.S. Department of Justice, lesbians and gay men "are probably the most frequent victims" of hate violence in the U.S.[3]

At least two studies have shown that lesbians and gay men of color are at greater risk for violent attack because of their sexual orientation.[4] Youth are also at greater risk. For example, of the 500 lesbian, gay, and bisexual youths who used the services of the Hetrick-Martin Institute of New York City in 1988, 40% had experienced violent attacks.[5]

Thirty-five states have enacted hate crimes statutes that mandate enhanced penalties for and/or the collection of official statistics on bias-motivated crimes. Only 21 of these statutes, however, include crimes motivated by bias against lesbians and gay men. Even in states with hate crime statutes that include sexual orientation, police routinely refuse to investigate or act on violent crimes against lesbians and gay men and are themselves the third most common perpetrators of violence against lesbians and gay men, which includes rape and sexual assault.[6] Similarly, district attorneys frequently refuse to prosecute violence against lesbians and gay men as hate crimes, even when the perpetrators acknowledge a homophobic motivation, and courts often view lesbians and gay men as undeserving of protection. In 1989, Dallas judge Jack Hampton stated that "I put prostitutes and queers at the same level…and I'd be hard-put to give somebody life for killing a prostitute."[7]

Not surprisingly, most lesbians and gay men who are victimized by hate crimes never report the assault, for fear of being disregarded or victimized further by the police or criminal justice system. A recent study found that 72% of white lesbian and gay victims of assault and 82% of lesbian and gay people of color victimized by assault did not report such incidents.[8] Although comprehensive studies have not yet been done, lesbians appear to be particularly unlikely to report hate crimes. Because assaults on lesbians are usually based on gender as well as sexual orientation, reports by lesbians are especially liable to be minimized or dismissed as incidents of "routine" male hostility toward women.

According to Women, Inc., a California organization serving battered women, domestic violence occurs in one in four lesbian relationships—roughly the same percentage as in heterosexual relationships. However, few domestic violence agencies have created services for battered lesbians.

FAMILY RIGHTS

Child Custody and Visitation

As a group, lesbians and their children are systematically denied the basic rights and protections guaranteed to other American families. Although the U.S. Supreme Court has recognized that "the rights attached to parenthood are among the 'basic civil rights,'"[9] state courts routinely view lesbian and gay parents as undeserving of the rights afforded to other parents. As a result, the estimated six to 14 million children with a lesbian or gay parent[10] have little protection against judicial decisions that arbitrarily dissolve or disrupt their families.

State courts generally discriminate against lesbians in custody and visitation determinations. A minority of states consider a parent's sexual orientation to have bearing on a custody determination only if there is some evidence of harm to the child. Most state courts, however, either deem lesbian and gay parents per se unfit to raise children or deny normal custody and visitation rights based on unfounded bias and stereotypes about lesbian parents.[11] In states with statutes that criminalize private consensual sexual acts between adults, some courts subject lesbian and gay parents to invasive questioning about their private sexual practices or deprive lesbian parents of custody or normal visitation on the supposition that they have violated the state sodomy statute. In a highly publicized case in 1994, a Virginia trial court removed Sharon Bottoms' two-year-old son from her custody based solely on the judge's belief that Sharon Bottoms' lesbianism was "immoral" and "illegal." In April 1995, the Virginia state supreme court upheld this ruling.[12] Every year, hundreds of lesbian mothers across the nation lose custody of their children on similar grounds.

Adoption

Lesbians confront numerous legal and administrative barriers to adoption, both as single parents and as couples. In Florida and New Hampshire, legislation absolutely prohibits lesbians and gay men from becoming adoptive parents. Even in the absence of a statutory prohibition, courts have denied adoption petitions by lesbians and gay men solely because of the petitioner's sexual orientation.[13] Many state and private adoption agencies engage in a more subtle form of discrimination by refusing to initiate adoption proceedings on behalf of a prospective lesbian or gay parent.[14]

Lesbian couples who wish to adopt a child as a couple face even more formidable obstacles. Because the overwhelming majority of states prohibit joint adoptions by unmarried couples, and because same-gender couples cannot marry, lesbian and gay couples are effectively barred from bringing a joint adoption petition. To date, only Massachusetts has granted a joint adoption petition on behalf of a lesbian couple. Finally, many lesbian couples have formed families in which both partners raise and care for a child who is the biological or adoptive child of one of the partners, but who has no legal relationship to the other parent. In a small but growing number of states, courts have allowed the nonlegal or "second parent" to adopt the couple's child without terminating the parental rights of the first parent.[15] In most states, however, there are virtually no legal means of protecting the relationship between the nonbiological or nonadoptive parent and the child. If the legal parent dies or becomes incapacitated, the child does not automatically remain with her or his other parent and may be left without a legal parent. Even if the legal parent has drafted a nomination of guardianship or conservatorship, it is up to the discretion of the court whether the child will be allowed to stay with her or his nonlegally recognized parent. The children of such couples are also deprived of numerous other legal rights and protections afforded by having two legal parents, such as the right to inherit property from both parents, and to receive family-related benefits such as health insurance and Social Security.[16]

Foster Parenting

Lesbians also face extreme discrimination in their efforts to serve as foster parents. In New Hampshire, a state statute prohibits placement of foster children in homes with lesbians or gay men.[17] In 1994, the Nebraska Department of Social Services also adopted a formal policy prohibiting placement of children in lesbian or gay foster homes.[18] While most states do not have explicit policies regarding lesbian and gay foster parents, states that discriminate against lesbians and gay men in custody and adoption proceedings are extremely unlikely to certify lesbians as foster parents.[19]

The pervasive discrimination against lesbians and gay men in the foster system has a particularly devastating impact on lesbian and gay youth in the child welfare system, for whom finding a supportive foster placement is frequently difficult or impossible. The tragedy of denying lesbians and gay men the opportunity to provide supportive foster homes for lesbian- and gay-identified youth was brutally illustrated by the immediate aftermath of the Nebraska policy described above. The day following the announcement of Nebraska's policy prohibiting placement of children with gay and lesbian foster parents, E.J. Byington, a 17-year-old openly gay foster child recently placed with a gay couple, committed suicide after expressing fear that he would be removed from his foster parents' home.[20]

Access to Donor Insemination

Because most state laws governing donor insemination are designed to protect married women and their husbands, lesbians who conceive children through a known sperm donor are vulnerable to paternity suits by donors. As a result, access to anonymous or confidential donor insemination services is the only way for most lesbians to protect the integrity of their chosen families against interference by donors and courts.[21] Currently, no state prohibits lesbians from using insemination services, although such legislation was proposed in Oregon in 1995. In practice, however, lesbians seeking insemination services face significant discrimination, including widespread denial of services by doctors, sperm banks, and other health care providers,[22] and the refusal of insurance companies to reimburse lesbian couples for insemination and other fertility-related expenses.

Domestic Partnership and Same-Sex Marriage

Currently, there is no jurisdiction in the U.S. in which lesbian or gay couples can legalize their relationships through marriage. The landmark case currently underway in Hawaii, however, may open the door to a state-by-state consideration of whether the "different-sex" restriction on marital choice amounts to unconstitutional sex discrimination.[23] If Hawaii permits same-gender marriage in that state, many lesbians and gay men will marry in Hawaii and return to their home states expecting full legal recognition of their marriages. Utah has already passed state legislation refusing to recognize same-gender marriages from other states, and opponents of same-gender marriage are organizing to pass similar "gay exceptions" to equal marriage rights in other states.

A small number of cities and counties permit lesbian and gay couples to register as "domestic partners" and in some cases to become eligible to receive some of the benefits afforded to legal spouses. Because of the inability to marry and given the very limited scope of domestic partner benefits, lesbian couples and their children are still effectively denied numerous significant rights afforded to married couples, including the right to inherit property, the right to obtain family-related employment benefits such as health insurance and family leave, the right to visit one's partner in prison or in the hospital, the right to tax exemptions, the right to make medical decisions on behalf of an incapacitated partner, and the right to bring one's non-U.S. citizen spouse into the U.S. on a permanent basis. In a well known case, for example, Karen Thompson was forced to fight a seven-year legal battle to gain guardianship of her partner, Sharon Kowalski, after Kowalski was severely disabled in a 1983 car accident.[24] Although the Kowalski case garnered national attention, lesbian and gay couples continue regularly to confront similar circumstances.

DISCRIMINATION IN EMPLOYMENT

Employers in the United States must comply with numerous state and federal statutes that prohibit discrimination in employment on the basis of race, sex, religion, national origin, or disability. In the overwhelming majority of jurisdictions, however, sexual orientation is not a protected category. Employers in these jurisdictions are free to fire or otherwise discriminate against lesbian and gay employees solely on the basis of their sexual orientation. In practice, moreover, discrimination against lesbians and gay men is extremely widespread. As many as two-thirds of gay corporate employees have witnessed some sort of hostility toward gay people on the job.[25] The impact of this discrimination falls hardest on lesbians, and particularly on lesbians of color, who are also subject to discrimination on the basis of gender and race.

Gains for lesbians in the private employment sector have been slow. In 1993, the National Gay and Lesbian Task Force sent surveys to the 1,000 largest companies in the country. Of the 98 companies that returned the survey, only five offer domestic partner benefits to same-sex partners. However, half of those companies do include sexual orientation issues in diversity training; more than two-thirds offer some type of support for people with HIV, and in February 1992, Levi-Strauss & Co., with 23,000 workers, became the largest U.S. employer to offer health insurance to partners of lesbians and gay men.

Lesbians have slightly greater protection from discrimination in public employment than in the private arena, since government employers must comply with civil service regulations and with state and federal constitutions that often provide some protection against arbitrary termination or other penalties. Nonetheless, traditional civil rights litigation strategies in federal and state courts have not been very successful in establishing protection against discrimination. The impact of discrimination in the public employment arena is especially egregious in public education, where lesbian teachers are extremely vulnerable to the loss of their jobs on the basis of their sexual orientation.

In 1994, Congress failed to enact the Employment Nondiscrimination Act, a proposed national law that would have banned job discrimination on the basis of sexual orientation. Prospects for enactment of any such bill in the near future are dim. In addition, voters in nine states proposed statewide anti-gay ballot initiatives that would repeal all existing anti-discrimination protections for lesbians and gay men. Seven of these initiatives never reached the ballot, and the remaining two were defeated, in Oregon and Idaho. Organized anti-gay movements throughout the country continue to confront state and local governments with similar attempts to deny equal protection to lesbians and gay men.

As the largest employer in the nation, the U.S. military's policy of discriminating against lesbians and gay men has caused profound economic and personal injury to thousands of lesbian service members. It is also a devastating symbol of the U.S. government's refusal to afford lesbians and gay men equal treatment under the law. The official policy of the U.S. military is that "homosexuality is incompatible with military service." Despite the widely publicized "Don't Ask, Don't Tell" compromise enacted into law following a great deal of media attention and political debate,[26] lesbian military personnel remain routinely subject to harassment and discharge. The Code of Military Justice still prohibits same gender sexual conduct, and lesbians continue to be court-marshalled and discharged for violating the code. Under the new policy, lesbians may also be discharged merely for disclosing their sexual orientation to others, even to personal friends or family members.[27]

Both historically and under the new policy, the military's ban on lesbian and gay service members has a dramatically disproportionate effect on lesbians. Between 1980 and 1990, women accounted for 6% of all personnel serving in the armed forces and for 20% of all discharged for homosexuality.[28] The primary explanation for this disproportionate impact is the pervasive sexual harassment faced by women in all levels of military service. Regardless of their actual sexual orientation, female service members who reject sexual overtures from male soldiers are vul-

---

Lesbian youth confront systematic isolation, rejection, hostility and violence.

---

nerable to the accusation of lesbianism and to being singled out for investigation and discharge.

LESBIAN YOUTH

As a group, lesbian youth confront systematic isolation, rejection, hostility, and violence. Parents and other family members frequently reject or abuse their lesbian and gay children. A recent study found that 46% of teenagers reporting violent physical assault said that the assault was related to their sexual orientation; of these, 61% reported that the violence came from within their own families.[29] Nationally, studies show that as many as 25% percent of homeless urban youth are lesbian, gay, bisexual, or transgender runaways or "throwaways," pushed out of their families of origin because of parental homophobia.[30] Lesbian youth also confront an extremely high level of harassment and abuse in the school system, both from other students and from teachers and other school staff. A 1984 study by the National Gay and Lesbian Task Force, for example, found that 20% of lesbians reported being verbally or physically assaulted in high school.[31] No federal statute protects lesbian and gay youth against discrimination in public schools; only one state (Massachusetts) has such a statute.

Lesbian youth face profound discrimination in the child welfare and juvenile justice systems, due to the nearly complete lack of social services and safe placements (e.g., foster homes or group homes) and to open hostility and prejudice on the part of many attorneys, judges, probation officers, and social service providers. Lesbian youth are also extremely vulnerable to forced psychiatric confinement by parents, school officials, social welfare personnel, and juvenile courts, many of whom perceive lesbian youth as "confused" or "deviant" and in need of psychiatric treatment. Within the mental health system, lesbian youth are frequently labeled and "treated" for their sexual orientation. In particular, lesbian youth are vulnerable to being labeled with so-called "gender identity disorder," a psychiatric diagnosis that pathologizes girls and young women who "display intense negative reactions to parental expectations or attempts to have them wear dresses or other feminine attire," who "prefer boy's clothing and short hair," who "prefer boys as playmates, with whom they share an interest in contact sports, rough-and-tumble play, and traditional boyhood games," and who "show little interest in dolls or any form of feminine dress up or role-play activity."[32] Lesbian youth diagnosed with this homophobic and misogynist "disorder" are frequently subjected to invasive behavior modification treatments that attempt to force them to conform to gender stereotypes and to adopt a heterosexual orientation.

HEALTH CARE

The major problem facing lesbians seeking access to health care is lack of information on the part of providers, which in turn causes many lesbians to avoid the health care system altogether. Homophobia is widespread; in a recent national survey of physician attitudes towards lesbian and gay patients conducted by the American Physicians for Human Rights, nine out of 10 physicians reported observing anti-gay bias and more than two-thirds knew of lesbian and gay patients who had received poor care or were denied care because of their sexual orientation. While nearly all agreed that a physician's knowledge of a patient's sexual orientation was important to ensure that specific medical needs were met, two-thirds believed that patients who revealed their sexual orientation would receive inferior care as a result. Finally, cost and lack of health insurance are major barriers to care; more than one out of three lesbians in a large 50-state study reported having no health insurance.[33]

Many lesbians avoid seeking or cannot afford gynecological care. In a large national study, 35-45% of lesbians received no gynecological care, and in a 1988 study of lesbians' relationships with their health-care providers, 72% recounted negative experiences.[34] Doctors often presume that lesbians are not at risk for sexually transmitted diseases, and they often fail to provide routine screening. Research is limited, but has shown that syphilis, herpes, and chlamydia can be passed between between women.[35] Most research on HIV transmission has neglected to study woman-to-woman transmission.

Lack of preventive care often fails to identify treatable conditions, including hypertension, diabetes, substance abuse, and early stage cancers. Undetected gynecological cancers in lesbians, which could be identified through routine screening, ultimately become life threatening. According to the latest national study of lesbian health concerns, one out of 20 lesbians over age 55 has never had a pap smear, and one out of six has never given herself a breast self-examination.

NOTES

1 National Gay and Lesbian Task Force Policy Institute, *Anti-Gay/Lesbian Violence, Victimization and Defamation in 1992*, Washington, D.C., 1993.

2 Id.

3 National Institute of Justice, U.S. Department of Justice, "The Response of

the Criminal Justice System to Bias Crime: An Exploratory Review," 1987.

4 Gregory M. Herek and Kevin T. Berrill, eds., *Hate Crimes: Confronting Violence Against Lesbians and Gay Men*, 1992.

5 Id.

6 Gary David Comstock, *Violence against Lesbians and Gay Men*, 1991.

7 Pamela Reynolds, "Judge creates uproar in Texas," *Boston Globe*, 26 February 1989.

8 Id.

9 See Stanley v. Illinois, 405 U.S. 645 (1972).

10 Charlotte J. Patterson, "Children of the Lesbian Baby Boom: Behavior Adjustment, Self Concept, and Sex-Role Identity," in *Contemporary Perspectives on Gay and Lesbian Psychology: Theory, Research, and Applications* 156, 164 (Beverly Greene & Gregory Herek, eds., 1994).

11 David K. Flaks, "Lesbian Families: Judicial Assumptions, Scientific Realities," 3 *Wm. & Mary Bill of Rts.* J. 345 (1994).

12 *Bottoms v. Bottoms*, 18 VA App. 481; 444 S.E.2d 276.

13 In a 1986 Arizona case, for example, an appellate court denied an adoption petition from a bisexual man on the grounds that "It would be anomalous for the state on the one hand to declare homosexual conduct unlawful and on the other create a parent after that proscribed model, in effect approving that standard, inimical to the natural family, as head of a state-created family." *In re Pima County Juvenile Matter*, 727 P.2d 830, 835 (Ariz. Ct. App. 1986).

14 Ricketts and Achtenberg, "The Adoptive and Foster Gay and Lesbian Parent," in F. Bozett, ed., *Gay and Lesbian Parents*, 1987.

15 "Second parent" adoptions have been granted in Alaska, California, D.C., Illinois, Massachusetts, Michigan, Minnesota, New York, New Jersey, Oregon, Pennsylvania, Texas, Vermont and Washington. Only two states, however, have upheld the validity of second parent adoptions at the state supreme court level (Massachusetts and Vermont). In the other states listed here, second parent adoptions are still vulnerable to legal challenges.

16 National Center for Lesbian Rights, *Lesbians Choosing Motherhood: Legal Implications of Donor Insemination and Co-Parenting*, 1991.

17 N.H.Rev. Stat. Ann. @ 161:2 (IV)(Supp. 1988). In upholding the policy, the court noted: "as a matter of public policy, the provision of a healthy environment, and role models for our children, the New Hampshire policy should exclude homosexuals." Opinion of the Justices, No. 87-080, Supreme Court of New Hampshire, 129 N.H. 290; 525 A.2d 1095.

18 See *The New York Times* 29 January, 1995 p.17, col. 1. "Nebraska Moves to Bar Homosexuals from being Foster Parents," noting that "Foster children in Nebraska can no longer be placed in the homes of people who identify themselves as homosexual or in homes where unrelated, unmarried adults live together."

19 Wendell Ricketts, *Lesbians and Gay Men as Foster Parents* (National Child Welfare Resource Center, 1991).

20 Elise Harris, *OUT*, May 1995.

21 National Center for Lesbian Rights, *Lesbians Choosing Motherhood: Legal Implications of Donor Insemination and Co-Parenting*, 1991.

22 A 1988 federal government study found that homosexuality was among the top four reasons given by doctors and clinics for refusing to provide insemination services. United States Department of Commerce, Office of Technology Assessment, "Artificial Insemination: Practice in the United States: Summary of a 1987 Survey,"1988.

23 In May 1993, the Hawaii Supreme Court ruled that the state's denial of a marriage license to three couples—two lesbian, one gay—presumptively violates Hawaii's constitutional guarantee of equal protection (*Baehr v. Lewin*, 852 P.2d 44, Hawaii 1993). The Hawaii Supreme Court sent the case back to the trial court, directing it to examine the state's policy under "strict scrutiny." If the state fails to demonstrate a "compelling" interest for discriminating, it must stop refusing marriage licenses to same-sex couples.

24 *In re Guardianship of Kowalski*, 478 N.W.2d, 790 (Minn. 1991).

25 Mark D. Fefer, "Gay in Corporate America," *Fortune*, 16 December, 1991.

26 Under the old policy, there were three separate grounds for separation: statements of sexual orientation, acts, and marriage or attempted marriage. The grounds for separation under the new directive are substantially the same, with the important caveat that all three bases are now defined under one category as "Homosexual Conduct." "Homosexual Conduct" includes statements of sexual orientation, or words to that effect, acts, marriage, or attempted marriage. Unlike the old policy, the new directive imposes a rebuttable presumption on servicemembers who say they are lesbian, gay, or bisexual. The presumption is that servicemembers who make such statements engage in, have a propensity to engage in, or intend to engage in homosexual acts. The regulations place the burden of disproving this presumption on servicemembers.

27 Memorandum, Servicemembers Legal Defense Network, 27 January, 1994.

28 General Accounting Office, "DOD's Policy on Homosexuality," June 1992.

29 Joyce Hunter, "Violence Against Lesbian and Gay Male Youths," *Journal of Interpersonal Violence*, Vol. 5, No. 3 (1990), p. 295.

30 *U.S. Dept. of Health and Human Services*, "Report of the Secretary's Task Force on Youth Suicide," 1989.

31 *National Gay and Lesbian Task Force*, "Anti-Gay/Lesbian Victimization," 1984.

32 *Diagnostic and Statistical Manual of Mental Disorders*, 4th Ed., 1994.

33 "What Every American Needs to Know About Health Care Reform," Human Rights Campaign Fund, 1994.

34 P.E. Stevens and J.M. Hall, "Stigma, Beliefs and Experiences with Health

Care in Lesbian Women," *Image: Journal of Nursing Schools* 29 (no.2), 1988.

35 "What Every Lesbian and Gay American Needs to Know About Health Care Reform," HRCF, 1994.

ABOUT THE AUTHOR

Shannon Minter is staff attorney at the National Center for Lesbian Rights, where she is the director of the Youth Project and the Immigration Rights Task Force.

Uruguay

· · · · · · · ·

Ana Martínez

LESBIANS AND THE LAW

The Uruguayan Constitution contains several provisions that, in theory, protect lesbians from discrimination and persecution. These include:

> Chapter I, Section II, Art. 8: "All people are equal before the law which recognizes no distinction among them other than that of talent and virtue."

> Art. 10: "The private actions of persons which in no way assail public order nor harm a third party are exempt from the authority of the magistrates."

> Art. 39: "All persons have the right of association, regardless of the end they pursue, as long as that association has not been declared illicit by the law."

> Chapter II, Art. 44: "The state will legislate on all questions of health and public hygiene to assure the physical, moral and social well-being of all inhabitants of the country."

Nevertheless, lesbians lack any functional protection from discrimination in the Uruguayan legal system and are vulnerable to many different forms of abuse and harassment. Such violations of lesbians' human rights have rarely been documented. While one of the founders of El Servicio de Paz y Justicia (SERPAJ) has acknowledged the importance of including "all those excluded, the marginalized, beggars, prostitutes, street children, homosexuals, the shadows of those who were tortured or disappeared, all those forgotten by the 'human rights' community,"[1] there are currently no organizations in Uruguay which document human rights violations against lesbians and gay men.

The following information was gathered through informal discussions with approximately 50 lesbians in Montevideo in 1994-95. After a brief discussion of several general themes, five specific cases are described. Because of the discrimination that lesbians face in Uruguayan society, the women whose experiences are discussed here never sought to make their experiences public. Thus, much of this information is general in nature and does not identify specific actors. Names have been omitted in order to protect identities.

POLICE HARASSMENT

During the military dictatorship (1973-1984), and even during the first restored democratic government, raids, called *razzias*, were very common. During these raids young people, and especially lesbians, gay men, and transvestites, were taken into detention. Several gay bars were closed in such raids, and lesbians and gay men were often detained for 24 to 48 hours.[2] Transvestites were often kept in small roach and rat infested rooms for up to seven days with little food or water. People detained in such raids were photographed, and records were taken of all their personal information: identification card number, home address, place of work, profession, parents' profession, etc. This information was kept in special files in police headquarters. Frequently anonymous telephone calls were made to families or employers informing them of the person's homosexuality.

During this same period it was common for lesbians and gay men to organize meetings in their own homes, since the right of free association had been expressly forbidden. Even within private homes, however, they were still subject to police harassment. Many lesbians and gay men who attended such meetings were detained by the police while their records were checked.

Even now with "democracy" returned, it is not uncommon for ordinary citizens to pretend to be policemen in order to intimidate lesbians and gay men and extort money from them. These "policemen" threaten to take individuals to police headquarters unless they are paid a fee. This sort of extortion is only possible because lesbians and gay men know that they are more likely to encounter harassment than protection at the hands of the police.

Homophobic attitudes can be found across a broad spectrum of political opinion. For example, the Communist Party achieved notoriety in the lesbian and gay community when it expelled the daughters of several of its militants in the late 1970s after learning that they were lesbians.

CUSTODY

Another arena in which lesbians encounter discrimination is in the courts. It is common for lesbian mothers who have been married and divorced to receive threats from their ex-husbands that their sexual orientation will be raised as an issue in child custody disputes. It is not unusual for doctors, psychiatrists, psychologists, and sexologists to support the demands of the fathers in such cases by testifying that lesbians do not have the moral character to keep the children.

HEALTH CARE

An evident violation of lesbians' right to health is the complete lack of information about woman-to-woman transmission of HIV in the AIDS prevention materials produced by the Uruguayan Ministry of Public Health. This omission denies lesbians access to potentially life-saving information.

The following five cases demonstrate the specific ways in which lesbians experience persecution and discrimination:

1. In 1984, the last year of the dictatorship, a kiss on the mouth between two women (L. and P.) saying good-bye at a bus stop resulted in the following: a policeman approached them, asked them for their identity cards, and ordered them to accompany him as suspects to the local police station. They were released only when L. said to him, "Let's go to headquarters, if you like, but it's going to get you into trouble. I am the daughter of an army general and she (P.) is the daughter of a colonel."[3]

2. In June, 1977, M.L., a lesbian from Uruguay, was arrested in Buenos Aires in a "military operation" along with two other Uruguayan women with whom she shared an apartment. In a few days, M.L.'s companions were released. One of them states that she heard M.L.'s voice as she was being tortured in Automotoras Orletti. She was never seen again. M.L. is one of Buenos Aires' desaparecidos ("disappeared") from Uruguay. Familiares is an organization in Montevideo for the mothers and family members of desaparecidos; it is part of Fedefam, the Latin American union of all such organizations. However, once Familiares learned of M.L.'s sexual orientation they began to ignore her and her family. They abandoned all efforts to find her and no longer carried her picture in the marches they organized.

3. In 1985 a group of lesbians were leaving a gay bar. They were followed and harassed by a gang of young men on motorcycles. Two of the lesbians got away and told a police patrol what was happening. The police did nothing to intervene. A week later, in a separate incident not involving lesbians, one of the young men was arrested as the leader of a gang. This example makes clear that while such gangs are not completely above the law, they are able to harass lesbians with impunity.

4. Two lesbians who went to Brazil for a vacation were surprised by a telephone call telling them that their house in Montevideo had been robbed. A friend who lived in the same block passed by and saw several police cars in front of their house. One of the policemen told her what had happened and asked her to call someone who could draw up a list of what was in the house so that they could determine what was missing. Two days later the friend returned to the house and discovered that many additional items were missing. The explanation was simple: while

the two women were still in Brazil, the house had been under police guard. Now two bicycles, a radio, a toaster, shoes, and several other items were missing. One of the two women went to the police commissioner to complain of the theft perpetrated by the police who were guarding the house. The commissioner was very clear. "It would be better if you didn't make any accusations. You have a single double bed in your bedroom. You have photographs of yourself being embraced by another woman. If you make a complaint against the police this is going to come out and you and your friend could lose your jobs. Think about it." The commissioner's threat had its desired effect; they did not make a complaint.

5. On September 7, 1994, Susana Fernández and Marianela Arnaud, both lesbians, were arrested after robbing one taxi driver and attempting to rob a second. Their statements were taken separately in the Larceny and Robbery Department of the Montevideo Police Headquarters. When asked where they had met, they stated that they knew each other from their involvement in Homosexuales Unidos (H.U.), a lesbian and gay organization in Montevideo. From then on the questions of the

"Since we truthfully stated our sexual orientation, we were confined to two different cells, located on different floors."

police focused on their lesbianism: What was H.U.? What went on there? Were there orgies? Were the two of them married to each other? Who played the part of the man? They were both subjected to verbal abuse and have continued to be specifically targeted for harassment because of their lesbianism. They are currently awaiting sentencing in the women's prison.

In a letter written from jail, Susana Fernández described the discriminatory treatment that lesbians receive:

> Once imprisoned in the women's jail, we were asked [once again] whether we were lesbians. This was not a chance question; the main objective of the system is to prevent lesbianism....Since we truthfully stated our sexual orientation, we were confined to two different cells, located on different floors. As new couples are discovered they are separated as well. It is forbidden to stay in a sector other than the one we are assigned. Watchfulness is more severe during the night. Lights remain lit everywhere since darkness is considered a sign of promiscuity. No prisoner is above suspicion.
>
> Having a male partner and children guarantees certain privileges which are only intended for heterosexual women and mothers.... They are given the opportunity to go out at the weekends and to have their children with them. They give priority to preserving the family institution since it is considered the unit reproducing the system....Lesbians are treated in a different way. They are confined in cells if they do not have children. According to prison regulations cells are punishment. It is forbidden to have more than one person per cell. Gates are locked from 11 p.m. to 8 a.m. Every time we hear the doors are being locked we feel tormented with loneliness.

LESBIAN ORGANIZATIONS

Lesvenus, the only existing lesbian organization in Uruguay, is a part of the larger group Homosexuales Unidos. A lesbian group called Las Mismas existed for a brief period between April and August 1991. During this time, the group carried out a survey which was answered by 49 lesbians broken down into two groups: A) 19 to 36 years old, and B) 38 to 47 years old. [4] In particular, the responses to two questions reveal a great deal about the lives of lesbians in Uruguay. When asked if their family and friends knew about their lesbianism, out of the 35 women in group A, 18 said yes, 15 said no, and 2 declined to answer; out of the 14 women in group B, 7 answered yes, 6 no, and one did not respond. When asked about the conditions that lead to negative attitudes and indifference toward lesbians within Uruguayan society, the answers of both groups together, ranked from the most to least common, were:

1. Lack of sex education/lack of knowledge about the subject.
2. Male chauvinist prejudices based on the historical subordination of women.
3. Low esteem for women/women are ignored.
4. Male prejudices women have themselves adopted.
5. Self-marginalization of lesbians.
6. Lack of visibility of lesbians in society.
7. The influence of the Catholic religion.

Thus, over half of lesbians who responded had not revealed their sexual orientation even to their own friends and family, a figure which suggests the strength of anti-lesbian prejudice in Uruguay. As the responses to the second question indicate, many experience this discrimination not only in isolated cases, such as bar raids, but as an added dimension of the everyday discrimination that they face as women.

NOTES

I wish to thank the International Gay and Lesbian Human Rights Commission and all of the women who made this report possible, in particular Elvira Lutz; Ana Coreta, member of Lesvenus, for unfailing dedication; and my companion, Sandra, for her advice:

> *"Según el prognóstico para
> hoy, habrá vendabales de
> irreverentes verdes y
> precipitaciones de cuidados
> ocres, por lo que se
> recomienda salir desnudas a
> la calle"*

I dedicate this work to Susana Fernández and Marianela Arnaud; among other things they have taught me to disobey.

1 Luis Perez Aguirre, *If I Speak of Human Rights*, p. 13. SERPAJ has been an important agent in the defense of human rights both during the dictatorship and afterwards.

2 Raids are known to have taken place at the following bars and discos: Summer Gay (1980). New York City (1982), Moulin Rouge (1983), Don Quien (1983).

3 Article 361, which prohibits acts against public decency, is often selectively

enforced against same-sex couples in such situations.
4 Evaluation by Elsa and Ana Coreta, Lesvenus.

ABOUT THE AUTHOR

Ana Martínez is active in Lesvenus and Homosexuales Unidos. She is particularly interesting in bringing the struggle for sexual choice together with other human rights struggles.

Zimbabwe

● ● ● ● ● ● ● ● ● ●

Bev Clark

In 1982, the first lesbian group in Zimbabwe, which consisted of about twelve white women, began to hold weekly meetings in Harare. This group existed primarily as a lesbian support group and meetings provided an opportunity for lesbians to discuss various issues, such as isolation, "coming out," and relationships. The meetings took place at a different venue each week and slowly the number of women participating increased. As time went by and the discussions started to flag, the support group began to be replaced by cultural evenings. These evenings became very popular and bisexual and straight women began to attend.

The Monday night lesbian group also encouraged the formation of a support group for bisexual women, which began to meet regularly. The original group stopped meeting in 1984, and in 1988, the Women's Cultural Club (WCC) was formed to fill the gap that was felt in the lesbian community. The membership of the WCC was predominantly white but also included some Black women. The WCC stopped meeting after a few years, but since 1994 it has been revived and the group currently organizes parties and cultural events for lesbians.

In 1988 Gays and Lesbians of Zimbabwe (GALZ) was formed by a group of people who were interested in providing social events for lesbians and gay men. The birth of GALZ gave rise to a new energy in the lesbian and gay community in Zimbabwe. GALZ began publication of a regular newsletter, introduced a membership structure, and started to organize social events of various kinds.

Lesbians have been very visible in the administration of GALZ and through this have been able to maintain a lesbian presence in the magazine and at social functions. Unlike earlier groups, GALZ has a large number of Black members; while most are male, the number of Black lesbians in GALZ has been steadily increasing as the organization becomes more visible.

LEGAL SITUATION

Male homosexual acts are illegal under the Zimbabwe penal code. Although lesbians could in theory be subject to arrest under the statute (which prohibits "unnatural offences"), there are no known cases of it being enforced against lesbians. Even without legal prohibition, however, widespread social prejudices against lesbians serve to keep them silent. Many women will not receive mail from GALZ, or do so under pseudonyms; they fear that the discovery of their lesbianism may jeopardize their jobs or subject them to arrest. Many are similarly afraid to write checks to GALZ in case they can somehow be traced.

The Minister of Home Affairs, Dumiso Dubengwa, has said publicly on several occasions that "homosexuality is abhorrent and should not be allowed."[1] In 1993-94, the homes of a number of GALZ members were raided by police, and Mr. Dabengwa was quoted as saying that the police were "anxious" to make arrests: "We are going to arrest them. It is illegal in this country."[2] The Zimbabwe Human Rights Association has issued written statements opposing this campaign of harassment and threats, but few others in Zimbabwe have come to the defense of GALZ. In this climate of fear, few individuals will publicly acknowledge that they are lesbian or gay. There are a number of well-known figures in the media and the entertainment industry who could provide a public face for lesbian and gay concerns, but they will not speak out for fear of losing their jobs.

THE NEWS MEDIA AND LESBIANS

Currently, GALZ has been shut out of the media completely. In 1994, the organization attempted to run a counseling advertisement in the *Herald*, a national newspaper. The notice, which read "For advice, support and counselling contact Gays and Lesbians of Zimbabwe," was refused on the grounds that the *Herald* is a "family newspaper." GALZ has issued numerous press statements in response to a recent spate of sensational press coverage featuring homophobic statements from President Robert Mugabe, Minister of Home Affairs Dumiso Dubengwa, and other government officials; however, these statements have rarely been printed.

The media attention on homosexuality has focused almost exclusively on the issue of sodomy, and lesbians are very seldom mentioned. A rare exception to this rule is an occasional article such as the one which appeared in the June 1992 issue of a tabloid-style women's magazine called *Just for Me*. While the veracity of the "lifestories" included in the article is perhaps questionable, the preface gives a clear sense of the prevailing attitudes toward and stereotypes of lesbians within Zimbabwean society: the author confessed that she was hesitant to take the assignment and expected to be "groped and molested (and threatened)" by the lesbians she interviewed.[3]

CULTURAL REPRESENTATION OF LESBIANS

At the same time that the mainstream media is failing to provide positive images—or any images at all—of lesbians, lesbian publications are subjected to strict censorship. Images of gay men have filtered into Zimbabwe through films such as *Philadelphia*. In contrast, lesbians never get to see a positive portrayal of their lives unless they are sent material directly from friends overseas.

The *Penguin Book of Lesbian Short Stories* was recently banned, as was the British lesbian magazine *Diva*, which GALZ had submitted to the Censor Board for approval to mail to GALZ's lesbian members. When the homes of several GALZ members were raided by the police in 1993-94, the material seized by the police was all non-pornographic but the

T.M.'S STORY

I am twenty-four years old and I was born in Gokwe.

[My girlfriend and I] are always on the run because my parents are against what I am. When they found out that I was a lesbian, they tried to force me to find a boyfriend but I could not fit in with what they wanted.

My parents decided to look for a husband on my behalf so they brought several boys home to meet me but I was not interested so in the end they forced an old man on me. They locked me in a room and brought him everyday to rape me so I would fall pregnant and be forced to marry him. They did this to me until I was pregnant after which they told me I was free to do whatever I wanted but that I must go and stay with this man or else they would throw me out of the house. They did throw me out eventually thinking that, as I was not employed, I would end up going to this man's house. Instead, I went to stay with my friends.

I went for an abortion and I was in the hospital for a month. After that, I used to hide whenever I saw my relatives. I did not contact them for six months. The police were looking for me so I used to move during the night only. In the end, the police found me and took me home where I was locked up and beaten until I could not even lift my arms or get up.

I stayed in that room for months pretending I was sick so they would not bring the horrible man again but they did and I fell pregnant again. I ran away and went to stay with my girlfriend. I did not go for an abortion this time because I was scared it would kill me. The first time had been really painful. I kept the pregnancy until I had a miscarriage at seven months and the baby died. Now I am always on the run. As soon as I know my parents have found out where I am staying, I move on to another place. They are still after me. I have not seen my family in about seven months. I am scared this time they will put chains on me so I am in hiding.

—excerpted from the *GALZ Newsletter*, December 1994

words "lesbian" and "gay" were enough to result in their seizure. Items seized included a book of lesbian and gay poetry, an international directory of bisexual groups, and a catalog from a South African art gallery. Although GALZ is planning to take part in an upcoming annual book fair, the group's request to participate was initially refused despite this year's theme of Human Rights and Justice.

EMPLOYMENT

Few lesbians are open about their sexual orientation at their jobs. Although little research has been done on the subject, a recent informal poll confirmed their fears. In researching its article on lesbians in Zimbabwe, *Just for Me* magazine asked 20 employers if they would employ a woman whom they knew to be a lesbian. Fourteen said no, citing the following reasons: a bad reputation for the firm; she might make passes at other female employees; she must be unstable if she chooses that way of life; women with a husband and children are more stable. Three said they would do so only if she remained silent about her lesbianism, and all of them said they would not allow her partner to participate in company functions. Two said they would do so only if her qualifications were outstanding and there were no one else suitable for the job; both stated that they would choose equally qualified people, particularly men, if given the choice. Only one—a British man who had lived in Zimbabwe for four years—said yes unconditionally.

HEALTH CARE

GALZ launched an initiative in 1992 to try and educate medical practitioners about lesbians and gay men. This project was begun in response to reports from lesbians that some of their problems were being attributed to use of the contraceptive pill; they were being placed in a position of either having to lie to their doctor or "come out" as a lesbian. With regard to mental health workers, GALZ has a general sense that the majority do not try to convert lesbians and gay men into heterosexuals, although a few have been known to use biblical arguments against homosexuality.

PRESSURE TO MARRY

Many Black women face great pressure from their families to marry. GALZ has documented cases of families trying to "cure" lesbians (see sidebar). A large majority of white people still living in Zimbabwe after Independence are ultra-conservative, and while white lesbians may not experience as much direct pressure to marry, they are pressured to conform to society's expectations of "proper" feminine appearance, and their relationships with women are often harshly condemned.

PARENTING

Lesbian mothers receive little support from society as a whole or, unfortunately, from the lesbian and gay community. Lesbian mothers are not yet visible or vocal enough to have created room within the lesbian and gay movement to discuss the particular issues that they face.

Most lesbian mothers in Zimbabwe have children from previous relationships with men. Lesbians seeking to become pregnant through donor insemination face numerous difficulties. One couple approached a female gynecologist in Harare who was so vehement and disapproving that she reduced one of the women to tears. GALZ took this matter up with the Health Professions Council (a government body) and asked them to investigate the matter. As with all of GALZ's communication with the authorities, this request went unanswered. In this area as in many others, the relevant government body has failed to address the discrimination that lesbians face within Zimbabwean society.

NOTES

[1] See, for example, "ZCC urged to help process missionaries' permits," *Herald*, 12 January 1995.

[2] "Police Warn Homos," *Daily Gazette*, 24 January 1994.

[3] "Lesbians," *Just For Me*, June 1992, pp. 18-21.

ABOUT THE AUTHOR

Bev Clark has been active in Gays and Lesbians of Zimbabwe (GALZ) for the past five years.

Appendices

▲▲▲▲▲▲▲▲▲▲▲▲▲▲▲▲▲▲▲▲

Appendix A:

PUT SEXUALITY ON THE AGENDA AT THE WORLD CONFERENCE ON WOMEN

In Beijing in September 1995, the Member States of the United Nations will convene the Fourth World Conference on Women, where they will adopt a Platform for Action that will set goals for achieving gender equality over the next decade. We, the undersigned, call upon the Member States to recognize the right to determine one's sexual identity; the right to control one's own body, particularly in establishing intimate relationships; and the right to choose if, when, and with whom to bear or raise children as fundamental components of the human rights of all women regardless of sexual orientation. We support the inclusion of lesbians in governmental delegations and as non-governmental observers at the conference and we call upon all delegates to insure that adequate recognition and protection of these rights are included in the final version of the Platform for Action and all other conference documents. We base these demands on the Universal Declaration of Human Rights, which recognizes the "inherent dignity and...the equal and inalienable rights of all members of the human family," and guarantees the protection of the fundamental rights and freedoms of all people "without distinction of any kind, such as race, color, sex, language ...or other status" (art. 2).

ENDORSED BY:

Acadia Women's Centre (Canada) • Advice Desk for Abused Women, University of Durban (South Africa) • AL-HAQ Palestinians for Human Rights (Palestine) • Anjaree (Thailand) • APADOR—Comitetul Helsinki (Romania) • Arkadija-Lesbian and Gay Lobby (Serbia) • [San Francisco] Asian/Pacific AIDS Coalition (USA) • [San Francisco] Asian Women's Shelter (USA) • Asia Monitor Resource Center (Hong Kong) •Asociación Civil

Labor (Peru) • Asociación Colombiana de Lesbianas y Homosexuales (Colombia) • Asociación Venezolana para una Educación Sexual Alternativa (Venezuela) • Association for Civil Rights in Israel (Palestine) • Astraea National Lesbian Action Foundation (USA) • Austrian Coalition for Women's Human Rights (Austria) • Awakening Foundation (Taiwan) • B.a.B.e.-Women's Human Rights Group (Croatia) • Bagnoud Center for Health and Human Rights (USA) • Brazilian Association of Gays, Lesbians, and Transvestites (Brazil) • B'Tselem (Israel) • Cal State Northridge Women's Center (USA) • Cal State Sacramento Lesbian-Feminist Alliance • Campaign Against Pornography (UK) • Canadian Labour Congress (Canada) • Cape Cod Lesbian Social & Support Group (USA) • CAFRA - Caribbean Association for Feminist Research and Action (Tunapuna, Trinidad & Tobago) • Casa de la Mujer (Peru) • CEM (Argentina) • CEMINA (Brazil) • Center for the Study of Human Rights (USA) • Center for Women War Victims (Croatia) • Center for Women's Global Leadership (USA) • Centro de Estudios Sociales y Publicaciones (Peru) • Centro de la Mujer Panameña (Panama) • CIDEM - Centro de Infomación y Desarrollo de la Mujer (Bolivia) • Centro de Documentacón sobre el Tema Mujer (Argentina) • CIMDC (Mexico) • CIRE (Mexico) • CLADEM - Comité de América Latina y el Caribe para la Defensa de los Derechos de la Mujer (Peru) • CLIC—Can't Live in the Closet (Philippines) • El Clóset de Sor Juana (Mexico) • Coalition Against Trafficking of Women-Asia/Pacific Chapter (Philippines) • Colectivo Ataba (Mexico) • Colectivo Mulher Vida (Brazil) • Colectiva 25 de Noviembre (Costa Rica) • Colombia Human Rights Commission (USA) • CONNECT (USA) • Coordinardora Gai-Lesbiana (Spain) • COVAC (Mexico) • Creatividad y Cambio (Peru) • CSUN Women's Center • Deneuve Magazine (USA) • Department of Women's and Gender Studies, Amherst College (USA) • Difusion Cultural Feminista (Mexico) • Equality Now (USA) • Eurostep Network (Belgium) • Federation for Women and Family Planning (Poland) • FIRE (Costa Rica) • Foundation Against Traffic in Women (Netherlands) • The Foundation for Women's Solidarity (Turkey) • Foundation Stop Violence Against Women in Suriname (Suriname) • Frente por el Derecho a la Alimentacion (Mexico) • Fundación Ecuatoriana de Ayuda Educación y Prevención del SIDA (Ecuador) •Fundación para Estudio e Investigatcion de la Mujer (Argentina) • Fundación Xochiquetzal (Nicaragua) • [Santa Barbara] Gay and Lesbian Resource Center (USA) • Gay People's Health Forum (South Africa) • GENDER-Center for Women's Studies (Romania) • GLEN - Gay and Lesbian Equality Network (Ireland) • Global Focus: Women in Art and Culture (USA)• Ground Zero (USA) • The Group (Philippines) • GLOW - Growing, Learning, Organized Women (Barbados) • Grupo de Educación Popular con Mujeres (Mexico) • Grupo de Estudios Ambientales (Mexico) • Grupo Dignidade (Brazil) • Grupo Esperança (Brazil) • Grupo Estação Mulher (Brazil) • Grupo Liberdade (Brazil) • Harvey Milk Gay/Lesbian/Bisexual Democratic Club-San

Francisco (USA) • Hetrick-Martin Institute (USA) • Homosexuelle Initiative Wein (Austria) • Human Rights Watch • Humanistic Committee on Human Rights (Netherlands) • ILLA, Centro de Educación y Comunicación (Peru) • Images Asia (Thailand) • Institute for Social Studies and Action (Philippines) • Instituto Latina Americana de Prevención y Educación en Salud (Costa Rica) • Instituto Latino Americano de Servicios Legales Alternativos (Colombia) • International Committee of Lawyers for Tibet/Women's Committee • International Gay and Lesbian Human Rights Commission (USA) • International Human Rights Law Group (USA) • International League for Human Rights (USA) • International Lesbian and Gay Association • International Lesbian Information Service • International Women's AIDS Caucus (Argentina) • International Women's Health Coalition • International Women's Human Rights Clinic at CUNY Law School (USA) • International Women's Tribune Center (USA) • Isha L'Isha/Haifa Feminist Center (Israel) • ISIS International (Philippines) • ISIS - WICCE (Switzerland) • ISIS - WICCE (Uganda) • Juniper House (Canada) • Kadin Dayanisma Vakfi - The Foundation for Women's Solidarity (Turkey) • Katipunan ng Kababaihan para sa Kalayaan (Philippines) • Kilawin Kotektibo (USA) • Kokusai Bian Renmei (Japan) • KLAF-Community of Feminist Lesbians (Israel) • The Korean Council for Women Drafted for Military Sexual Slavery by Japan (South Korea) • Lambda Legal Defense and Education Fund (USA) • Lesbian and Gay Liberation Front Cologne (Germany) • Lesbian Equality Network (Ireland) • Lesbians Organizing Together (Ireland) • [Seattle] Lesbian Resource Center (USA) • Lesbian Rights Advocates (Thailand) • Libreria de Mujeres (Argentina) • LLH-Nat'l Organization for Lesbian and Gay Liberation (Norway) • London Lesbian and Gay Switchboard (England) • LLEGO - National Latino/a Lesbian and Gay Organization (USA) • MADRE (USA) • Mount Holyoke College Women's Studies Committee (USA) • Movimiento Homosexual de Lima (Peru) • Mujeres para el Dialogo (Mexico) • Mujeres por la Salud en Acción (Mexico) • Mujeres Trabajadores Unidas (Mexico) • National Abortion Rights Action League (USA) • National Center for Lesbian Rights (USA) • National Coalition Against Domestic Violence (USA) • National Coalition of Feminist and Lesbian Cancer Projects (USA) • National Women's Network for International Solidarity (UK) • Necessities/Necesidades, Inc. (USA) • Network of Belgrade Autonomous Women's Groups (Serbia) • New York Men Against Sexism (USA) • North-South Institute (Canada) • Northwest Immigrant Rights Project (USA) • Northwest Women's Law Center (USA) • Norwegain Tibet Komite (Norway) • Nova Scotia Association of Women and the Law (Canada) • Oasis (Mexico) • Oficina Juridica para la Mujer (Bolivia) • Outlet (Canada) • OutRage!/Queer Progressive Network (USA) • P-FLAG - Parents and Friends of Lesbians and Gays (USA) • Palestinian Human Rights Information Center (Palestine) • Pictou County Women's Clinic (USA) • Planned

Parenthood of Pictou County (USA) • Programa Universitario de Estudios de Genero-UNAM (Mexico) • Regumi Studio Tokyo (Japan) • Romanian Helsinki Committee (Romania) • Seattle Lesbian and Gay Chorus (USA) • Seattle Women's Commission (USA) • SETA (Finland) • Shirkat Gah (Pakistan) • SIGLA (Argentina) • SOGA-Sociedad Gay y Lésbica (Ecuador) • South Brazilian Association of Gays and Lesbians (Brazil) • Society for the Protection of Personal Rights (Israel) • Solidarity With Foreigners (Japan) • Southern California Women for Understanding (USA) • Students Organizing Students (USA) • Sydney Asian Lesbians (Australia) • Taller Permanente de la Mujer (Argentina) • Tibetan Women's Association (India) • Tibetan Women's Association (Switzerland) • Township AIDS Project (South Africa) • Ukrainian Center for Women's Studies (Ukraine) • USPDA - Union Suisse Pour Decriminaliser l'avortement (Switzerland) • Vrouwenberaad Ontwikkelingssamenweiking (Netherlands) • War Resisters League (USA) • Wolfville Lesbian Group (Canada) • Women and Media Collective (Sri Lanka) • Women for Women's Human Rights (Turkey) • Women Living Under Muslim Laws • WEDO-Women's Environment and Development Organization (USA) • Women's Global Network for Reproductive Rights • Women's Crisis Center (Philippines) • Women's Education Development Productivity and Research Organization (Philippines) • Women's Legal Bureau, Inc. (Philippines) • Women's Legal Service (Australia) • Women's Media Circle (Philippines) • Women's Party (Netherlands) • Women's Research and Action Group (India) • Women Supporting Women Committee (Philippines) • Young Amazons (Canada)

This petition has been signed by thousands of women from over 60 countries representing every region of the world. Signatures were presented in March 1995 to the UN Commission on the Status of Women and to Gertrude Mongella, Secretary-General of the UN Fourth World Conference on Women.

▲▲▲▲▲▲▲▲▲▲▲▲▲▲▲▲▲▲▲▲▲▲▲

Appendix B:

STATEMENT READ AT THE NOVEMBER 1993 NGO SYMPOSIUM

Manila, Philippines

The lesbians of the Asia-Pacific Region are happy to be in this crucial meeting of women's NGOs in Women in Development. However, except for one person, we are all here not as lesbians but as women activists and members of groups involved in issues of violence, health, human rights, culture, education and media, family, labor, economic empowerment, political empowerment, environment, science and technology, indigenous women and agriculture. Lesbians have been at the core of the women's movement all over the world. And yet, most of us have had to hide a large part of our humanity because of fear of disempowerment and discrimination. We had hoped that this Asia-Pacific symposium of NGO's in WID would provide all women a forum of brave, free and encouraging discussions. But this is not necessarily the case for lesbians in Asia and the Pacific region, and that is why we have decided to forward this resolution from the floor.

RESOLUTION AGAINST THE ASSUMPTIONS OF HETEROSEXUALITY AND THE MARGINALIZATION OF LESBIANS IN THE SYMPOSIUM

A group of more than twenty-five women from the Asia and Pacific region met on the 18th of November to discuss their concern over assumptions of heterosexuality and the marginalization of lesbians in this symposium.

We therefore request that the UN ESCAP, Secretariat of this symposium and the organizers of all activities in preparation for the 1995 World Conference of Women in Beijing acknowledge the disadvantaged position of a large number of women who choose to have primary relationships with women by ensuring:

1) That a proper analysis and documentation be made of discrimination against lesbians in policies and programmes which either by omission or commission exclude, marginalize and discriminate against lesbians.

2) That reference to lesbians not be removed from documents and the wording of these documents and resolutions not covertly or overtly disadvantage or marginalize lesbians.

3) That there is recognition of the right of women to choose lifestyles and partners without discrimination.

4) That the treatment of women's issues does not silence individual women who choose not to marry and not to live with a male partner.

5) That violence and discrimination against lesbians perpetuated by homophobia and sanctioned by institutions of the state, of religious and of cultures be condemned and, further, that steps be taken to stop this violence.

We therefore conclude by saying that should this forum, all other fora and the women's movement continue to remain silent about homophobia and discrimination against lesbians, we leave open the possibility for all women to be discriminated against.

This resolution was read by Anna Leah Sarabia of the Philippines, on behalf of the lesbian community in the symposium.

Appendix C:

LATIN AMERICAN AND CARIBBEAN LESBIANS SATELLITE MEETING STATEMENT

Lima, Peru
May 27-29, 1994

Considering that:

1. The UN Fourth World Conference on Women:Action for Equality, Development, and Peace is an important opportunity to establish equal relationships in all aspects of society;

2. There are still diverse forms of discrimination against lesbians in the whole region;

3. This specific form of discrimination limits lesbians in the full exercise of their civil, political, economic, social and cultural rights as enshrined in many international and national declarations;

4. There are still countries like Ecuador, Chile and Nicaragua that criminalize homosexuality and lesbianism, which limits the access of lesbians to their rights as citizens and therefore allows for violations of their human rights;

5. Social prejudice still prevails that stigmatizes lesbians and limits their participation at all levels of social, political and economic life;

6. Diverse forms of repression against free sexual orientation impede the

rights of lesbians to freely associate and the creation of organizations;

7. There still is a high incidence of physical and psychological violence in public as well as in private life;

8. The right of reproduction, their right to adopt children and to be mothers and have custody of their children is not recognized;

9. There still is discrimination in the fields of employment, education, housing, health, etc.;

10. The mass media promotes violence against lesbians;

11. Religious institutions, especially the Catholic Church, instigate repression and reproduction of prejudices against lesbians and homosexuals;

12. The repression on account of sexual orientation limits lesbians' right to open political participation.

We reaffirm:

• Our conviction in the importance of strengthening democratic processes to guarantee real mechanisms of political, social and economic participation for all women alike in all spheres of power and decision-making in society, within a legal framework, and with respect to diversity of sexual orientation;

• All women are entitled to exercise their full citizen's rights including economic, social, political and cultural rights;

• We want to keep contributing to the construction of a society based on relations of peace and equality.

Based on these convictions we:

1. State that the objective of the Satellite Meeting on Lesbians from the whole region prior to the World Conference on Women is to make proposals towards the establishment of international instruments and mechanisms to secure the full exercise of lesbian rights in all spheres of social life;

2. Request that the concept of the lesbian family be included as a legal option in social legislation, concerning for instance access of partners to medical insurance, life insurance, inheritance, etc.;

3. Request that social and educational institutions include in their educational and awareness raising programs realistic and positive images of lesbian life;

4. Demand the freedom of sexual orientation to be established as an inalienable human right;

5. Recommend that UN organizations urge governments to implement international human rights' declarations and treaties to all persons in order to allow full exercise of individual and collective rights as well as the right of lesbians to associate and organize freely and to participate in political parties and other political institutions;

6. Recommend that UN organizations urge governments to apply different international instruments and treaties to guarantee the free right of association, organization and public gathering of lesbians, as well as their right to participate in political activities and parties;

7. Recommend that lesbians be guaranteed their free and open political participation in the women's movement, in national and international political sectors as well as at all levels of the United Nations;

8. Demand that the UN recommend to all multilateral development cooperation organizations that they include education programs about freedom of sexual orientation in their aid programs and that

they open their aid and cooperation programs towards projects presented by lesbian organizations;

9. Create a monitoring system to be administered by the International Lesbian and Gay Association (Information Pool for the Beijing Conference and the ILGA Secretary General) and the Regional Joint Committee, in charge of ensuring proper implementation of the objectives of this Satellite Meeting of the WCW and different national, sub-regional and world organizations.

This statement was drafted by representatives of the following organizations: Tal para Cual (Ecuador), Colectiva Neconi (Nicaragua), Colectiva Ayuquelen (Chile), Colectiva Ciguay (Dominican Republic), Las Lunas y las Otras (Argentina), Rede Um Otro Olhar (Brazil), Las Entendidas (Costa Rica), Movimiento Homosexual de Lima (Peru), El Clóset de Sor Juana (Mexico).

▲▲▲▲▲▲▲▲▲▲▲▲▲▲▲▲▲▲▲▲▲

Appendix D:

STATEMENT OF THE INTERNATIONAL GAY AND LESBIAN HUMAN RIGHTS COMMISSION, THE INTERNATIONAL LESBIAN INFORMATION SERVICE, AND THE NATIONAL CENTER FOR LESBIAN RIGHTS

Presented to the United Nations Economic Commission for Europe and to all Governments of Europe and North America present at the ECE High Level Regional Preparatory Meeting for the Fourth World Conference on Women
Vienna, Austria
17-21 October 1994

At the Fourth World Conference on Women, the Member States of the United Nations should take steps to reverse their historical failure to include lesbians in action for the advancement of women. The Vienna Declaration adopted at the World Conference on Human Rights affirmed that women's rights are inalienable human rights. The Fourth World Conference on Women should affirm that lesbian rights are fundamental components of the human rights of women. We urge the Governments of the ECE Region to take the opportunity presented by this preparatory meeting to examine the following issues:

REVIEWING THE FORWARD-LOOKING STRATEGIES

In reviewing progress made since the Third World Conference on Women, this preparatory meeting should recognize the failure of the Nairobi Forward-Looking Strategies to address the human rights abuses that lesbians experience in every country in the world. These abuses cover a wide range of violations, including murder and other forms of violence, discriminatory legislation, employment discrimination, and denial of the freedom of expression. Fear of persecution or discrimination ensures that the vast majority of lesbians remain silent about their sexual orientation and are denied the right to determine their most basic life choices. Nearly twenty years after the first United Nations World Conference on Women, the majority of countries lack any form of legislation protecting lesbians from discrimination on the basis of sexual orientation.

PUTTING LESBIAN ISSUES ON THE AGENDA FOR THE WORLD CONFERENCE

The ECE Draft Regional Platform for Action includes as one of its basic principles that the promotion, protection and realization of the human rights of women must "reflect the full diversity of women, recognizing that many women face additional barriers because of such factors as their race, language, ethnicity, culture, religion, sexual orientation, disability, socio-economic class or status as indigenous people."

We urge the governments of the ECE Region to ensure that this diversity is reflected in both the Critical Areas of Concern and the Strategic Objectives outlined in the Platform for Action. In particular, four of the Critical Areas of Concern identified in the ECE Regional Draft Platform for Action, along with their corresponding Strategic Objectives, should be revised to include lesbian-specific language: (1) Insufficient promotion of the human rights of women, (2) Feminization of poverty, (3) Insufficient de facto gender equality in employment and economic opportunity and insufficient policies and measures to reconcile employment and family responsibility, and (4) Insufficient participation of women in public life. Specific recommendations for these four areas are included below.

This preparatory meeting should affirm that the agenda of the Fourth World Conference on Women will include the human rights of lesbians. At the Conference, Governments should commit to taking action to make those rights a reality. Governmental delegations should include lesbians, and lesbian organizations should be accredited to participate as non-governmental organizations in the Conference.

RECOMMENDATIONS TO THE ECE HIGH-LEVEL PREPARATORY MEETING:

We urge the Governments of the ECE Region to include lesbian-specific language in the following four Critical Areas of Concern:

Insufficient promotion of the human rights of women:

• Governments should repeal all national laws that discriminate against lesbians, including "public decency" laws that are used disproportionately against lesbians and gay men.

• Governments should enact laws and policies to ensure the human rights of lesbians in economic, social, cultural, civil, and political life. Lesbian partnerships should be afforded the full protection of the law in the areas of pension and inheritance rights, taxation and social security, custody rights, adoption rights, access to donor insemination, and equal treatment with regard to freedom of movement and immigration.

• Governments should ensure that all girls have access to truthful, informative, and bias-free education on all issues relating to sexuality. Information about lesbianism should be included in all sex education curricula.

• Governments should recognize that lesbians have the right to receive health care free of judgment or discrimination. Lesbians should be included in all public health campaigns, including AIDS education. Lesbians should not be subject to any form of persuasion or coercion from health care providers, teachers, or anyone else to undergo alteration "therapy" for their sexual orientation.

• Governments should take action against the perpetrators of violence against lesbians, and should implement public education campaigns to eliminate the prejudice and intolerance that enables such violence to occur.

Feminization of poverty:

• Governments should recognize that lesbians are particularly vulnerable to poverty due to job discrimination and the fact that lesbians often lack the financial support of family members.

Insufficient gender equality in the access to employment and insufficient policies and measures for reconciling employment and family life:

• Governments should pass legislation protecting lesbians from discriminatory hiring and employment practices. Lesbians should be protected against workplace harassment on the basis of their sexual orientation.

Insufficient participation of women in public life:

• Governments should take steps to counter the invisibility of lesbians in public life, and should recognize that widespread societal prejudice severely constrains the ability of lesbians to participate in civic and political life.

• Governments should recognize that the media are integral to forming public opinions about lesbians. Governments should take steps to ensure that lesbians have equal access to the media to secure fair, accurate, and diverse portrayals of lesbians.

▲▲▲▲▲▲▲▲▲▲▲▲▲▲▲▲▲▲▲▲▲▲

Appendix E:

STATEMENT OF THE INTERNATIONAL LESBIAN AND GAY ASSOCIATION TO THE UN ECONOMIC COMMISSION FOR EUROPE TO ALL GOVERNMENTS OF EUROPE AND NORTH AMERICA PRESENT AT THE EUROPEAN AND ATLANTIC GOVERNMENTAL PREPARATORY CONFERENCE

Vienna, Austria
17-21 October 1994

The principles of human rights, upon which the Universal Declaration was created 45 years ago, are those for which the International Lesbian and Gay Association has been fighting since 1978. A worldwide federation of organizations throughout Africa, Asia and the Pacific, Europe, North America and Latin America and the Caribbean, the ILGA work is to overcome all legal, social, cultural and economic discrimination against lesbian women (and gay men) on grounds of their sexual orientation. Lesbian women have always played a very active role in the women's movement around the world, promoting women's human rights issues. They now call upon the government delegations present at the European and Atlantic Governmental Preparatory Conference to confront the violation of human rights and freedoms on the grounds of their sexual orientation and to put this issue on the agenda of the UN World Conference on Women in 1995.

The lack of attention of the appropriate UN bodies and in particular of the bodies which deal explicitly with the elimination of all forms of discrimination against women is in contrast to the developments at the national and regional levels, particularly in Europe, at which the human rights of lesbian women (and gay men) have become increasingly a focus of attention.

POSITIVE DEVELOPMENTS

The Parliamentary Assembly of the Council of Europe (Recommendation 924/81 and Motion for recommendation 6348/90) as well as the European Parliament (Resolution of Sexual Discrimination at the Workplace 1984) have urged their member states to entirely equate lesbian women and gay men with heterosexual women and men in all fields of legislation. In 1993 the Parliamentary Assembly adopted the Written Declaration No. 227 stressing the necessity to end the practice of discrimination against homosexuals in former communist countries.

In February 1994 the European Parliament adopted a Resolution with regard to equal rights for lesbians and gays in matters such as age of consent, social security benefits, custody and adoption rights, anti-discrimination legislation and measures against violence against lesbian women and gay men. A growing number of European countries have adopted laws prohibiting discrimination on grounds of sexual orientation over the last decade: Denmark, Norway, Sweden, The Netherlands, France and Ireland.

In 1991 the European Commission adopted a Recommendation and a Code of Practice on the protection of the dignity of women and men at the workplace, which explicitly states that harassment on the grounds of sexual orientation undermines the dignity of those affected and that it is impossible to regard such harassment as appropriate workplace behavior.

In the past year a number of European countries have ended their criminal prohibitions of homosexual activity, such as the Russian Federation, Lithuania and Ireland.

We also note the publication of the study "Homosexuality, A European Community Issue," funded by the European Commission and coordinated by the European Human Rights Foundation. In November 1993 a pilot study on lesbian visibility by LBL Denmark and ILGA was completed, funded by the European Commission and LBL, the Danish Association of Gays and Lesbians.

These positive developments indicate that the human rights of lesbian women (and gay men) are an issue the United Nations Forum can no longer avoid addressing. The fact that the Economic Social Council has granted ILGA the roster consultative status in 1993 is an indication that the United Nations is aware of this. The ILGA feels that the governments in the European and Atlantic Region should play a leading role in enhancing this process within the United Nations. The European and Atlantic Preparatory Conference is an ideal platform to put this issue on the UN agenda and to explicitly mention the human rights of lesbian women in their proposal for the Platform for Action.

EQUAL RIGHTS FOR LESBIAN WOMEN

Notwithstanding the positive developments mentioned above, the specific needs of lesbian women are inadequately addressed by existing legislation, be it on global, European or national level and lesbian women (and gay men) are denied equal legal access.

In democratic societies where the majority rules, the treatment of minorities is one of the principal tests of how far respect for the human rights and the rule of the law is observed. Discrimination is not only about gender, color or religion but also about sexual orientation. Proclaiming that all forms of discrimination should be eliminated, means that governments should be willing to respect the rights of lesbian women (and gay men).

At this moment, lesbian women are denied the right to self determination, a right which has been the focus of the women's movement around the world. Lesbian women do not enjoy the right to be respected and protected because of their sexual orientation.

This is not in agreement with the fact that self determination is internationally acknowledged as being a fundamental human right for women. Since lesbian women do not share the traditional marital status, they are discriminated against in many different ways.

VIOLENCE AGAINST LESBIAN WOMEN

It is well known that sexual violence and harassment of women is a serious and major problem. But so far very few studies have dealt with sexual violence and harassment of lesbian women. The studies that do exist (the Netherlands, United Kingdom, Germany) indicate that sexual orientation is an important factor when dealing with sexual harassment and violence in e.g. the workplace and public spaces, the educational system and the health system.

FAMILY

In spite of the growing variety of actual family structures, personal relationships and lifestyles, family legislation in most European countries does not consider lesbian (and gay) couples as family. The denial of equal rights for lesbian (and gay) families has a number of discriminatory legal and economic consequences in terms of pension and inheritance rights, taxation and social security, custody rights, adoption rights, the right to receive artificial insemination, equal treatment with regard to freedom of movement and immigration.

LABOUR MARKET

In many European countries identified lesbian women run the risk of being excluded from access to "sensitive sectors" of the labour market such as the diplomatic and military service, education and other jobs that imply contact with children and youth. In some countries they are dismissed whenever their sexual orientation becomes known.

FREEDOM OF SPEECH AND FREEDOM TO ORGANIZE

Various countries use their laws on "public decency" and "obscenity" against lesbian women (and gay men) who show affection in public or apply provisions on "public morals" against publications by lesbian and gay organizations. Lesbian women like heterosexual women should have the right to freedom of expression and to receive and impart information and ideas without interference by public authority. The opportunities for lesbian women to meet and organize (either for political or recreational purposes) have been reduced by different legal restrictions in various countries. Often organizations of lesbian women experience great difficulty in getting funding, charitable status and commercial credit.

Whereas other forms of bigotry and hatred toward individuals and groups based on their identity, such as sexism, racism, and anti-Semitism, have been the concern of public authorities in statements, legislative and administrative action, no corresponding attention, in kind and degree, has been given to the position of lesbian women. Prejudice by certain parts of the population is no excuse for denying same sex couples social recognition. Legal equality and recognition will contribute to the elimination of prejudice and to pluralistic societies in which next to traditional family life new ways of single and collective living are emerging. Eventually legal recognition for lesbian women (and gay men) will be of benefit for all democratic societies.

We therefore call upon the governments and international bodies to eliminate all forms of de jure and de facto discrimination of women on grounds of their sexual orientation and to explicitly include sexual orientation in existing equal treatment provisions on a par with anti-gender discrimination and to include sexual orientation in any new initiative.

We call upon the governments and international bodies present at the European and Atlantic Governmental Preparatory Conference to explicitly address the issue of human rights for lesbian women on par with the human rights for heterosexual women in their proposals for the Platform for Action, the UN document to be adopted at the UN World Conference on Women in 1995.

We call upon the Economic and Social Council and the Commission on the Status of Women to initiate a study on all forms of discrimination and oppression of lesbian women and to present in cooperation with NGOs like the ILGA proposals for the improvement of their social and legal situations worldwide.

The International Gay and Lesbian Human Rights Commission, founded in 1991, is a San Francisco-based non-governmental human rights organization. IGLHRC's primary work is to monitor, document and mobilize responses to human rights abuses against lesbians, gay men, bisexuals, transgendered people, people with HIV and AIDS, and those oppressed due to their sexual identities or sexual conduct with consenting adults.

Publications

Secreto a Voces: Orientación Sexual y Derechos Humanos de las Mujeres. Spanish edition of *Unspoken Rules: Sexual Orientation and Women's Human Rights.* Contains 30 country reports from around the world documenting human rights violations against lesbians. $15.00.

Epidemic of Hate: Violation of the Human Rights of Gay Men, Lesbians, and Transvestites in Brazil / A Epidemia do Odio: Violação dos Direitos Humanos dos Gays, Lesbicas e Travestis no Brasil. By Luiz Mott. Available in Portuguese and English editions. $12.00.

No Human Being is Disposable: Social Cleansing, Human Rights and Sexual Orientation in Colombia. By Juan Pablo Ordoñez. Foreword by Noam Chomsky. Available in Spanish and English editions. $12.00.

The Rights of Lesbians and Gay Men in the Russian Federation. By Masha Gessen. Foreword by Larisa Bogoraz. Available in special bilingual English-Russian edition. $12.00.

(Forthcoming) *Asylum Based on Sexual Orientation: A Resource Guide.* Contains articles on various issues relating to political asylum for sexual minorities and people with AIDS, as well as contact lists of attorneys and organizations.

Emergency Response Network *Action Alert.* A bi-monthly publication which goes out to over 4000 individuals and organizations worldwide. Contains current information about specific cases of human rights violations against sexual minorities and people with HIV/AIDS as well as addresses and information to mobilize protest letters. Published in Spanish, French and English.

Shipping and handling within the United States: $2.00 for first book, $1.50 each additional book. International shipping and handling: $5.00 per book. For more information, to order reports, or to join the Emergency Response Network, please contact:

**INTERNATIONAL GAY AND LESBIAN
HUMAN RIGHTS COMMISSION**
1360 Mission Street, Suite 200
San Francisco, CA 94103 USA

Tel: +1-415-255-8680
Fax: +1-415-255-8662
E-mail: IGLHRC@igc.apc.org